Royal Commission on Civil Liability and Compensation for Personal Injury
Chairman: Lord Pearson

REPORT
Volume Two

Statistics and Costings

Presented to Parliament by Command of Her Majesty
March 1978

LONDON
HER MAJESTY'S STATIONERY OFFICE
£3·60 net

Cmnd 7054–II

Royal Commission on Civil Liability and Compensation for Personal Injury

Chairman: Lord Pearson

REPORT
Volume Two

Statistics and Costings

Presented to Parliament by Command of Her Majesty
March 1978

LONDON
HER MAJESTY'S STATIONERY OFFICE
£3.00 net

ISBN 0 10 170542 5

Table of contents

List of tables

CHAPTER 1

Introduction

1   From the outset of our work it was clear that detailed statistics would be needed, first in order to assess the numbers and characteristics of people injured and the coverage of existing methods of compensation, and secondly as a basis for costing alternative schemes.

2   We set up a statistics working party to review the data available and to consider what further statistics needed to be obtained. The Central Statistical Office provided a summary of existing statistical material. This showed that although information was available from a number of sources, it was limited to particular classes of injured people or to particular categories of injury. Among the main sources were the Department of Health and Social Security, who could provide information about injuries to the working population leading to payment of social security benefits, and also – from the Hospital In-Patient Enquiry – about injuries leading to a stay in hospital; the Department of the Environment (now the Department of Transport), who had information about casualties on the roads reported to the police; and the Registrars General, who produced analyses of deaths.

3   We examined the data assembled and the estimates made by earlier committees and by independent investigators who had been concerned with parts of our field. This previous work gave us useful initial guidance, but it too provided only part of the information we needed.

Special surveys

4   We concluded that we should ourselves seek fuller information covering injuries of all kinds, distinguishing so far as possible those within our terms of reference. Additional information was obtained in three principal ways. We arranged with the Office of Population Censuses and Surveys for a survey to be carried out of injured people in a sample of households; this survey was called the personal injury survey. We took up an offer of assistance from the British Insurance Association, and obtained from them analyses of insurance companies' accounts relating to personal injury business, and of a sample of claims for personal injury, to the second of which Lloyd's underwriters contributed. We asked the Lord Chancellor's Office and the Scottish Home and Health Department to analyse personal injury cases which had been the subject of court proceedings. At later stages, other special surveys on a smaller scale were carried out on our behalf. Information from all these surveys is given in later chapters.

Arrangement of the volume

5   Besides giving the results of the surveys specially carried out, we bring together in this volume statistics relating to personal injury, or to death following injury, from a variety of sources. The material consists partly of the original data, and partly of derived estimates, often made by using data from a number of sources, including the special surveys.

6   The first section is concerned with injuries of all kinds. Chapter 2 gives general summary figures, and Chapters 3 to 5 deal respectively with injuries compensated through tort, through social security, or in other ways. (The term tort is used to include delict in Scotland.) Chapters 6 to 13 give statistical information relating to particular categories of injury. Chapters 14 to 21 report on the personal injury survey, and Chapters 22 to 26 on the other surveys specially carried out. Chapters 27 and 28 contain material relating to the assessment of tort compensation. Chapters 29 and 30 give cost estimates.

Notes on the statistics

Reliability

7   Many of the statistics in this report are estimates, which vary in accuracy. Where appropriate, uncertain estimates of magnitudes of significance are given rather than none at all. Indications of the degree of accuracy are given for the most important sets of figures in Chapter 2 and in Chapter 30. They represent a judgment, not a statistical calculation, that there is a 90 per cent probability that the figures given do not differ from the true values by more than:

A   2 per cent
B   5 per cent
C   10 per cent
D   25 per cent

8   Estimates of national aggregates based on the personal injury survey had to allow for a degree of under-recording in the survey, and are subject to sampling error; they are of reliability D.

Coverage

9   All figures relate to the United Kingdom except where otherwise stated.

Dates

10   The figures given are for the most recent period or date for which they were available, which is stated in the tables. Where appropriate, figures for two or three years were averaged. Information derived from the surveys commissioned at the outset relates to 1972, 1973 or 1974.

Basis of value figures

11   Where appropriate, amounts and benefit rates are at January 1977 levels. But in the reports on the surveys specially carried out, and in some quotations from other sources, other dates are used.

Relationship to terms of reference
12   Some classes of injury or accidental death, in particular those relating to work and transport, are within the terms of reference. But for other classes, and for injuries and deaths in total, it was not possible to make a clear distinction in the statistics between those within and those outside. Many of the figures given therefore relate to all injuries or deaths resulting from injury, or to all those of a particular kind. The classification on which the main estimates are based is described in Chapter 15.

Definition of injury
13   Where possible the definition of injury adopted is that leading to 4 or more days off work, or an equivalent degree of severity for those not at work. This corresponds to the period after which national insurance sickness or injury benefit ordinarily becomes payable. References to 'serious' injuries mean injuries appreciably more serious than this.

14   The personal injury survey used the wider definition of injury leading to 4 or more days' incapacity for activity of any kind normally undertaken. The insurance survey covered all injuries and deaths which had led to tort claims. Some of the other sources quoted used other definitions of injury. Where these can be easily described, they are given; otherwise, they are to be found in the sources quoted.

Rounding
15   Where figures have been rounded the sums of constituent items may not be exactly equal to the totals shown.

Standard abbreviations
..   means not available
–   unless otherwise stated means nil, or less than half the final digit shown.

PART I

Statistics relating to injuries of all kinds

CHAPTER 2

General information

16   Each year in the United Kingdom some 3 million people are injured and over 20,000 die as a result of an injury.

Death from injury

17   Statistics of death from accidental or purposely inflicted injury are compiled by the Registrars General for England and Wales, Scotland and Northern Ireland. Details are available about deaths involving road, rail, water and air transport. For all accidents to employees at work, the number has been estimated from DHSS statistics of industrial death benefit with an allowance for cases where there were no dependants entitled to benefit.

18   Table 1 gives an analysis of deaths following injury. The figures are for deaths classified as being due to accidents, poisonings or violence, excluding those identified as suicides. More than one third of the deaths are caused by motor vehicles and nearly 30 per cent occur in private homes. 6 per cent occur at work, and over 3 per cent result from homicide.

19   More men than women die as the result of accidental or other injury. The disparity is greatest in respect of deaths at work. Twice as many men as women are killed on the roads, where for young adults the ratio of male to female deaths is more than 4 : 1. Men are also more likely than women to die in other transport accidents, or by violence. But more women than men die in private homes, or in the other ways included in the residual category in the table. Elderly women are more likely than men of the same age to die from injuries such as accidental falls, both in absolute numbers and in relation to their numbers in the population.

20   In all categories, deaths of boys outnumber those of girls.

21   Just over 3 per cent of all deaths result from accident, poisoning or violence. The incidence of death from these causes is highest among the elderly, who may often die where a younger person might recover. But deaths from injury are proportionately commonest at younger ages. For people under 35, for whom the overall death rate is low, injury represents the commonest cause of death, accounting for 24 per cent of all deaths in this age range. This proportion has increased as fatal diseases which used to be common have become rarer.

Numbers of injuries

22   How many injuries are recorded depends on how injury is defined. Many different definitions are in use. If injuries requiring no more than first aid

7

treatment were to be included, a substantial proportion of the population would be reckoned as suffering injury each year. In order to eliminate trivial injuries, the basis adopted in this chapter is injury sufficiently serious to lead to 4 or more days off work, or an equivalent degree of severity for people not at work.

Table 1 Deaths following injury

United Kingdom: averages in round numbers for 1973, 1974 and 1975   Numbers

	All	Males 15 and over	Females 15 and over	Boys under 15	Girls under 15
At work[1]	1,300	1,270	30	–	–
Motor vehicle[2]	7,220	4,330	2,080	540	270
Other transport[3]	460	350	70	30	10
Violence	720	420	190	60	50
In private homes[4]	6,200	2,080	3,480	380	260
Other	5,520	2,250	2,800	360	110
All deaths	21,420	10,700	8,650	1,370	700

1 Employees only, excluding the self employed.
2 Excluding an estimated 400 deaths of employees while at work – 390 men and 10 women.
3 Excluding an estimated 50 deaths of employees while at work – 45 men and 5 women. The total of 510 comprises 72 deaths in traffic accidents involving only non-motor vehicles, and 438 involving air, water or rail transport.
4 Not in previous categories.

Source: Reports of the Registrars General (Reliability A), except injuries at work, which were estimated by the Commission (Reliability D).

23   Information about those who draw sickness or injury benefit as the result of an injury covers the working population only, and, even within this group, not everyone who is injured is entitled to draw benefit, or makes a claim. The personal injury survey covered injuries of all kinds; but comparisons of its results with other data showed that not all injuries within the scope of the survey were reported at interview. Estimates of the numbers injured among the whole population grossed up directly from survey data would therefore understate the true number of injuries.

24   In order to overcome these deficiencies, the method used to estimate total numbers of injuries in the population was to take the survey estimates and to adjust them by approximate allowances for the likely degree of under-recording. For those in work, an indication of the extent of under-recording was obtained by comparing survey estimates with social security benefit statistics. For those not in work, the adjustments were made partly on internal evidence from the survey results and partly by analogy with the adjustments for the working population.

25 Table 2 gives estimated annual numbers of injuries by type of injury, sex and broad demographic group. The classification of injuries is that used in the personal injury survey, and differs from the classification of deaths in Table 1. A description of the criteria used to classify injuries by type is given in Chapter 15.

Table 2   Annual numbers of injuries by broad demographic group

United Kingdom: estimates in round numbers
based on data for 1973, 1974 and 1975   Thousands

	All injuries	At work	Motor vehicle[1]	Other injuries Possibly due to the act or omission of another	Not due to the act or omission of another
Working population					
Males[2]	1,390	630	150	250	360
Females[2]	390	90	50	70	180
People not in work					
Children under 15 and students					
Males	490	–	30	280	180
Females	320	–	20	180	120
Housewives[3]	140	–	10	30	100
Others					
Men[2]	60	–	10	10	40
Women[2]	260	–	20	60	180
All injuries	3,050	720	290	880	1,160
Of which:					
Males	1,940	630	190	540	580
Females	1,110	90	100	340	580
In private homes					
Males	310	–	–	55	255
Females	510	–	–	95	415

1 Moving or stationary; excluding about 55,000 injuries while at work, which are included in the previous column.
2 15 and over. Including students injured at work.
3 Married women under 60 not at work.

Estimated by the Commission from the personal injury survey and DHSS data. Reliability D.

26 Of all injuries as here defined, well over half are to the working population, who account for less than half the total population. Children under 15 and students accounted for about their proportionate share of injuries, housewives and others – principally the retired – for less.

27   Nearly a quarter of all injuries were sustained at work. Less than 10 per cent were caused by motor vehicles. Together these categories accounted for nearly one third of all injuries. Less than half the remainder were classified as being possibly due to the act or omission of another, leaving more than one third of the total number of injuries as clearly not caused by anyone other than the injured person himself.

28   There were more injuries to males than to females, both among adults and children. But there were many more injuries to women than men among the elderly who make up the bulk of the others not in work; and also among those injured in private homes. In all these respects, the pattern for injuries is similar to that for deaths from injury.

29   Injuries resulting from violence, which are not distinguished in the table, probably number some 50,000 a year.

30   The total number of injuries can be taken as being accurate to within 15 per cent either way, with 90 per cent probability. The figures for the working population are subject to less uncertainty, and those for other groups to more.

31   Besides injuries and deaths following injury, the subjects considered included work illnesses and ante-natal injuries. Statistics of work illnesses are to be found in Chapters 6 and 19, and of ante-natal injuries in Chapters 10 and 20.

Trends in the numbers of injuries

32   Many of the figures which might provide a guide to trends in the numbers of injuries are obtained as a by-product of administration, and changes in the level of injuries may be capable of several interpretations. For instance, the number of patients in hospital suffering from injuries may be partly determined by the number of beds available; the number of spells of incapacity for work may be influenced by readiness to take time off for minor injuries, which in turn may be affected by the increasing provision of sick pay.

33   Qualifications of this kind apply least to figures for deaths from injury. Table 3 shows that there has been a decline in motor vehicle deaths, and in accidental deaths at work leading to payment of industrial death benefit. Deaths from other kinds of injury show no particular trend.

34   Among the series relating to injury, there has been a downward trend in recent years in the numbers of accidents at work. However, as explained in Chapter 6, the factors which led to the reduction in work accidents are unlikely to be repeated to the same extent in the future. In contrast, injuries to the insured population elsewhere than at work, leading to receipt of sickness benefit, have increased.

The contribution of injury to incapacity

35   The proportion which the injured make up of all those incapacitated by injury or disease can be derived from a number of sources. Some estimates are given in Table 4. Those which relate to the whole population lie fairly

close to 10 per cent, whatever the measure of incapacity used. The proportion is higher for people incapacitated for work and claiming sickness or injury benefit, since those eligible for benefit are predominantly males aged 16 to 64, for whom injury is a more common cause of incapacity than for women or the retired.

Table 3 Trends in the number of injuries and deaths from injury

Thousands

	1965	1966	1967	1968	1969	1970	1971	1972	1973	1974	1975
Deaths from injury (UK)											
In motor vehicle accidents	8·5	8·5	8·2	7·4	7·8	7·9	8·2	8·1	8·3	7·6	7·0
Other deaths from injury	13·7	14·2	13·5	13·8	13·4	14·0	13·7	13·5	13·7	13·8	14·0
All deaths from injury	22·2	22·6	21·6	21·2	21·2	21·9	21·9	21·6	22·0	21·3	21·0
Accidental deaths leading to payment of industrial death benefit (GB)	1·29	1·31	1·11	1·14	1·19	1·09	1·02	0·98	1·00	0·95	0·82
Hospital in-patients (GB)											
All injuries[1]	480	486	505	526	562	572	591	596	594	..	..
Sickness benefit (GB)[2]											
New spells of absence through injury											
Males	750[3]	769	802	839	843	898	886[3]	839	908	953	..
Females	144[3]	144	142	145	141	143	138[3]	138	152	158	..
Injury benefit (GB)[2]											
Fresh industrial accidents											
Males	755[3]	757	734	739	716	710	612[3]	556	562	555	509
Females	89[3]	92	90	85	87	86	73[3]	66	68	68	68

1 Spells in hospital resulting in discharge during the year.
2 Year starting on first Monday in June of previous year.
3 53 weeks.

Sources: Registrars General: Reliability A. Department of Health and Social Security: Reliability B.

Duration of incapacity

36 Most incapacity resulting from injury is of relatively short duration. This is evident both from the personal injury survey, which covered a sample of all the injured, and from social security statistics of incapacity for work.

37 Table 5 shows the distribution of incapacity for work among people receiving sickness or injury benefit in the three years from June 1972 to June 1975. Injury is less likely than sickness to lead to very short or very long spells of incapacity. Nevertheless, almost 90 per cent of the injured were back at work within 8 weeks of their injury.

11

Table 4   Contribution of injury to incapacity

Source	Measure of incapacity	Percentage of incapacity due to injury	Reliability
General Household Survey (GB) (OPCS)	Any restriction of activity in a 2 week reference period	12	B
Sickness and injury benefit statistics in Great Britain (DHSS)	Days of certified incapacity for work among the insured population	14	B
Hospital In-patient Enquiry (England and Wales) (DHSS)	Spells of in-patient treatment	10	B
Survey of handicapped and impaired in Great Britain (OPCS)	Permanent handicap	10[1]	B

1 Estimated by the Commission.

Table 5   Duration of spells of incapacity for work due to injury and sickness

Great Britain: averages for the three years June 1972 to June 1975

	Injury[1]		Sickness	
	Percentage of spells terminating in period	Cumulative percentage of spells terminating by end of period	Percentage of spells terminating in period	Cumulative percentage of spells terminating by end of period
4 days–1 week	18·5	18·5	28·0	28·0
Over 1 week–2 weeks	27·4	45·9	30·3	58·4
Over 2 weeks–4 weeks	27·5	73·5	21·5	79·9
Over 4 weeks–8 weeks	16·0	89·5	10·7	90·6
Over 8 weeks–3 months	5·5	94·9	4·5	95·0
Over 3 months–6 months	3·4	98·3	2·7	97·8
Over 6 months	1·6		2·2	

1 Obtained by combining statistics of injury benefit and of sickness and invalidity benefit following injury. Where injury benefit is followed by sickness or invalidity benefit, the spells for the two types of benefit are both included; in consequence of this duplication, the percentages shown for the longer durations may be slightly overstated.

Source: Based on DHSS statistics. Reliability B.

Long term incapacity

38 Invalidity benefit, which is payable after 28 weeks' incapacity for work, usually ceases after a time. The Government Actuary's Department (GAD) has agreed to publication of the following estimates, though making it clear that they are approximations which do no more than indicate the likely pattern.

Table 6 Approximate percentages of payments of invalidity benefit for injury continuing after the periods shown

Great Britain: 1970 to 1975

Period since award (years)	$\frac{1}{2}$	$1\frac{1}{2}$	$2\frac{1}{2}$	$3\frac{1}{2}$	$4\frac{1}{2}$
Percentage of payments continuing	46	21	14	8	5

Source: GAD. Reliability D.

39 The estimates are based on statistics of payments of invalidity benefit for absence from work due to accidents, poisonings or violence. The period since the injury is just over half a year longer than the period shown in the table.

40 It has been estimated in Table 5 that about $1\frac{1}{2}$ per cent of the injured are still unable to work after 6 months, and go on to receive invalidity benefit. Although Table 6 reflects cessation of payment because of death or the attainment of retiring age as well as through resumption of work, it can be concluded that the proportion of those injured who remain permanently unable to do any work at all is extremely small – probably no more than 1 in 1,000. A much larger proportion, however, would be unable ever to resume their normal occupations, and many would be able only to do a little part-time work, though sufficient to lose them their entitlement to invalidity benefit.

Long term disability

41 Durations of disability following injuries at work have also been analysed by the Government Actuary. Many of the disability pensions initially awarded cease after a time because the disability is reassessed at less than 20 per cent (when gratuity is awarded), or disappears altogether. Details are given in Table 7.

Table 7 Percentages of industrial disablement pensions for injury or industrial disease[1] continuing in payment after the periods shown

Great Britain: 1970 to 1975

Period since award (years)	$\frac{1}{2}$	$1\frac{1}{2}$	$2\frac{1}{2}$	$3\frac{1}{2}$	$4\frac{1}{2}$	5
Percentage of pensions continuing	71	39	32	29	28	28

1 Excluding pneumoconiosis, to which special arrangements apply.

Source: GAD. Reliability C.

42   Disability pensions are paid on return to work or after 26 weeks, so that the period since the injury is up to half a year longer than that shown in the table.

Long term tort cases

43   The British Insurance Association (BIA) have estimated that in about $2\frac{1}{2}$ per cent of cases where tort compensation was paid for personal injury, the injured person had still not been fit to return to work after two years. A higher percentage was to be expected than in all cases of injury, since injuries in tort cases tend to be of more than average severity.

44   This estimate is consistent with the estimate derived from the BIA's survey that $5\frac{1}{2}$ per cent of tort payments in injury cases included compensation for future loss of earnings. Most awards are made between a few months and three years after the injury. Adding in fatal cases, representing 2 per cent of the total number, in all about $7\frac{1}{2}$ per cent of tort payments include provision for future pecuniary loss.

Injuries to the self employed

45   The figures for injuries to the working population in Tables 2 and 5 include injuries to the self employed. Information about the self employed is less full than for employees, since the self employed are not eligible for industrial injuries benefits, although they may be eligible for sickness and invalidity benefit. There was evidence from the personal injury survey that not all the self employed who were incapacitated for work claimed benefit. In particular the great majority of self employed women are not entitled to benefit since they do not pay national insurance contributions. The estimated annual number of injuries to the self employed is therefore based on survey data rather than DHSS benefit statistics.

46   The estimate is that there are about 85,000 injuries to the self employed each year. About one half of them occur in the course of work. Injuries to self employed women account for less than a fifth of the total (Table 8).

47   The incidence of injury to men who are self employed is lower than for male employees, both at work and elsewhere. The lower incidence at work is partly explained by differences in the ranges of occupations which are followed.

48   The pattern of incapacity for work due to injury among the self employed differs from that for employees. An analysis of DHSS records shows that the self employed, when absent from work four days or more, tend to be away longer than employees. It would seem that the self employed are less likely to take relatively short periods off work for minor injuries.

49   A comparison based on DHSS data for employees and the self employed is given in Table 9. It covers injuries both at work and elsewhere. It is limited to one year since the analysis distinguishing durations of sickness and invalidity benefit for employees and for the self employed – which was specially prepared – was made only for that year.

14

Table 8   Incidence of injury to employees and the self employed

United Kingdom: averages or estimates in round numbers for 1973, 1974 and 1975

	Annual number of injuries	Number in employment	Incidence of injury
	Thousands		Rate per 1,000 employed
Employees			
Male	1,320	13,650	97
Female	375	9,070	42
Both sexes	1,695	22,720	74
Self employed			
Male	70	1,560	45
Female	15	370	41
Both sexes	85	1,930	44

Sources: Department of Employment and estimates made by the Commission. Reliability D.

Table 9   Duration of spells of incapacity for work following injury for employees and the self employed

Great Britain: June 1973–June 1974

	Employees[1]		Self employed	
	Percentage of spells terminating in period	Cumulative percentage of spells terminating by end of period	Percentage of spells terminating in period	Cumulative percentage of spells terminating by end of period
4 days–1 week	18·7	18·7	9·3	9·3
Over 1 week–2 weeks	27·7	46·4	25·0	34·3
Over 2 weeks–4 weeks	27·5	73·9	28·7	63·0
Over 4 weeks–8 weeks	15·7	89·6	22·4	85·4
Over 8 weeks–3 months	5·4	95·0	8·3	93·7
Over 3 months–6 months	3·5	98·5	4·5	98·2
Over 6 months	1·5		1·8	

1 See footnote 1 to table 5.

Source: Based on DHSS statistics. Reliability B.

Sources of compensation

50   Table 10 gives broad estimates of the numbers of cases in which compensation is obtained from the main sources in respect of fresh injuries each year. It is estimated that of 3,070,000 casualties a year, no more than about 1,700,000, or 55 per cent, obtain financial compensation for them. Of those who do, many receive compensation from more than one source. Some injured people already receiving retirement or widow's pensions may not be entitled to any additional benefit on account of their injuries, and if so would not be included in the table.

Table 10   Numbers obtaining compensation from different sources

Injuries and deaths following injury in the United Kingdom: estimates in round numbers based on data for 1973, 1974 and 1975	Number of new beneficiaries a year
	Thousands
Social security	1,550
Tort	215
Occupational sick pay	1,000
Occupational pensions	4
Private insurance[1]	200
Criminal injuries compensation	18
Other forms of compensation	150
All forms of compensation	1,700[2]

1 Excluding life insurance, for which no estimate can be made.
2 Excluding duplication.

Estimated by the Commission.

51   Most of the payments under almost every heading go to employees. In part, this is because compensation has aimed to replace a breadwinner's lost earnings in the forms for example of injury, sickness and invalidity benefits and occupational sick pay. But compensation for non-pecuniary loss also has gone mainly to employees. This is true both of state benefits for disablement as distinct from incapacity for work, and of tort compensation – most of which is for non-pecuniary loss. One third of all tort compensation is paid to employees on employer's liability claims, but most other claims also are made by those in work, probably because non-earners tend to be injured at home or in other circumstances where no tort claim arises.

52   The personal injury survey showed that over 80 per cent of those receiving tort compensation for injury were in work. Not all of them would have been eligible for social security benefits, and in particular about half the women injured elsewhere than at work might be expected to have opted out of the

general insurance scheme. After taking out those ineligible for benefit, it is estimated that about three quarters of the recipients of tort compensation would also be receiving social security benefits. If the system continues unaltered this proportion may be expected to rise as the proportion of married women covered by the general national insurance scheme increases.

53 Many of the injured receive both social security and occupational sick pay. Married women again are the main category who might receive the latter and not the former. Sick pay is usually not paid independently of social security benefits but by way of a supplement to them, and so in this instance the overlap between forms of compensation is more apparent than real.

54 Nevertheless, it is true to say that employees can receive compensation from two or three sources, or even more, whereas non-earners such as house-wives, children or the retired often receive no compensation at all. The intro-duction in recent years of attendance and mobility allowances and of non-contributory invalidity pensions has not had a large effect on the numbers of non-earners entitled to benefits, when they suffer an injury, since help has been concentrated on the relatively small proportion who are severely disabled, or incapacitated for a long period.

CHAPTER 3

Tort claims

55   Little quantitative information has hitherto been available about the system of tort compensation in this country. There have been some small-scale surveys, notably a survey of the financial consequences of motor vehicle accidents carried out by Harris and Hartz[1] in Oxford, and a survey of solicitors' personal injury cases in England and Wales made by Ison[2]; and some information about cases in the courts in England and Wales was collected for the Winn Committee On Personal Injury Litigation.[3]

56   The information in this chapter comes principally from three sources: the insurance survey carried out by the British Insurance Association with the co-operation of Lloyd's, the analyses of court records, and the personal injury survey. Greater detail is to be found in chapters 18, 22, 23 and 24. Together these sources provide a picture of the tort system which is both fuller and more reliable than that hitherto available.

57   The data quoted from the insurance survey and the analyses of court records cover injuries, work illnesses and deaths; those from the personal injury survey relate to injuries only.

Annual number of claims

58   The number of personal injury claims made each year could not be estimated directly from any of these sources. In the course of interviewing for the personal injury survey, it was found that people did not always know whether a formal claim had been made by the solicitor or trade union in whose hands the matter had been placed, or were uncertain how far the claim had progressed. The insurance survey was based on a four week period; but because of seasonal and other factors, the claims files analysed were known to represent a good deal less than the 1 in 13 of the annual total which might have been expected.

59   The best estimates that could be made, relating the insurance survey figures to those provided by the analyses of court records and other data, were that about 250,000 tort claims in respect of personal injury were dealt with in the United Kingdom during 1973, and that about 215,000 payments had been made (Table 11). Some 4,500 of these payments related to deaths following injury. There is a 90 per cent probability that these estimates are within 15 per cent of the true figures.

60   The total amount of tort compensation paid was about £200 million, expressed in January 1977 prices.

61   Just under 90 per cent of all personal injury claims are dealt with by insurers. Most of the remainder are claims against organisations which carry their own risk – mainly public bodies. In addition there are claims in respect of professional negligence, for which insurance is provided by mutual indemnity associations, and small numbers of claims involving uninsured or untraced motorists which are dealt with by the Motor Insurers Bureau. These claims are included in the total given above. Finally, there is a small number of claims against other uninsured individuals, for which no estimates have been made.

62   Among those making tort claims there will be a few with injuries not sufficiently severe to fall within the definition of 4 or more days' incapacity for work or an equivalent degree of incapacity for injured people not in work. It is therefore not possible to estimate numbers of claims or payments in respect of injury to correspond with the estimates of numbers of injuries given in the previous chapter.

Trends in the numbers of personal injury claims

63   There is no direct evidence of changes in recent years in the number of personal injury claims made annually. Some statistics of legal proceedings in respect of personal injury claims in England and Wales are now published by the Lord Chancellor's Office, but have not been available for a sufficient length of time for any trend to have become apparent.

Table 11   Annual numbers of tort claims and payments for personal injury or death by type of claim

United Kingdom: estimates in round numbers for 1973

	Claims		Payments	
	Numbers	Percentages	Numbers	Percentages
Employers' liability				
Injury	114,700	46·0	90,500	42·0
Disease	2,900	1·2	1,700	0·8
Motor vehicle	102,200	40·9	98,300	45·7
Other transport	1,100	0·4	900	0·4
Products and services (excluding medical services)	2,200	0·9	1,700	0·8
Medical services[1]	700	0·2	300	0·1
Occupiers' liability	12,200	4·9	10·800	5·0
Other	14,000	5·6	11,200	5·2
Totals	250,000	100·0	215,400	100·0

1 Claims on doctors, dentists and pharmacists.

Sources: Insurance survey.
Survey of organisations carrying their own risk.
Information from medical indemnity associations.

Types of claim

64   Altogether 88 per cent of claims are under employers' liability or motor policies.

Stage at which claims are settled

65   About 86 per cent of claims are settled without the issue of a writ, and only 1 per cent reach the courts (Table 12).

Table 12   Stage at which tort claims were settled

United Kingdom: 1973

Number of claims	250,000
	Percentages
Disposed of:	
Without the issue of a writ	86
After writ, before being set down	11
After setting down, before trial	2
In court, including at door of court	1
Total	100

Source: Insurance survey.

Payments of compensation

66   Some payment is made in respect of about 86 per cent of all personal injury claims. The proportion is higher in the case of motor vehicle claims, and lower for claims involving employers' liability.

67   The majority of payments of tort compensation are of small sums. More than half the payments in the insurance survey were for less than £400 at January 1977 prices, though these accounted for only 10 per cent of the total amount paid (Table 13).

68   The average payment for all types of claim was about £1,000 at January 1977 prices – over £900 for injuries, and about £5,000 for deaths. Payments tended to be higher in Northern Ireland than in Great Britain.

69   More than a half of the amount paid in tort compensation was for non-pecuniary loss.

Adequacy of payment

70   About three quarters of respondents to the personal injury survey whose claims had been settled by the time of interview (8–24 months after their injury) thought that the amount obtained covered their total pecuniary losses.

20

But it is likely to have been mainly the smaller claims which were settled by the time of interview, and there is evidence from the survey in Oxford[1] and from the United States[4][5] that small pecuniary losses are relatively more fully compensated than larger ones. It is possible therefore that the response to this part of the survey exaggerates satisfaction with tort awards among all claimants receiving payment.

Table 13   Distribution of amounts paid in tort compensation

Great Britain: 1973

Size of payment	Percentage of total number of payments	Percentage of total amount paid
£		
1 – 100	17	1
101 – 200	15	3
201 – 300	11	3
301 – 400	9	3
401 – 500	7	3
501 – 1,000	19	14
1,001 – 2,000	11	16
2,001 – 5,000	7	22
5,001 – 10,000	2	13
Over 10,000	1	21
Total	100	100

Source: Data from insurance survey, revalued at January 1977 prices.

71   Most of the people interviewed in the personal injury survey who received tort payments spent at least some of the money on the repayment of debts incurred during their incapacity or on general living expenses. Only a small proportion invested any.

72   The 1973 claims which had been settled showed average tort compensation of £249 compared with average financial losses of £180 at 1973 prices. The Oxford survey showed 13 cases out of 27 of tort compensation exceeding financial losses where these were less than £1,000, but only 2 cases out of 11 where the financial loss amounted to £1,000 or more. In each case, the comparison is made between tort compensation for both pecuniary and non-pecuniary loss, and the estimated pecuniary loss.

Proportion of injuries and deaths for which compensation is paid

73   Tort compensation is paid in respect of about a fifth of all deaths from injury. The proportion may be as much as one half for deaths at work or

involving a motor vehicle; there are few claims in respect of death from other kinds of injury.

74   Altogether about 6–7 per cent of people with non-fatal injuries receive some payment through the tort system in compensation for their injuries. The proportion varies according to the type of injury. A much higher proportion of people injured by motor vehicles receive tort compensation than for any other kind of injury (Table 14).

Table 14   Proportions of injured people who receive some
tort compensation by type of injury

Great Britain: 1973   Percentages

All injuries	6½
Injuries at work	10½
Motor vehicle injuries[1]	25
Other injuries	1½

1 Including injuries in the course of work.

Source: Personal injury survey.

75   These percentages are based on the personal injury survey, which provided comparable data for tort claims and for numbers of injuries, albeit including some injuries leading to less than 4 days' incapacity for work or the equivalent. It was not possible to exclude these less serious injuries; if it had been, slightly larger percentages would have been obtained. The percentages based on the survey however provide better measures than those obtained by relating estimates of total numbers of tort claims in respect of injuries of any degree of severity to total numbers of injuries which exclude minor injuries.

76   People at work are more likely to obtain compensation for their injuries than those not in work, and men than women. Children under the age of 15 stand a particularly poor chance of obtaining compensation through tort (Table 15).

77   Judging from data for the working population, the proportion receiving some compensation through tort rises steadily with the severity of injury.

78   It is to be expected therefore that the percentage of people severely injured in motor accidents who receive tort compensation would be a great deal higher than the 25 per cent given in Table 14. The survey results are not necessarily inconsistent with the higher figure of 44 per cent recorded in the Oxford survey of motor vehicle injuries, which was based on a sample of 90 serious injuries. Evidence from surveys carried out in Canada and the United States suggests that in those countries the proportions of injured people obtaining tort compensation for motor vehicle injuries may be somewhat higher than in this country (Table 16).

Table 15 Proportions of injured people who receive some
tort compensation by sectors of the population

Great Britain: 1973   Percentages

All injured people	$6\frac{1}{2}$
Working men	10
Working women	8
Other men	5
Other women	4
Children under 15	1

Source: Personal injury survey.

Table 16 Proportion of people injured in motor vehicle accidents obtaining
tort compensation in Great Britain and North America

Survey	Scope of survey	Percentage of injured obtaining tort compensation
Oxford[1] (Harris and Hartz, 1965)	Serious injury – 6 weeks off work or the equivalent or permanent disability	44
Personal Injury Survey 1973 (GB)	4 or more days incapacity for any normal activity	25
Michigan[4] (Conard et al, 1965)	'Serious' injury Including minor injuries	55 37
United States[5] Department of Transportation, 1970	'Serious' injury	48
Philadelphia[6] (Morris and Paul, 1962)	'Serious' injury	47
Ontario[7] (Osgoode Hall, 1965)	Includes minor injuries	43

Details of sources are given in the list of references at the end of this volume.

79 Evidence from employers showed wide variations in the proportions of
accidents at work giving rise to claims under employers' liability, ranging from
nearly a half of all lost-time accidents to about 1 in 10. One employer reported
large and consistent regional differences in the proportion of accidents which
led to a claim.

Attribution of fault

80 Whether an injured person makes a claim will depend not only on the objective circumstances of the injury, but also on how he feels about it, and particularly whether he considers anyone else to be at fault. Among those interviewed in the personal injury survey, blame was attributed to others in not more than a half of all cases, even in respect of transport accidents. For all other injuries someone else was thought to be at fault in no more than a third of cases, even allowing for cases where someone else was only partly at fault. Even when the injured person thinks someone else may have been responsible for his injury, he may not always take action or persevere in his claim.

Length of time before settlement

81 Nearly a half of all claims on insurers are dealt with within twelve months of the injury. Some payment is made in respect of 97 per cent of these claims. Generally the sums of money involved are small, accounting in all for less than a quarter of the total amount paid. As the length of time from injury to settlement increases, so the proportion of claims in which payment is made decreases, falling to about two thirds for claims not disposed of within two years of the injury. At the same time the average size of payment increases, reflecting the fact that it is the more serious cases which take the longest time.

Table 17 Distribution of numbers and amounts of claims on insurers by time taken from injury to disposal of claim

Great Britain 1973

Period in months from injury to settlement	Percentage of all claims made by number	Percentage of total amount paid	Percentage of claims in which payment made
0–3	4·6	0·5	99
3–6	12·6	4·0	98
6–9	16·6	8·2	97
9–12	15·1	11·0	96
12–24	31·6	35·4	81
24–36	12·4	21·8	68
36–48	4·9	12·4	63
48–60	1·5	3·1	66
over 60	0·9	3·6	66
All claims	100·0	100·0	86

Source: Insurance survey.

82 Information from a major construction company about claims in respect of employers' liability confirmed the link between the size of the payment and

the length of time taken to settle. The company thought that the length of time taken to settle larger claims indicated the complexities involved in assessing the medical consequences of the injuries.

Legal proceedings

83   In 1974, rather more than 3,000 personal injury claims reached court. They made up only a small proportion of civil actions, the majority being related to debt or divorce. In the Queen's Bench Division of the High Court, however, personal injury cases amounted to nearly 80 per cent of the cases heard.

84   In Great Britain, the majority of personal injury cases set down for hearing in the courts are withdrawn before hearing, whereas in Northern Ireland the commonest procedures are to settle at the door of the court, or in court without a full hearing.

85   In about three quarters of all cases in Great Britain in which the result is known (mainly those which proceed at least as far as the door of the court), the outcome is in favour of the plaintiff. In Northern Ireland the proportion is over 90 per cent.

86   Awards made in 1974 were on average highest in Northern Ireland and lowest in Scotland.

Table 18   Median awards in the courts

1974

England and Wales	£1,810
Scotland	£1,370
Northern Ireland	£2,230

Source: Data from surveys of the courts,
revalued at January 1977 prices.

87   The average time taken from injury to disposal for cases disposed of in 1974 was about three years in England and Wales and three years eight months in Scotland. The greater delay in Scotland is accounted for by the longer period between the injury and the issue of a writ. In the opinion of the Scottish Home and Health Department, the delay might reflect the cautiousness of Scottish lawyers in not initiating actions before the full effect of an injury is apparent, since in Scotland the amount claimed has to be specified.

88   The majority of hearings involving personal injury take no more than a day.

25

Appeals

89   Just over 2,000 actions in respect of personal injury reach judgment each year. Less than 10 per cent of these are the subject of appeal. Appeals to the House of Lords are rare, generally numbering no more than one or two a year.

Opinions of the legal system

90   About 30 per cent of those in the personal injury survey who had consulted a solicitor about making a claim were satisfied. Some 50 per cent were not altogether satisfied. The remainder gave no opinion. The most common complaints were that the system took too long and that it was hard to understand.

Legal costs

91   Data relating to legal costs were available from three sources, but they were not representative of costs in all personal injury cases handled by solicitors. A study by Professor Zander[8] was limited to taxed costs in 654 High Court cases, predominantly cases in which a writ had been issued. An unpublished study by The Law Society related to 222 cases handled by four firms of solicitors in which compensation had been obtained. An analysis made by the Lord Chancellor's Office, though covering larger numbers, was limited to legally aided cases in which a writ had been issued.

92   Both Professor Zander's and The Law Society's studies confirmed the existence of cases in which legal costs exceeded the value of the compensation obtained.

93   The most nearly representative figure for average costs is that derived from The Law Society's sample, which was the only one in which cases settled without the issue of a writ were properly represented. (They accounted for 150 of the 222 cases.) The average figure, for cases settled towards the end of 1975, was £196. Inclusion of unsuccessful claims might be expected to lead to a lower figure for all personal injury claims dealt with.

CHAPTER 4

Social security

94   This chapter contains a selection of statistics relevant to the consideration of compensation for injury compiled by the Department of Health and Social Security in Great Britain, and by the Department of Health and Social Services in Northern Ireland. (The Departments are referred to, together or separately, as DHSS.) Many of the figures have been used as the basis for estimates given elsewhere. They are produced as a by-product of the administration of the various benefits, and their coverage is determined by the nature of the social security system.

95   Most of the figures quoted relate to benefits paid in respect of injuries to people in insurable employment. Some of the statistical series quoted, however, do not distinguish between injury and illness. In particular, this distinction is not made in respect of national insurance widows' pensions. Information about deaths resulting from injury is limited to deaths caused by industrial accident, where there are dependants to whom industrial death benefit is paid. Deaths from industrial diseases are also identified.

96   Most of the statistics given relate to benefits paid to people who have suffered from injury or industrial disease. Such benefits are usually paid for no more than a few weeks. Numbers of fresh cases of injury, or fresh spells of absence, predominantly consist therefore of short term cases. Longer term cases account, however, for an appreciable proportion of the numbers incapacitated at any time. Notes follow describing the main features of the principal classes of statistics which are quoted.

Injury benefit
97   Injury benefit is paid to employees, but not to the self employed, in respect of injuries or diseases arising from work. It is paid for a maximum of 26 weeks, after which employees may be able to claim sickness or invalidity benefit. Those who do are recorded in the statistics both for injury benefit and for sickness and invalidity benefit.

98   The statistics distinguish industrial accidents from prescribed diseases. Injury benefit is not paid to those suffering from pneumoconiosis or byssinosis.

Industrial disablement benefit
99   Industrial disablement benefit is paid to those disabled by industrial injury or disease in addition to any benefits under the general national insurance

27

scheme to which the disabled person is entitled. It is paid when payment of injury benefit stops, either when the injured person is able to return to work, or when the 26 weeks' entitlement to injury benefit is exhausted.

100 The degree of disablement is expressed in terms of a percentage scale. For an assessment of less than 20 per cent, the benefit usually takes the form of a lump sum gratuity. For assessments of 20 per cent or more, a pension is paid, which continues as long as the disablement, even after retirement. Following payment of a gratuity, or in addition to a pension, certain allowances may be paid, of which the most important is special hardship allowance.

Special hardship allowance

101 Special hardship allowance can be paid to persons industrially disabled who because of their injuries are unable to follow their regular occupation or one of an equivalent standard. Like industrial disablement benefit, it is not paid during the initial period of absence from work. Broadly, the amount payable is the difference between the earnings in the regular occupation and those in an occupation which the claimant is capable of following, up to a maximum. About 90 per cent of the payments are at the maximum rate. Like an industrial disablement pension, special hardship allowance can continue to be paid for life.

Sickness and invalidity benefit

102 The figures quoted for sickness and invalidity benefit are for claims classified on the basis of doctors' certificates to the heading 'Accidents, poisonings and violence' in the International Classification of Diseases.

103 They predominantly relate to benefits paid for injuries to insured persons elsewhere than at work. But they include:

i Sickness and invalidity benefit paid to employees injured at work or suffering from industrial disease, following 26 weeks' receipt of injury benefit; these cases represent about 1 per cent of all new spells of absence recorded. The period recorded is that during which sickness or invalidity benefit was paid.

ii All payments of benefit for injury to the self employed, whether at work or elsewhere. Injuries to the self employed at work represent 1 to 2 per cent of all new spells of absence recorded.

Numbers within the scheme

104 There are about 16 million men in the working population, including about 1 million registered as unemployed, and about 1½ million self employed. All but a few with low earnings are in the general national insurance scheme, and all employees are covered by the industrial injuries scheme.

105 There are roughly 10 million women in the working population, including the self employed and those registered as unemployed. Employees, covered by the industrial injuries scheme, number over 9 million. The coverage of the general

national insurance scheme is less, since most married women have opted out of the scheme (an option which will not be open in future). The number covered by the general national insurance scheme is about 4 million, including the self employed; the number of self employed included is less than 100,000, since many self employed women have opted out and others, e.g. those working part time or as outworkers, earn less than the minimum required for participation.

Note on the DHSS statistics

106 Some of the figures quoted are based on large samples, not on complete counts.

Table 19 Numbers receiving benefits and allowances at a given date

United Kingdom: June 1975

	Both sexes		Male injuries and industrial diseases		Female injuries and industrial diseases	
	Total number	Percentage following injury	Total number	Percentage following injury	Total number	Percentage following injury
	'000		'000		'000	
Industrial injuries benefits						
Injury benefit	46·2	..	39·1	..	7·1	..
Industrial disablement pensions	204·1	78·6[1]	184·0	78·6[1]	20·2	78·4[1]
Special hardship allowance Supplementing pension	79·1	70·1[1]	..	..	..	..
Following gratuity	65·7	88·5[1]	..	..	..	..
Industrial death benefit pensions	31·4	..	31·4	..	–	–
Sickness benefit	444·3	15·7[2]	337·3	17·9[2]	107·0	8·8[2]
Invalidity benefit	475·4	5·7[2]	390·4	6·0[2]	84·9	4·1[2]
Widow's national insurance benefit	523·5	..	523·5	..	–	–
Attendance allowance	217·0	..	88·9	..	128·1	..
Non-contributory invalidity pension[3]	69·2	..	..	..	..	..

Figures are not yet available for mobility allowance, which was introduced in January 1976, or for invalid care allowance, introduced in July 1976.

1 Percentage of benefits for injury caused by accident, not by disease.
2 Great Britain only.
3 The figure relates to December 1975. The pension was introduced in November 1975, and extended in November 1977 to housewives.

Numbers receiving benefits

107   Tables 19 and 20 give the numbers who were receiving benefits and allowances of various kinds at a given date, usually June 1975. Table 19 gives the total numbers of benefits and allowances in payment, whether for injury or for disease. A second column gives the percentage of the total which relate to injury, where that is available. For industrial disablement pensions and special hardship allowance, the percentages are for those receiving benefit for industrial accidents and not because they were suffering from a prescribed disease. Accident cases greatly out-number cases of prescribed disease.

108   The proportion of injury cases in Great Britain among all sickness benefit cases was 15·7 per cent, and among invalidity benefit cases 5·7 per cent. The difference reflects the fact that injury leads to proportionately fewer cases of long term incapacity than illness.

Table 20   Persons receiving benefit for injury at a given date

United Kingdom: June 1975   Thousands

	Both sexes	Male injuries and industrial diseases	Female injuries and industrial diseases
Injury benefit[1][2]	46·2	39·1	7·1
Industrial disablement benefit			
Pensions for pneumoconiosis and byssinosis	37·8	35·0	2·8
Other pensions			
Accidents	160·4	144·5	15·8
Prescribed diseases[3]	6·1	4·6	1·6
Special hardship allowance[4][5]			
Accidents			
With pensions	54·5	47·8	6·6
Following gratuities	57·3	..	..
Prescribed diseases			
Pneumoconiosis and byssinosis (with pension)[6]	19·0	18·7	0·2
Other diseases[7]			
With pensions	4·5	2·3	2·3
Following gratuities	7·0	..	..
Industrial death benefit	31·4	31·4	–
Sickness and invalidity benefit for accidents, poisonings and violence[6]	92·3	80·2	12·1

1 Accidents at work and prescribed diseases other than pneumoconiosis and byssinosis.
2 Claimants incapacitated at 31 May 1975.
3 Other than pneumoconiosis and byssinosis.
4 At 30 September 1975.
5 Great Britain only. For Northern Ireland, the number receiving special hardship allowance was 1,875, of which 1,607 were males and 268 females.
6 Great Britain only.
7 Great Britain only. For Northern Ireland the number receiving benefit was 673, of which 480 were males and 193 females.

109   The figure given for non-contributory invalidity pension relates to a date only two months after its introduction. By 1978, the number of these pensions in payment will be appreciably larger, both because of late applications from those entitled to this pension when it was introduced in November 1975, and as the result of its extension to incapacitated housewives in November 1977.

110   Table 20 gives details of benefits in payment to people who had been injured, or who were suffering from prescribed diseases incurred at work. Because industrial disablement pensions are paid, once injury benefit has

Table 21   Injuries to the insured population in a year for which benefit is paid

United Kingdom: 3 June 1974–31 May 1975   Thousands

	Both sexes	Male injuries and industrial diseases	Female injuries and industrial diseases
Injury benefit			
Accidents at work			
New spells of absence	608·9	536·3	72·6
Fresh injuries	590·8	520·8	70·1
Prescribed diseases[1]			
New spells of absence	14·4	10·8	3·6
Fresh developments of disease	12·8	9·6	3·2
Industrial disablement benefit			
Pneumoconiosis and byssinosis			
Cases diagnosed[2]	1·2	..	..
Pensions – initial assessments			
Accidents at work	11·6	10·0	1·7
Prescribed diseases[1]	2·1	1·9	0·2
Gratuities – initial assessments			
Accidents at work	78·2	66·7	11·5
Prescribed diseases	2·0	1·4	0·6
Special hardship allowance – initial assessments			
Accidents at work	5·5	4·5	1·0
Prescribed diseases	0·4	0·3	0·1
Industrial death benefit			
Accidents at work	0·9	0·9	–
Prescribed diseases[3]	0·8	0·8	–
Sickness and invalidity benefit for accidents, poisonings and violence[4]			
New spells of absence	1,089·3	936·3	153·0

1 Excluding pneumoconiosis and byssinosis.
2 In the calendar year 1975.
3 The disease may have been contracted long before death resulted.
4 Includes accidents to employees at work only if incapacity lasts for over 28 weeks and invalidity benefit is received.

stopped, irrespective of whether the injured person is able to go back to work or not, and because they can continue for life, these pensions greatly outnumber other forms of benefit for personal injury.

Table 22 Adjudication

Great Britain: 1975
i Industrial Injury Benefit   Numbers

	Total	Outcome in claimant's favour
Claims on local insurance offices	648,000	..[1]
Appeals to local tribunals against rejection of claim	1,558	563
References to regional medical services		
Relation of condition to injury	5,500	3,300
Period of incapacity longer than to be expected	69,500	32,400
Appeals to national insurance commissioners[2]	429	135

1 Proportion estimated to be at least 98 per cent.
2 Includes industrial disablement benefit and industrial death benefit.

ii Industrial Disablement Benefit   Numbers

	Total	Outcome in claimant's favour
Accidents and prescribed diseases (other than pneumoconiosis and byssinosis)		
Medical boards		
First examinations	115,000	..[1]
Reassessment and reviews	122,000	..[2]
Other examinations[3]	11,000	..
Medical appeal tribunals		
Appeals	8,129	3,416
References by Secretary of State	3,069	1,123
Pneumoconiosis and byssinosis		
Pneumoconiosis medical panels		
First examinations	3,057	771[4]
Re-examinations[5]	1,842	366[4]
Reassessments	14,728	..
Appeals on points of law to national insurance commissioners	61	48

1 Proportion estimated to be about 85 per cent.
2 Proportion estimated to be 70–80 per cent.
3 Mainly in connection with awards of special hardship or other allowances.
4 Disease diagnosed, giving entitlement to benefit.
5 Disease not previously diagnosed.

Injuries in a year

111 Table 21 contains a set of figures for cases arising in a year. In respect of injury benefit, figures are given both for fresh cases, and for the number of separate spells of absence, whether resulting from those or from earlier cases. The DHSS statistics make use of both concepts, though numbers of spells are more commonly recorded since they are more directly related to the payment of benefit.

Adjudication

112 Table 22 gives details of the numbers of cases dealt with at various stages of the adjudication procedures in 1975. A large part of the table relates to industrial disablement benefit, where medical examination is always necessary to establish the degree of disablement, and further examinations may be required at intervals.

Rates of benefit

113 Table 23 sets out the principal rates of benefit and allowances. The first column shows the rates in force from November 1976 to November 1977, which are those used in this report, in particular as the basis for estimates of cost. A second column gives the rates which came into force in November 1977.

Table 23 Principal rates of benefits and allowances

£ per week

	15 November 1976 to 13 November 1977	From 14 November 1977
Industrial injuries benefits		
Injury benefit		
Personal benefit	15·65	17·45
Adult dependant	8·00	9·10
First child	3·05[2]	3·50[3]
Other child	2·55[2]	3·00[3]
Industrial disablement benefit		
100% disability pension	25·00	28·60
Special hardship allowance		
Maximum rate	10·00	11·44
Constant attendance allowance		
Normal maximum	10·00	11·40
Industrial death benefit[1]		
Widow's pension for first 26 weeks	21·40	24·50
Subsequent widow's pension	15·85	18·05
First child	6·45[2]	7·40[4]
Other child	5·95[2]	6·90[4]
Sickness benefit		
Men and single women: 18 and over	12·90	14·70
Adult dependant	8·00	9·10
First child	3·05[2]	3·50[3]
Other child	2·55[2]	3·00[3]

Table 23—*continued*   £ per week

	15 November 1976 to 13 November 1977	From 14 November 1977
Invalidity pension		
Personal benefit	15·30	17·50
Adult dependant	9·20	10·50
First child	6·45[2]	7·40[4]
Other child	5·95[2]	6·90[4]
Invalidity allowance		
Up to 34	3·20	3·70
35–44	2·00	2·30
45–59 (men)	1·00	1·15
45–54 (women)	1·00	1·15
Widow's national insurance benefits[1]		
Widow's allowance for first 26 weeks	21·40	24·50
Widow's pension, standard rate	15·30	17·50
First child	6·45[2]	7·40[4]
Other child	5·95[2]	6·90[4]
Attendance allowance		
Lower rate	8·15	9·30
Higher rate	12·20	14·00
Mobility allowance[1]	5·00	7·00
Non-contributory invalidity pension		
Personal benefit	9·20	10·50
Adult dependant	5·60	6·30
First child	6·45[2]	7·40[4]
Other child	5·95[2]	6·90[4]
Invalid care allowance	9·20	10·50
Increase for adult dependant	5·60	6·30
Child benefit		
First child	1·00[2]	1·00
Each other child	1·50[2]	1·50
One-parent families: each child	1·50[2]	1·50
Retirement pension	15·30	17·50
Adult dependant	9·20	10·50

1 Taxable.

2 From April 1977.

3 From April 1978 rates will be £2·20 a week for each child, assuming child benefit is raised to £2·30 a week for each child.

4 From April 1978, rates will be £6·10 a week for each child, assuming child benefit is increased to £2·30 for each child.

Further information

114 Further information is contained in Social Security Statistics published annually by the Department of Health and Social Security, or can be obtained from their Statistics and Research Division, Friars House, 157–168 Blackfriars Road, London SE1 8EU. For Northern Ireland, information is obtainable from the Department of Health and Social Services, Statistics Branch, Castle Buildings, Stormont, Belfast.

CHAPTER 5

Other forms of compensation

115   The sources of compensation dealt with in this chapter are:

Occupational sick pay
Occupational pensions
First party insurance
Other sources of financial assistance, for example trade unions, friendly societies
and charities.

116   The basic information about occupational sick pay, occupational pensions
and some forms of insurance does not distinguish payments following injury
from those following disease.

Occupational sick pay

117   Information is available from a sample survey carried out by DHSS of
entitlement to occupational sick pay in September 1974.[9]

118   That survey showed 80 per cent of male employees and 73 per cent of
female employees as being covered by arrangements, formal or informal, for
pay during sick absence. Some of the employees covered would not have been
in their jobs long enough to have qualified for payment, and the proportions
who would have received any pay if sick or injured were about 70 per cent of
males and 64 per cent of females.

119   The proportion covered by sick pay schemes was lower for manual than
for non-manual workers. Details are given in Table 24. The percentages quoted
are for full time and part time workers, taken together.

120   Sick pay is usually paid for a limited time, and may be received for only
part of the period of sick absence. Table 25 gives estimates of the proportions
away sick at any one time who would be receiving sick pay. It distinguishes
those who had been away for six months or less. Even this group would include
some who had exhausted their entitlement to sick pay, and so the percentages
are lower than those quoted above for those receiving any sick pay. After 6
months it is probable that less than 10 per cent of employees would still be
receiving sick pay.

121   The table distinguishes those receiving 'full pay', though this might exclude
overtime pay or bonuses and commissions which were normally payable. The
table shows also the proportion of cases in which the payment would be

35

reduced by the amount of any national insurance benefits payable; the benefits deducted would normally include sickness, invalidity or injury benefit, but not industrial disablement benefit or the allowances associated with it.

Table 24 Coverage of sick pay

Great Britain: September 1974   Percentages

	Proportion covered by sick pay scheme	Proportion entitled to receive any sick pay
Males		
Manual	73	
Non-manual	94	
All	80	70
Females		
Manual	58	
Non-manual	87	
All	73	64
Both sexes		
Manual	69	
Non-manual	91	
All	77	68

Source: DHSS.

122   The DHSS survey did not cover some employments, for example in the civil service and the Post Office, with better than average sick pay entitlements. The percentages shown would therefore need to be increased to obtain those applicable to all employees.

123   On the other hand, downward adjustments would be needed to arrive at percentages appropriate to those who had suffered injury. The incidence of injury is greatest among manual workers, and also in certain industries, such as construction and transport, with below average entitlements to sick pay.

124   The second adjustment would outweigh the first. A broad estimate allowing for both is that roughly half those off work on any day as a result of injury sustained no more than 6 months earlier would be receiving some sick pay from their employers. Nearly 40 per cent would be receiving sick pay, full or partial, from which national insurance benefits had been deducted. This percentage provides the basis for the estimate made in Chapter 30 of the extent to which improvements in benefits might be offset by reductions in occupational sick pay.

Table 25 Estimated proportions of employees absent through sickness at any given time who would be entitled to sick pay

Great Britain: September 1974   Percentages

| | Proportion entitled to | | | |
| | Any pay | | Full pay | |
	All	With NI deductions	All	With NI deductions
Males				
In first 6 months	60–62	46–48	37–39	33–35
After 6 months	4–15	2–11	0– 2	0– 1
At any time	33–39	25–30	20–21	17–18
Females				
In first 6 months	52–54	41–43	39–41	33–35
After 6 months	2–10	1– 8	–	–
At any time	32–36	25–29	24–25	20–21

Source: DHSS.

Occupational pensions

125 The Government Actuary's Department carry out surveys of occupational pension schemes every few years. This summary makes use of the survey relating to the end of 1971.[10]

126 The results quoted may not necessarily indicate what the position is likely to be in the future. Changes are being made in occupational pension schemes to fit in with the new state pensions introduced by the Social Security Act 1975. In particular, any occupational scheme which is contracted out will have to provide pensions at or above a minimum level.

Membership of occupational pension schemes
127 About one half of all employees are members of occupational pension schemes. Membership is proportionately higher among men than among women, and among non-manual than among manual workers. Details are given in Table 26.

Premature retirement
128 Nearly all occupational schemes provide for pensions to be paid to members who have to give up work because of ill-health. The provisions, however, for the most part apply only to those who have been in the scheme for a minimum qualifying period.

129 The total numbers who retire from work early through injury are not exactly known. The number awarded occupational pensions is still more uncertain, but is probably not greater than 1,000 a year.

Table 26   Membership of occupational pension schemes
United Kingdom: 1971

	Number of employees	Members	
		Number	Percentage
	Millions	Millions	%
Men			
Manual	8·2[1]	4·1	50
Non-manual	5·8[1]	4·6	79
All	14·0	8·7	62
Women			
Manual	3·8[1]	0·6	16
Non-manual	4·9[1]	1·8	37
All	8·7	2·4	28
Both sexes			
Manual	12·0	4·7	39
Non-manual	10·7	6·4	60
All	22·7	11·1	49

1 Obtained by dividing the total in the proportions of manual
  to non-manual shown in table 2 of the GAD report for 1971.
Sources: Government Actuary's Department (GAD) and
         Department of Employment.

130   There are several ways in which pensions may be assessed. The member may receive from the date of his premature retirement the pension which has then accrued, but with a deduction to allow for its being paid earlier than the normal pension age. He may receive the accrued pension without any deduction. Or he may in certain circumstances receive more than the accrued pension, e.g. by being credited with 20 years' service when his actual service had been less. Table 27 shows how entitlements to pension were divided between these classes.

131   Schemes restricted to manual workers alone tend to have a rather poorer provision than other schemes; in particular enhancement of the accrued pension is far less common. Since manual workers suffer injury more frequently than other groups of employees, the benefits of those retiring early on account of injury would, in many cases, be less favourable than those indicated by the table.

Benefits following death
132   Occupational schemes usually provide for lump sum payments to be made following death in service. In many cases there is provision for pensions to be paid to widows, and more rarely, to widowers. Pensions usually continue

38

until death or remarriage. Where the member has himself paid contributions, these are normally refunded, with or without interest. The refunds may, however, be incorporated in lump sum payments, or be withheld where a widow's pension is paid.

Table 27   Nature of pension entitlement

United Kingdom: 1971

	Percentage of scheme members
Accrued pension with enhancement	41
Accrued pension	20
Less than accrued pension	33
Other or no provision	6
All scheme members	100

Source: GAD.

133   The number of male employees who die as the result of injury each year is between 6,000 and 7,000. Approximately half would be members of occupational pension schemes, and not all of them would leave dependants or be entitled to benefits for them.

134   The division of benefits payable following deaths of male members between lump sums and widows' pensions is set out in Table 28. Benefits limited to the return of members' contributions are disregarded.

Table 28   Nature of death benefits

United Kingdom: 1971

	Percentage of male members
Widow's pension and lump sum	42
Widow's pension only	14
Lump sum only	59
Neither	5
All male members	100

Source: GAD.

135   Once again, provision for widows of men who have died following injury, predominantly manual workers, may be less favourable than that for all schemes taken together.

Other provision by employers

136　The occupational pensions schemes covered by the Government Actuary's reports do not represent the whole of the provision made by employers for injured employees. Additional *ex gratia* payments may be made, especially in respect of injuries at work. In particular, special provision has been made for those working in some especially dangerous occupations in the public sector who are forced to retire by injury sustained while on duty; arrangements of this kind apply to policemen and firemen, and to coal miners forced to retire by pneumoconiosis.

Magnitude of benefits

137　Occupational pensions paid following retirement or death through injury are usually a good deal smaller than state benefits. Many of those entitled to them have had only a few years' membership in a particular scheme. In 1974, the median weekly payment was £5·80 for married couples and less than £5 for single persons.[11]

138　The aggregate amount paid by employers to the injured or their dependants cannot be estimated with any accuracy from the information available, but is unlikely to be more than £5 million a year at January 1977 prices.

139　Some 80 per cent of all occupational pensions are increased from time to time to allow for changes in the cost of living. This percentage may not apply exactly to pensions paid following early retirement, or to widows' pensions, considered separately. In the private sector, increases have not generally kept pace with the increases in the cost of living.

First party insurance

140　The survey of personal injuries showed that about 10 per cent of those injured had private insurance cover, and about 7 per cent made successful claims. Most of these claims would have been under personal accident insurance.

Personal accident insurance

141　Personal accident insurance is usually taken out for a short period such as a year, though it may be renewed. In the event of accident it usually provides benefits in the form of periodic payments for a fixed period together with a lump sum.

142　The aggregate amount paid out under personal accident insurance was £36·1 million in the twelve months ending in August 1975.

Permanent health insurance

143　Permanent health insurance provides cover against loss of income. Cover is provided for an extended period – often until retirement age – on payment of an annual premium. Payments are made if the insured person is unable to follow his normal occupation either because of sickness or accident.

144   Statistics compiled by the Life Offices Association, which may not be quite complete, show 784,000 persons covered by permanent health insurance in 1975. A substantial proportion of them were covered by group policies taken out by employers on behalf of their employees to fill the gap between sick pay and occupational pensions. Permanent health insurance has been expanding rapidly in recent years.

145   Total payments under permanent health insurance in respect of injury are estimated to have amounted to about £1 million in 1975.

Life insurance
146   The family expenditure survey for 1975 showed that 79 per cent of households were paying premiums on life policies.

147   The majority of life policies are so-called industrial policies for relatively small sums.

148   Information provided by the Life Associations shows 85·8 million industrial policies in force at the end of 1976, with an average sum assured of £111, compared with 18·5 million ordinary life policies (including those linked to particular forms of investment), with an average sum assured of £3,865. The aggregate sum assured by ordinary life business was £71,500 million against £9,560 million for industrial business.

149   The number of industrial policies is greater than the number in the population, many people holding more than one policy. A substantial number are fully paid up policies on which no further premiums are being paid, which may have been issued after premium payments had lapsed. The plurality of policies is shown again by figures of claims published by the Chief Registrar of Friendly Societies,[12] from which it may be deduced that there were about 1¾ million claims in 1975, as compared with 646,000 deaths in Great Britain in that year. Assuming that those covered by life insurance represented 79 per cent of all those who died, they must have held on the average something like three industrial policies each. The average amount paid on each policy in 1975 was £52.

150   The average amount claimed following deaths is smaller than the average sum assured under policies in force since the policies on which payment is made tend to be those of older date.

151   This information does not make it possible to estimate the value of all payments on life insurance policies to those who are injured. There is no published information about the extent to which individuals are covered, distinguishing between industrial and ordinary life policies, between men and women, between manual and non-manual workers and non-workers, or between those of different ages. Nor are there any statistics giving the average amounts paid out on ordinary life policies following death.

152   For industrial policies, some kind of estimate can be attempted. If it were assumed that those who died following injury were covered to the same extent as the whole population, and that amounts paid on their policies – being

more recent – were above the average, it could be deduced that payments on their industrial life policies might approach £5 million a year at January 1977 prices; but that is only part of the story.

Other financial benefits

153 Other sources of financial assistance following injury consist principally of trade unions, friendly societies and charities. The personal injury survey recorded 5 per cent of all the injured, or not quite 10 per cent of injured employees, as receiving assistance from such sources. Trade unions accounted for the great majority of payments. The average amount received was small – less than £20 in 1973.

PART II

Statistics relating to injuries of particular kinds

CHAPTER 6

Work injuries and work illnesses

The working population

154 The working population of the United Kingdom stands at over 26 million. Just over 60 per cent of the work force are men. The number of men in the working population has changed little in recent years, but the number of women has been increasing. About 7 per cent of the work force are self employed.

Work injuries

Numbers of work injuries and deaths

155 Information about the number of people injured or killed each year as a result of accidents at work is available from two main sources: DHSS records of people receiving industrial injury benefit, and the numbers of accidents reported to the Health and Safety Executive. In addition the personal injury survey provides an estimate of the numbers injured at work during 1973. For most purposes the DHSS figures provide the most reliable information about employees injured at work; the numbers of injuries reported to the Health and Safety Executive are known to be incomplete, particularly in respect of the less severe injuries, and the same is true of the personal injury survey.

156 The results of the survey suggest, however, that the DHSS records may not include all employees who have injuries. This seems to be particularly true of

Table 29 Numbers of people killed or injured
in accidents at work

United Kingdom: Estimates in round numbers
based on data for 1972–1975

	Employees	Self employed
Death	1,300	..
Injury	680,000	40,000

Sources: Employees: Based on records kept by
DHSS, with allowance for those who do
not qualify or do not claim.

Self employed: Personal injury survey, 1973.

45

women. It may be that some people do not claim because they are unaware
of their entitlement, or because they continue to be paid by their employer.
The estimate of injuries to employees in Table 29 is based on a social security
figure of a yearly average of 610,000 people claiming industrial injury benefit
in the years 1972/73 to 1974/75, with an allowance made for those who have
injuries at work but do not claim benefit. The number of deaths among
employees is derived from the number of claims for industrial death benefit
for the same years, adjusted to allow for those who die leaving no dependants.
The number of injuries to the self employed comes from the personal injury
survey and relates to 1973. Over 85 per cent of the injured and almost all those
who die following injury are men.

Work injuries to the self employed
157   There are no official figures for injuries to the self employed while they
are at work since they do not qualify for industrial injury benefit. The personal
injury survey showed that self employed men were less likely than employees to
be incapacitated for normal activities for four days or more, through injury
either at work or elsewhere.

Work related injuries
158   There are two other categories of injury associated with work. Some
injuries occur on the way to or from work and others at the place of work
outside working hours – for example while attending a meeting or taking part
in sporting activities. The estimated annual numbers of work related injuries
are given in Table 30.

Table 30   Numbers of work related injuries

United Kingdom: Estimates in round numbers for 1973

	Employees	Self employed
On way to or from work	110,000	7,000
At place of work outside working hours	30,000	1,000

Source: Personal injury survey.

159   About 60 per cent of the accidents which occurred while travelling to or
from work involved motor vehicles.

Trends in work accidents
160   The number of accidents at work has been declining quite steeply. The
number of employees receiving injury benefit was 30 per cent lower in 1974/75
than 10 years earlier. In the same period, the number of accidental deaths
leading to payment of industrial death benefit fell by 36 per cent. (Figures are
given in Chapter 2.) Part of the decline was due to lower levels of employment
and output. The number of insured male employees recorded by DHSS fell

by 6 per cent during the 10 years, and the number who were at work, excluding the unemployed, by a further 2½ per cent. Unemployment has risen further since 1975.

161 Examination of the figures shows that the reduction in accidents was concentrated in particular areas. Most of it took place in the coal mining industry, where injuries in 1974/75 numbered hardly more than a quarter of those 10 years earlier. This was the result of both a reduction in the incidence of injury and a decline in the number of miners. The number of injuries in the construction industry also fell, though by a smaller proportion. Elsewhere, changes were relatively small. It seems unlikely that the fall in the number of work accidents which occurred in the last decade will be repeated in the next. The scope for further reduction in the coal mining industry is now more limited, and the decline in male employment should not go much further.

Duration of incapacity
162 Injuries to employees at work tend to lead to longer spells of absence than injuries elsewhere, with the exception that a slightly smaller proportion go over 6 months (Table 31). Even so, more than two thirds of the spells of absence following work injury last no more than 4 weeks.

Table 31 Duration of spells of incapacity for work following industrial and other injury

Employees in Great Britain: Averages for the three years June 1972 – June 1975

	Industrial injury[1]		Other injury[2]	
	Percentage of spells terminating in period	Cumulative percentage of spells terminating by end of period	Percentage of spells terminating in period	Cumulative percentage of spells terminating by end of period
4 days–1 week	13·8	13·8	21·3	21·3
Over 1 week–2 weeks	24·7	38·5	29·1	50·4
Over 2 weeks–4 weeks	29·4	67·9	26·5	76·9
Over 4 weeks–8 weeks	19·5	87·4	13·9	90·8
Over 8 weeks–3 months	7·0	94·4	4·6	95·4
Over 3 months–6 months	4·1	98·5	3·0	98·4
Over 6 months	1·5		1·7	

1 For which injury benefit paid.
2 For which sickness or invalidity benefit paid.

Source: Based on DHSS statistics.

Table 32 Injury rates by industry

Male employees in Great Britain: Averages for the three years June 1972 – June 1975

	Number of injuries at work[1]	Average number of insured employees[2]	Incidence of injury
		Thousands	Number of injuries per 1,000 employees
Agriculture, forestry and fishing	11	271	41
Mining and quarrying	76	383	198
Food, drink and tobacco	23	489	47
Coal and petroleum products	2	43	49
Chemical and allied industries	12	343	35
Metal manufacture	38	492	77
Mechanical engineering	37	1,114	33
Instrument engineering	1	105	13
Electrical engineering	11	567	19
Shipbuilding and marine engineering	10	176	57
Vehicles	18	703	26
Metal goods not elsewhere specified	21	441	48
Textiles	11	339	32
Leather, leather goods, fur	1	28	38
Clothing and footwear	1	127	11
Bricks, pottery, glass, cement, etc.	16	253	63
Timber, furniture, etc.	14	243	58
Paper, printing and publishing	11	414	27
Other manufacturing industries	9	226	42
Construction	72	1,309	55
Gas, electricity and water	10	323	31
Transport and communication	44	930	47
Distributive trades	38	1,148	33
Insurance, banking, finance and business services	2	526	4
Professional and scientific services	8	1,003	8
Miscellaneous services	18	855	21
Public administration and defence	24	740	32
Totals	542	13,592	40

1 Fresh accidents leading to payment of injury benefit.
2 These figures differ from Department of Employment figures.

Source: Based on DHSS statistics.

Disablement
163 Each year about a sixth of those who receive industrial injury benefit as a result of an accident at work go on to draw disablement benefit. The vast majority are assessed at less than 20 per cent disability, and receive a gratuity, the remainder drawing pensions.

Industrial analysis of injury
164 Table 32 gives an industrial analysis of injury rates for male employees only. Injury rates for females do not vary greatly between industries, averaging less than 10 per 1,000, and exceeding 20 per 1,000 only in food, drink and tobacco.

165 Within many of the industries or groups of industries listed above there may be occupations with widely differing risks of injury, particularly of severe injury. For instance, the group agriculture, forestry and fishing, which taken as a whole has an incidence of injury close to the average for all industries, includes deep sea fishing, which in terms of death is one of the most risky occupations. Some indication of the more dangerous occupations is given by the figures of deaths in Table 33. The figures are compiled from a number of sources and may therefore not be exactly comparable, particularly in respect of the definitions of numbers employed.

Table 33 Death rates in dangerous occupations

Number of deaths a year per 1,000 employees

Coalmining[1]	0·24	
Quarrying[1]	0·30	
Offshore oil installations[2]	2·8	
All manufacturing[1]	0·04	
Iron and steel making[1]		0·12
Shipbuilding[1]		0·13
Construction[1]	0·18	
Railways[3]	0·21	
Merchant shipping[4]	1·33	
Deep sea trawlers[4]	2·47	

Sources:
1 Health and Safety Executive: annual average for the years 1973–75.
2 Department of Energy: annual average for the years 1965–74.
3 Department of Transport: annual average for the years 1973–75.
4 Department of Trade: annual average for the years 1966–75.

Causes of injury
166 An indication of the extent to which work injuries might be prevented is given by an analysis of a random sample of accidents in factories and in the

construction industry during the second half of 1972, carried out by the Factory Inspectorate.[13] They found that for about half of all accidents, no reasonably practicable precautions were available. Where precautions were available but not taken, the failure to do so was more often the responsibility of management than work people.

167 The causes of accidents at work, as of other accidents, are, however, complex. A research paper[14] prepared for the Robens Committee on Safety and Health at Work, which reviewed the relevant literature, found that there was no agreed theory identifying the factors leading to work accidents.

Tort claims in respect of work injuries
168 About 115,000 tort claims were made in 1973 in respect of work injuries, of which about 90,000 resulted in some payment being made. Some claims were for injuries leading to less than four days off work, and consequently not included in the statistics of injuries given above. Evidence from employers showed wide variations in the proportions of injuries compensated through the tort system. In one case it was as much as a half of all injuries involving lost time. A nationwide employer indicated large regional variations in the proportion of accidents resulting in claims.

169 The average amount paid in tort compensation, at January 1977 prices, was nearly £900 in the case of injury and about £10,000 in fatal cases.

International comparisons
170 No international compilation exists of the incidence of work injury, and it is difficult to make useful comparisons from countries' own records because of widely differing definitions, both of injury and of numbers employed.

171 In respect of fatal accidents at work, the International Labour Office compiles comparative statistics. Table 34 gives death rates per 1,000 standard man years of 300 days for the year 1973 (or the nearest available equivalent). The figures for Great Britain are on a slightly different basis from those given elsewhere in this chapter. Death rates from accidents at work are lower in Great Britain than in most other industrialised countries. Although the data in the table are not all on an exactly comparable basis, the differences are unlikely to be sufficiently important to invalidate this conclusion. United States figures relate numbers of accidents to man hours, and are omitted as not being comparable.

Occupational diseases and work illnesses

Prescribed diseases
172 Each year in the United Kingdom 16,000 people contract an industrial disease prescribed under the Social Security Act 1975. The numbers in the main categories are given in Table 35. About a quarter of the total are women, a rather higher proportion than for industrial injuries.

Other work related illnesses
173   An investigation of other illnesses ascribed by the sufferer in some degree to conditions at work was carried out as part of the personal injury survey. The investigation is described in Chapter 19. The results suggested that there were substantial numbers of illnesses where there appeared to the sufferer to be a probable link between the illness and conditions at work, possibly amounting to five times the number of prescribed diseases recorded by DHSS.

Table 34   International comparisons of incidence of death from industrial accidents

Deaths per 1,000 standard man years of 300 days: 1973

Country	Coal mining	Manu-facturing	Con-struction
Great Britain	0·43	0·04	0·21
France	0·64	0·10	0·45
Federal Republic of Germany		0·17	0·37
Netherlands		0·04	0·12
Norway		0·08	0·11
Switzerland		0·13	0·63
Israel		0·22	0·29
Australia	1·69		
New Zealand	0·64	0·04[1]	0·26[1]
Canada	2·26	0·15	0·96

1 1970.

Source: International Labour Office.

Table 35   New cases of prescribed diseases

United Kingdom: Averages in round numbers for the three years June 1972 – June 1975	Numbers
Pneumoconiosis and byssinosis	900
Beat knee	1,000
Traumatic inflammation of the tendons of the hand or forearm	3,400
Non-infective dermatitis	10,000
Other	700
Total	16,000

Source: DHSS.

Trends in prescribed diseases

174   The numbers of people diagnosed as having contracted prescribed diseases other than pneumoconiosis and byssinosis have been falling steadily in recent years.

175   The numbers of people diagnosed as suffering from pneumoconiosis and byssinosis fell rapidly during the 1960's, but in recent years have become more stable. In 1975 and 1976, they were higher than in the immediately preceding years, possibly because a new compensation scheme introduced in the coal-mining industry in September 1974 led more miners to come forward for examination. Pneumoconiosis takes many years to develop and the smaller number of miners exposed to a lower degree of risk as the result of improved conditions should lead in the long term to a further reduction in the number of cases.

176   The numbers of cases of byssinosis recorded rose in 1974 and again in 1975, following a widening of the conditions of eligibility for industrial disablement benefit.

Table 36   Duration of spells of incapacity for work resulting from prescribed and other diseases

Employees in Great Britain: Averages for the three years June 1972 – June 1975

	Prescribed diseases[1]		All other diseases[2]	
	Percentage of spells terminating in period	Cumulative percentage of spells terminating by end of period	Percentage of spells terminating in period	Cumulative percentage of spells terminating by end of period
4 days – 1 week	5·4	5·4	28·1	28·1
Over 1 week – 2 weeks	20·2	25·6	30·3	58·4
Over 2 weeks – 4 weeks	29·2	54·8	21·5	79·9
Over 4 weeks – 8 weeks	24·8	79·6	10·7	90·6
Over 8 weeks – 3 months	9·8	89·4	4·5	95·1
Over 3 months – 6 months	6·8	96·2	2·7	97·8
Over 6 months	3·7		2·2	
Total	100·0		100·0	

1 Based on spells of incapacity for which injury benefit was paid. Pneumoconiosis and byssinosis are excluded.
2 Based on spells of incapacity (other than those due to injury) for which sickness benefit was paid.
Source: DHSS.

177   A recent increase in the number of cases of pneumoconiosis diagnosed in the asbestos industry may be due at least in part to an underlying increase in incidence in this industry. Another reason for it may be that publicity given to the dangers of absestos has encouraged people to come forward for examination. It is hoped that improvements in safety standards for those at risk will lead to a reversal in the upward trend in the number of cases diagnosed.

178   Occupational deafness was added to the list of prescribed diseases in February 1975, and some 3,000 awards of industrial disablement benefit have been made. There will be many more when resources permit the range of qualifying occupations to be extended.

Duration of prescribed diseases

179   Incapacity for work resulting from prescribed diseases generally lasts longer than that from illnesses not connected with work, or from industrial injuries (Table 36).

Tort claims in respect of industrial diseases

180   About 3,000 tort claims were made in 1973 in respect of industrial diseases, of which about 1,700 resulted in some payment. Although only 57 per cent of claims resulted in payment compared with 78 per cent for claims in respect of industrial injury, the average amount paid – £2,000 for non-fatal cases at January 1977 prices – was more than twice as much.

181   Coalminers do not now make tort claims for pneumoconiosis, and no such claims are included in the figures given above. Instead, special compensation is provided by the National Coal Board under an agreement made with the National Union of Mineworkers in September 1974.

CHAPTER 7

Road

Numbers of injuries and deaths

182   Statistics of road accidents reported to the police are published annually by the Department of Transport and by the Department of the Environment in Northern Ireland. Many of the injuries recorded are slight and do not fall within the definition adopted here, which includes only injuries leading to at least 4 days' incapacity for work or an equivalent degree of severity for people not at work. On the other hand, investigation has shown that not all injuries are reported to the police; one study suggests that 15 per cent of serious injuries and 30 per cent of slight injuries treated in hospital are not reported.[15] Injuries to pedal cyclists and bus passengers are particularly likely to go unreported.

183   For the sake of consistency with the estimates of injuries given elsewhere in this report, the estimates of numbers of road injuries given are based on information from the personal injury survey, with approximate allowance for under-reporting. The estimates go somewhat wider than the published figures. They include injuries involving road vehicles off the public highway, and injuries which are seldom reported to the police – for example, those involving only minor injury to the rider or driver of the vehicle. The classification of injuries is described more fully in Chapter 15.

184   For detailed analyses of the characteristics of the injured, and for an indication of trends in the number and rate of casualties, the official statistics have been used.

Table 37   Annual numbers of deaths and injuries involving road vehicles

United Kingdom: Estimates based
on data for 1973–75   Numbers

	Deaths	Injuries
Motor vehicle	7,624	349,000
Non-motor vehicle only	72	54,000
Total	7,696	403,000

Sources: Registrars General.
          Personal injury survey.

185 Figures for deaths are taken from those published by the Registrars General for England and Wales, Scotland and Northern Ireland.

186 Altogether about 7,700 people are killed and 400,000 injured by road vehicles in the United Kingdom each year. Almost all of the fatal accidents and about 85 per cent of the injuries occur on the public highway. The great majority of road injuries and deaths involve motor vehicles (Table 37).

187 About 13 per cent of injuries occur while the injured person is at work. A further 18 per cent take place on the way to or from work. Details are given in Table 38.

Table 38 Annual numbers of road vehicle injuries, by circumstances of injury

United Kingdom: 1973   Thousands

	Total	While at work	To or from work	Other
Moving motor vehicle	284	24	65	195
Stationary motor vehicle	65	29	4	32
Non-motor vehicle only	54	1	5	48
Total	403	54	74	275

Source: Personal injury survey.

Severity of injury

188 Apart from accidents in the air, accidents involving road vehicles are more likely to have serious or fatal consequences than those which occur in other ways. They account for about 13 per cent of all injuries, but for about 17 per cent of spells of hospital in-patient treatment for injury and as much as 34 per cent of all accidental deaths. People injured in road accidents are more likely to receive multiple injuries, and are likely to be incapacitated for a longer than average period.

Trends in the numbers of road traffic casualties

189 Since 1930 the number of motor vehicles on the road has grown more than sevenfold, but the annual number of injuries has not quite doubled and the number of deaths has fallen slightly. In terms of casualties per vehicle (and, for the period for which figures are available, casualties per vehicle mile also), there has been a substantial and continuous improvement in road safety. Factors which have contributed to this improvement include constantly improving road and vehicle design, and legislation to promote safety.

190 Since the mid-1960's there has been a slower rate of increase in the number of vehicles and in the mileage travelled than previously. The number of casualties dropped in 1968 following the introduction of the breathalyser,

and again in 1974 following the oil crisis, after which in each case it increased again, though remaining below its peak level in 1965 and 1966. For the future, it has been assumed that any tendency for casualties to increase as a result of the forecast growth in vehicle usage will be offset by developments in road and vehicle safety, and that the numbers of deaths and injuries may consequently be taken as approximately constant.

191 The statistics of road accidents in Great Britain published by the Department of Transport give a breakdown of injuries by class of road user. This information is restricted to accidents on the public highway reported to the police, and probably understates the proportion of pedal cyclists and bus passengers injured. The figures show that about a quarter of those injured are car drivers, a fifth are pedestrians and a similar proportion are car passengers. Most of the remainder are riders or passengers of two-wheeled vehicles.

Table 39   Road injuries and deaths by class of road user

Great Britain: Averages for 1973–75

	Killed		Injured	
	Annual number	Percentage	Annual number	Percentage
Pedestrians	2,600	37·8	72,040	22·0
Pedal cyclists	300	4·4	19,650	6·0
Two-wheeled motor vehicles:				
Riders	690	10·0	44,130	13·5
Passengers	90	1·3	4,480	1·4
Cars and taxis:				
Drivers	1,570	22·8	79,800	24·4
Passengers	1,170	17·0	72,500	22·1
Public service vehicle occupants	80	1·2	14,280	4·4
Goods vehicle occupants	340	4·9	18,660	5·7
Other classes of road user	40	0·6	2,000	0·6
Total	6,880	100·0	327,540	100·0

Source: Based on Department of Transport statistics.

192 At all ages, men are more likely to be injured than women. Among the groups most at risk are users of two-wheeled motor vehicles – predominantly males in the 16–29 age group. Among pedestrian casualties, there were proportionately more children and elderly people than people of working age. The personal injury survey showed, however, that of all those injured by road vehicles, a higher proportion were economically active, and a lower proportion were children, than among the injured population as a whole.

193 The most common type of road accident involves a collision between two vehicles (Table 40).

Table 40 Vehicle involvement

Great Britain: Averages for 1973–75   Percentages

Accidents involving	
Two vehicles	46
One vehicle and pedestrian	27
One vehicle only	20
More than two vehicles	6
All accidents	100

Source: Department of Transport.

Road accident statistics for Northern Ireland

194 The pattern of road accident casualties in the Northern Ireland statistics differs from that in Great Britain (Table 41). In total fewer casualties are recorded in relation to the population than there are in Great Britain, though the death rate is higher and the rate of serious injuries is close to that for Great Britain. Since car ownership is considerably lower in Northern Ireland than in Great Britain, casualty rates per vehicle would be higher there at all levels of severity.

Table 41 Casualties on the roads in Great Britain and Northern Ireland

Injuries reported to the police: Annual averages for 1973–75

	Great Britain	Northern Ireland
Numbers of:		
Deaths	6,880	320
Serious injuries	82,880	2,290
Slight injuries	244,680	5,110
Total casualties	334,440	7,720
Rates per 1,000 population:		
Deaths	0·13	0·21
Serious injuries	1·5	1·5
Slight injuries	4·5	3·3
Total casualties	6·1	5·0

Sources: Department of Transport (Great Britain).
              Department of the Environment (Northern Ireland).

195   The Department of the Environment, Northern Ireland suggested that although there were relatively fewer accidents in Northern Ireland than in Great Britain, those that occurred were likely to have more serious consequences. An alternative interpretation is that true casualty rates for all degrees of severity are higher in Northern Ireland than in Great Britain, but that a larger proportion of injuries, especially slight injuries, go unrecorded.

Causes of accidents

196   The Transport and Road Research Laboratory made a detailed study of 2,130 road accidents which took place in the Thames Valley police district between March 1970 and February 1974. It was found that human errors were the predominant cause of accidents, though often associated with other factors.

Table 42   Causes of accidents

March 1970 – February 1974   Percentages

Cause of accidents:	
Human errors alone	65
+ road environment	24
+ vehicle defects	$4\frac{1}{2}$
Road environment alone	$2\frac{1}{2}$
Vehicle defect alone	$2\frac{1}{2}$
Road environment + vehicle defect	$\frac{1}{4}$
All three factors	$1\frac{1}{4}$
All causes	100

Source: Transport and Road Research Laboratory.

197   In the same study, drivers or riders of vehicles were found to be at least partly to blame in nearly 60 per cent of accidents. Pedestrians were at least partly to blame in nearly 80 per cent of accidents to themselves. The commonest contributory faults were carelessness or lack of attention and, for motorists, driving too fast. As a cause of accidents, irresponsible or reckless driving was relatively infrequent, and deliberately aggressive driving extremely rare.

Alcohol and road accidents

198   Alcohol was found to have been the commonest cause of impairment of drivers in the accidents studied. Altogether 16 per cent of all drivers were known to have consumed alcohol shortly before their accident. Other studies by the Transport and Road Research Laboratory have suggested that the Road Safety Act 1967, which introduced the use of the breathalyser, brought about a substantial reduction in casualties, but that its effects have now largely worn off. The Blennerhassett Committee on drinking and driving stated in their

report[16] that, according to coroners' returns for England and Wales, a third of drivers who died in road accidents in 1974 had blood alcohol levels over the legal limit. This proportion was twice that in 1968, the first full year after the introduction of the breathalyser.

Tort compensation for road injuries

199   There are around 100,000 tort claims in respect of death or injury resulting from motor vehicle accidents each year. Motor vehicle accidents account for 70 per cent of all claims in respect of death and about 40 per cent of claims in respect of non-fatal injury. Altogether 96 per cent of motor vehicle claims result in the payment of some compensation. The numbers of claims and amounts paid in compensation are shown in Table 43.

Table 43   Tort compensation for motor vehicle injuries

United Kingdom: Estimates in round numbers for 1973

	Claims	Payments	Average payment[1]
	Numbers		£
Non-fatal injuries	98,300	94,600	1,080
Fatalities	3,900	3,700	4,300
Total	102,200	98,300	1,200

1 At January 1977 prices.

Sources: Insurance survey.
         Survey of organisations carrying their own risk.

200   Included in the figures given above are about 1,500 claims in which an award was made by the Motor Insurers' Bureau, because the motorist at fault was not adequately insured or could not be traced.

201   People injured in motor vehicle accidents are more likely to obtain tort compensation than people injured in other ways; 25 per cent of those with motor vehicle injuries obtain compensation as compared with $6\frac{1}{2}$ per cent of all injured people. Where death results, compensation is obtained for about half the motor vehicle fatalities as compared with 20 per cent of all accidental deaths.

No claim discounts

202   Insurance statistics indicate that the system of variable no claim discounts succeeds fairly well in classifying holders of motor policies according to their likely degree of accident involvement. Accident involvement, as measured by the average number of injury claims, increases fairly steadily as the number o' years of no claim discount decreases; for those allowed no discount the average number of injury claims is more than three times that for those allowed 4 or more years. The close correlation is mainly the result of identifying young and

inexperienced drivers. There is no firm evidence that experienced drivers who lose their no claim bonus are more likely to have an accident than those who do not, or that the system provides a deterrent effect.

International comparisons

203   Table 44 gives rates of car ownership and death from road accidents in 1974 for selected countries. Deaths from road accidents in Great Britain are, in relation both to population and to numbers of vehicles, among the lowest in the world.

Table 44   Road death rates in selected countries

1974

	Road motor vehicles per 100 population	Road deaths per 100,000 population	Road deaths per 10,000 vehicles	Car user deaths per 100 million car kilometres
Great Britain	32	13	4	1
Northern Ireland	25	20	8	..
Federal Republic of Germany	33	24	7	3
France	42	28	7	4
Netherlands	41	19	5	2
Sweden	35[1]	15	4[1]	1
Canada	45	28	6	..
United States of America	61	21	3	2[2]
Australia	47[1]	27	6[1]	..
New Zealand	49	22	5	3

1 Vehicle figures exclude mopeds.
2 1973.

Sources: Statistics of Road Traffic Accidents in Europe 1974. Economic Commission for Europe.
World Road Statistics 1975. International Roads Federation.
Department of the Environment, Northern Ireland.

CHAPTER 8

Other transport

204 Information about transport injuries other than the road and motor vehicle injuries considered in Chapter 7 is available from a number of sources, with varying coverage, and using different classifications.

Personal injury survey

205 The personal injury survey in principle covered the whole field of transport injuries. It provides the basis for an estimate that in 1973 there were about 60,000 transport injuries other than on the roads or involving motor vehicles designed for use on the roads. About half of them occurred in the course of sporting activities of various kinds. Most of these resulted from falls from horses. Others involved scrambler motorcycles and yachts. Non-sporting injuries in the residual category included injuries involving agricultural tractors when not on the road, and industrial trucks or mobile cranes, as well as air, sea or rail injuries.

Other information

206 The remaining information, including that derived from death registrations, is limited to casualties in the air, at sea or on inland waters, or on the railways. Such cases represent only a small proportion of all personal injuries – only 2 per cent of deaths, and a smaller proportion still of non-fatal injuries. For these forms of transport, as for motor transport, the ratio of deaths to non-fatal injuries is appreciably greater than for other kinds of activity. In air accidents indeed there are more deaths than serious injuries.

207 A substantial proportion of those injured on merchant ships or on the railways, and a smaller proportion in the air, are employees, and there is consequently a degree of overlap with work injuries.

Death registrations

208 The Registrars General distinguish air, water transport, and railway accidents, but not other transport accidents apart from road and motor vehicle accidents. Their figures cover deaths registered in the United Kingdom, and do not include deaths of British residents in sea or air accidents elsewhere in the world.

209 An analysis of deaths involving other forms of transport than motor vehicles, excluding suicides and homicides, is given in Table 45.

61

Table 45   Accidental deaths involving air, water or rail transport[1]

United Kingdom: Averages for 1973, 1974 and 1975   Numbers

	Total	Males	Females
Air transport	94	77	17
Water transport	158	149	9
Railways	182	151	31
Total	434	377	57

1 Including deaths at work. Excluding 4 deaths not classified.
Source: Registrars General.

210   Analyses of the deaths involving water transport in England and Wales in 1974 and 1975 show that over half of them were deaths by drowning from small boats.

211   The official death statistics show 182 deaths a year in railway accidents, averaged from 1973 to 1975, which is consistent with a figure of 208, excluding suicides, derived from Department of Transport statistics for the same period, with a wider coverage.

Air accidents

212   For aircraft on the British register, the average numbers killed and seriously injured in the ten year period from 1966 to 1975 were as shown in Table 46. About 90 per cent of the casualties were passengers and about 10 per cent crew members.

Table 46   Casualties in aircraft on the British register

Averages for 1966–1975   Numbers

	Killed	Seriously injured
Public services[1]	91	10
Other flights	30	10

1 Including air taxis.
Source: Civil Aviation Authority.

213   Statistics of numbers of accidents to aircraft are also published.[17] In the ten year period from 1966 to 1975, accidents to British registered aircraft on public services averaged about 15 a year, and on other flights about 150 a year. The accident rate per flying hour was much less on public services than on other flights – which include training and commercial flights as well as flights by private aircraft.

214   The number of accidents on public services was fairly stable, a declining rate of accidents per flying hour being offset by an increase in flying hours. For private aircraft, there was an upward trend in the number of accidents, although it was more than accounted for by the growth in flying hours.

Casualties on merchant ships
215   Deaths on ships registered in the United Kingdom are analysed by the Department of Trade.[18] They include deaths after discharge abroad, but not deaths ashore in the United Kingdom.

216   In most years no more than 10 passengers die on British ships as the result of accident. Accidental deaths among crews average about 75 a year. Deaths from accidents on board and through falling overboard are commoner than deaths resulting from damage to or loss of vessels.

217   Injuries to seamen are reported to the General Council of British Shipping. Their information excludes vessels under 200 tons, but includes United Kingdom owned ships registered abroad.

218   A special analysis limited to seamen resident in the United Kingdom showed about 1,500 injuries each year leading to four or more days off duty. (This criterion implies a somewhat greater degree of severity than it would ashore since an injured man at sea may continue working where a shore man with a comparable injury would not.) There are more accidents in port than at sea. Many arise from slips, trips, or falls, often from one level to another, or from being struck by moving objects.

219   The risk of death is nearly one a year for each 1,000 men at risk, a rate appreciably higher than for any industry ashore, though less than the rate of about $2\frac{1}{2}$ per 1,000 for deep sea trawlers. The incidence of injury, however, is no greater than for manufacturing industry. Casualty rates may be expected to be higher at sea than ashore to the extent that they include casualties during off-duty periods as well as during working hours.

Inland waters
220   The Report of the Home Office Working Party on Water Safety[19] gives an analysis of 1,069 deaths by drowning in Great Britain in the twelve month period from November 1974 to October 1975. They ranged from drownings in the bath to drownings at sea, and included 529 drownings in rivers, canals, locks, lakes or reservoirs, and weirs. Only a minority of these involved boats, the majority occurring while swimming, or resulting from falling in from the bank.

Railway casualties
221   Statistics for Great Britain compiled by the Chief Inspecting Officer of Railways and published by the Department of Transport[20] include injuries to railway employees only if they led to four or more days off work, but include all reported injuries to other people.

222   The statistics are summarised in Table 47. They show that the largest category of deaths on the railways consists of suicides, and the second largest of trespassers.

223   Apart from suicides and trespassers, railway deaths are about evenly divided between railway staff and passengers. For railway staff, they mainly arise from having to work on the line, and for passengers from falling out of trains in motion and from accidents when boarding or alighting. Accidents involving large numbers of passenger deaths are rare.

Table 47   Casualties on the railways

Great Britain: Averages for 1973, 1974 and 1975   Numbers

	Killed	Seriously injured	Slightly injured
Passengers	47	143	5,106
Railway staff	45	600[2]	5,140[2]
Trespassers			
Children[1]	20	45	4
Others	83	32	15
Suicides	166	–	–
Attempted suicides	–	27	11
Others	13	32	209
Totals	374	879	10,485

1 Aged up to 16.
2 Partly estimated.
Source: Based on Department of Transport statistics.

224   There are more injuries to railway staff than to passengers, especially when allowance is made for the recording of a wider range of injuries to the latter. The commonest type of passenger accident occurs while going up or down steps at a station. Among railway staff, accidents commonly occur while lifting or moving goods, or as a result of slipping, falling or tripping. Only a minority of injuries are caused by train accidents, or by the movement of trains or wagons.

225   The fatal accident rate for railway employees is about 0·2 a year per thousand employees – about the same as in the construction industry, or in the most dangerous of manufacturing industries. The rates are higher for some operational staff, rising to 0·5 a year per thousand for permanent way staff and the like – one of the highest fatality rates for any occupational group.

226   Examination of the run of figures since the war shows that there has been a downward trend in casualties per train mile.

CHAPTER 9

Products and services

227 Apart from medical injuries, considered later in this chapter, there is little information about injuries caused by defective products or services. The first report[21] on the home accident surveillance system recently set up by the Department of Prices and Consumer Protection identifies the kinds of product involved in home accidents which had led to hospital visits, but does not classify accidents by type. The personal injury survey gives only a broad indication of the possible numbers, whether at home or elsewhere, where products or services might have been faulty. Deaths, except those resulting from medical injury, are not distinguished.

228 The survey estimate, based on the descriptions given by those interviewed of the circumstances in which they had been injured, is that in 1973 about 70,000 injuries might have been caused by defective products or services, representing nearly $2\frac{1}{2}$ per cent of all injuries in the year. The number actually so caused would have been considerably less. About half the total number involved drugs or medical injuries.

229 Of the cases recorded in the survey, more were attributed to defective services than to defective goods. There was some degree of overlap with other categories of injury; some cases occurred at work, and others involved motor vehicles.

Non-medical injuries

230 Tort compensation was obtained for about 5 per cent of the non-medical injuries. The result compares with a proportion of about 10 per cent for all injuries where it was judged that there was any possibility of a tort claim.

231 The average amount paid in tort compensation on non-medical claims relating to defective products or services in 1973 was about half that for all payments in respect of personal injury – less than £500 when converted to the January 1977 price level as compared with about £900 for all types of injury not resulting in death. There are few fatal cases of non-medical injury – none at all in the four weeks covered by the insurance survey.

232 The proportion of cases reaching court was less than for other types of injury. Of the 12 cases reaching court in 1974, some compensation was awarded in 9.

Medical injuries

233   From the death registrations it is possible to distinguish deaths caused by the adverse effects of drugs, or from complications of medical or surgical care. From 1973 to 1975, deaths in England and Wales from these causes averaged 2,819 and 77 a year respectively.

234   The personal injury survey provides estimates representing an upper limit to the possible numbers of injuries, based on the patient's subjective impressions. They include injuries arising from errors in dispensing medicines, from failure to follow instructions or from self-medication, as well as some of those arising in the course of medical treatment. These include injuries resulting from accepted risks of medical treatment as well as from accident or error. The figures are given in Table 48.

Table 48   Estimates of maximum numbers of medical injuries

United Kingdom: 1973	Numbers
Adverse effects of medicines	24,000
Complications of medical or surgical care	13,000
Total	37,000

Source: Personal injury survey.

235   The majority of the medical complications would have arisen from unforeseen circumstances, not from negligence. Some were no more than incidental to the treatment of an injury, and were recorded in the survey only because the injury was reported.

236   As with other kinds of injury, only a proportion of medical injuries lead to the payment of compensation through the tort system. It is not possible to estimate the proportion accurately, since there is no firm information about claims on health authorities, or the extent to which they are combined with claims on doctors. But if, as seems likely, the cases handled by medical defence societies or other professional organisations represent the majority of those brought, the proportion of injuries in which claims are made, or compensation obtained, is appreciably lower than for other classes of injury.

Claims on doctors and dentists

237   Medical and dental practitioners in the United Kingdom insure against tort claims in respect of medical negligence with one of three medical defence societies. Table 49 gives approximate estimates based on information provided by the societies in respect of 1974 and 1975.

238   Just over a third of the claims led to the payment of compensation, a much lower proportion than for other personal injury claims. The average payment, converted to the price level of January 1977, was about £8,000, or about eight times as much as the average figure of £1,000 for all payments of tort compensation for personal injury or death.

Table 49   Claims on medical defence societies

United Kingdom: Estimates in round numbers
based on data for 1974 and 1975   Annual averages

	Number
Number of negligence claims referred to legal advisers	500
Number where compensation paid	175
Out of court	170
In court	5
Number of claims abandoned	305
Number of claims where judgment given for defendant	20
	Value
Total value of compensation	£1,000,000

Estimates made by the Commission from data supplied by the medical defence societies.

239   The societies make no analysis of injuries by type or severity. The examples quoted in their annual reports, which may not be representative, give the impression that most of the cases lie at one or other of two extremes; a substantial number of relatively trivial injuries involving only discomfort and inconvenience, and a smaller number of serious injuries, such as brain damage during anaesthesia, for which large payments are made.

Claims against other professions
240   Claims for medical injury are sometimes made also against members of professions such as pharmacists or opticians. These too are usually handled by a professional organisation. The National Pharmaceutical Union deals with about 130 claims a year, and payment is made in about 80 cases. The average payment is less than £100 at January 1977 prices.

Legal proceedings
241   A relatively high proportion of medical injury claims lead to the issue of a writ, or to a court hearing. The analyses of court records in Great Britain show that 46 cases were set down in 1974 of which 18 proceeded to trial. This latter figure is close to that obtained from the medical protection societies for 1974, suggesting that there are relatively few claims against health authorities alone, or at any rate few which reach court. Of the small number of medical injury cases which reached court, only a minority resulted in the payment of compensation. This is the only kind of case of which this is true.

242   At all stages, medical negligence cases took longer than other personal injury cases. The average interval between the date of injury and the date when the claim was disposed of was nearly 5 years, compared with 3 to 4 years for all personal injury claims.

Vaccine damage

243 Vaccination can lead to adverse reactions, and in exceptional cases these can be serious. Measurement of such effects is difficult, especially in investigations carried out retrospectively. It is not always possible to be certain whether an adverse reaction following vaccination has been caused by it, or whether it has occurred spontaneously or from another cause. Reports to the Committee on Safety of Medicines provide an indication of the types of adverse reaction which may occur, but not a measure of their extent.

244 In the past, adverse reactions have been associated with vaccination against smallpox. This form of vaccination is no longer routinely recommended, because the risk of contracting the disease is now considered to be less than the risk of adverse reactions, and it no longer presents a serious problem.

245 The main subject of public concern now is of adverse reactions, in particular of brain damage, following vaccination against whooping cough. The Association of Parents of Vaccine Damaged Children said that they knew of 356 children whom they believe to have been seriously injured as a result of vaccination, of whom 240 were said to have been injured by whooping cough vaccination.

246 Partly in consequence of adverse publicity, the proportion of children vaccinated, especially against whooping cough, has been falling, as is shown in Table 50.

Table 50 Proportions of children vaccinated

Great Britain   Percentages[1]

	1967	1968	1969[2]	1970	1971	1972	1973	1974	1975	1976
Diphtheria	75	78	67	64	65	65	64	57	57	56
Whooping cough	74	76	66	63	64	63	62	51	32	32
Poliomyelitis	71	74	65	63	64	64	63	57	57	56
Tetanus	75	78	67	64	65	65	64	57	57	56

1 Percentages of children born in the previous year who were vaccinated by end of year stated.
2 Change in the recommended schedule of vaccination.

247 There is at present no reliable estimate of the incidence of brain damage following whooping cough vaccination in the United Kingdom, but the risk of damage is slight. Two recent studies of large numbers of immunised children quoted in the report on whooping cough vaccination by the Joint Committee on Vaccination and Immunization[22] had found no cases of severe or permanent brain damage. A measure of the incidence of damage may be provided by the National Childhood Encephalopathy Study, which began in July 1976 under the auspices of the Committee.

248   Some of the evidence reviewed in the Committee's report suggests that the incidence of adverse reactions may have been reduced since the 1960's, following the introduction of improved types of vaccine.

249   Data from other countries quoted in an appendix to the Committee's report provide some confirmation that the risk of brain damage is extremely small, although the significance of the data depends on how completely adverse effects are reported. In some countries, no cases had been recorded, and in others the number of reported cases was in single figures, even over a period of several years. The highest figure was for the Federal Republic of Germany, where it was estimated that one case of brain damage occurred for every 100,000 doses of whooping cough vaccine.

250   Indications of the possible incidence of damage resulting from vaccination other than against whooping cough are provided by information collected in the Federal Republic of Germany and in France. In the Federal Republic, compensation is paid on the basis of a probable causal connection between the vaccination and the injury; from 1962 to 1969 there were on average 34 payments a year, excluding cases arising from smallpox vaccination, some of them in relation to injuries which were not permanent. In France, compensation was paid in 30 cases, excluding smallpox vaccination, on claims arising from 1966 to 1975, or an average of 3 a year; the make up of the 30 cases is given in Table 51.

Table 51   Payments of compensation for
vaccine damage[1] in France

Claims made from 1966 to 1975	Numbers
Polio	4
Diphtheria/polio	7
Tetanus/diphtheria	3
Tuberculosis	14
Tetanus	1
Rabies	1
Total	30

1 Excluding smallpox.

Source: Ministre de la Santé, Paris.

CHAPTER 10

Children

251   Apart from a short introductory section, this chapter is concerned with birth defects, and with children who are severely disabled, whether congenitally or otherwise.

252   There are about 14 million children under the age of 16 in the United Kingdom, and about 1½ million full time students aged 16 or over. The number of children under 16 is at present declining, and the decline is expected to continue until the 1980's, after which numbers may again increase.

253   Children and students sustain just over 800,000 injuries each year, the incidence of injury – averaged over all ages – being much the same as for all adults. Some analysis of these injuries is given in Chapters 2 and 15. Only a few children and students were injured while doing part time work, and the proportion injured by motor vehicles was less than for adults, although the proportion killed was larger. Consequently a relatively small proportion of injuries to children fell under the two main headings of the terms of reference – work and road.

254   It is rare for tort compensation to be obtained on behalf of injured children, the proportion of injuries where tort payments are made being only 1 per cent. This small proportion is partly due to a high proportion of cases where the injury is not anyone else's fault, and partly to the difficulty a child may have in giving a coherent account of an accident on which a claim could be based. In respect of children with congenital defects, tort claims are also rare because it is only exceptionally that the defect can be attributed to a specific harmful agent or to a negligent act.

Congenital defects

255   Statistics of the incidence of congenital defects depend on how the term is defined, and also on the age at which assessment is made. Some defects are not apparent until some time after birth; some disappear spontaneously or can be corrected (e.g. by surgery); some result in early death.

256   Three distinct kinds of measures are considered below. The first relates to defects identifiable at or shortly after birth; the second, to defects at age seven; the third, to children under 16 who suffer from severe congenital disabilities. All three use data from studies made by the National Children's Bureau of the '1958 cohort' – some 17,000 children born in the week of 3–9 March 1958.

Defects identifiable at or shortly after birth

257 The incidence of defects reported at or soon after birth in the 1958 cohort was 17·5 for each 1,000 live and still births.[23] Congenital malformations in England and Wales discovered within seven days of birth and notified under a voluntary scheme to OPCS represented an incidence of 21·0 for each thousand in 1976.[24] The difference is more likely to result from differences in classification or improved methods of diagnosis than to represent an increase in incidence.

Defects identified by age seven

258 The incidence of serious defects in the 1958 cohort detected at any time up to age seven[25] which were congenital or had arisen shortly after birth, excluding defects of sight or hearing, was 30·8 for each 1,000 births. At the age of seven, after allowing for defects which had been remedied, and for children who had died, the incidence was 19·6 in each 1,000 children. Details of the defects are given in Table 52.

Table 52 Incidence of congenital defects identified by age seven

Children born 3–9 March 1958   Number per 1,000

	At birth	At age seven
Anencephaly	1·8	–
Spina bifida and/or hydrocephalus	4·2	1·1
Heart or blood vessels	6·6	3·6
Cleft palate	1·5	1·5
Club foot	4·1	3·1
Dislocated hips	1·1	1·1
Other bones or joints	2·1	1·6
Other malformations	8·9	2·2
Down's syndrome	2·0	0·8
Other severe subnormality	1·4	1·5
Cerebral palsy	2·5	2·3
Cancer, leukaemia etc.	0·8	0·2
Other congenital disorders	2·3	1·9
Children with defects[1]	30·8[2]	19·6[2]

1 Excluding defects of sight or hearing. Some children had
  more than one of the defects listed.
2 Figures revised since original publication.

Source: National Children's Bureau.

259 The study does not state how many children with congenital defects alive at age seven were handicapped in consequence, but it may be inferred from the text that the proportion would be about one half.

260 Defects of sight and hearing at age seven were analysed separately.[26] None of the cohort children was wholly blind, but some 9 per 1,000 of the sample suffered from very poor sight (i.e. a severe defect in the better eye), though many could have the defect corrected to some degree by wearing glasses. About 1 child in 1,000 was assessed as severely deaf and a further 2 in 1,000 suffered sufficient loss of hearing to qualify for special educational treatment. Because no information is given about how many of the defects of sight or hearing were congenital, or the extent to which they overlapped with other congenital defects, it is not possible to combine these figures with those given above.

Severe congenital disabilities
261 It is estimated that about 6 in 1,000 children under 16 suffer from congenital disabilities sufficiently severe to entitle them to help from the Family Fund (described below). That is to say, nearly one third of the children with congenital defects of the kinds shown in Table 52 would be eligible for help of this kind.

International comparisons
262 There are no closely comparable figures of the incidence of congenital defects in other countries. The statistics of deaths from congenital defects shown in Table 53 give some indication, but need to be treated with caution because of differences in definition and in the way in which deaths are classified.

Table 53 International comparison of deaths from
congenital malformations

1972   Number of deaths per 1,000 live births

	Neonatal period (0–27 days)	Post neonatal period (28 days–1 year)	Under 1 year
France[1]	1·6	1·1	2·7
West Germany	2·6	1·4	4·0
Netherlands	1·9	1·1	3·0
Sweden	2·3	1·0	3·3
Switzerland	2·4	1·1	3·5
United Kingdom:			
England and Wales	2·6	1·2	3·8
Scotland	3·1	1·2	4·3
Northern Ireland	3·3	1·6	4·9
Canada	..	..	3·8
United States	2·0	0·9	2·9
New Zealand	1·8	1·3	3·1

1 Live-born babies who died before registration of births are not included.
  Registration may take place up to three days after birth.

Sources: World Health Organisation.
         Annual Report of the Registrar General for Scotland, 1972.

263   Nevertheless, the figures suggest that the incidence of death from congenital defects may be higher in the United Kingdom than in most of the other countries in the table, particularly in the neonatal period. This seems to be due to the much higher incidence of death from spina bifida in the United Kingdom than elsewhere. The incidence of death from spina bifida in Canada and New Zealand also was higher than average, though lower than in the UK. The incidence of death from defects other than spina bifida in the UK was not very different from that in other countries, with the exception of France, where the figures are not comparable except for the post-neonatal period.

Trends in congenital defects
264   A number of factors can affect the incidence of birth defects. New harmful agents may be introduced, or existing ones may be identified and eliminated. Developments in medical practice can reduce the incidence of defects, in particular the development of techniques to detect defective foetuses, combined with abortion.

265   This factor may have contributed to a fall since 1973 in the incidence of some of the congenital defects of the central nervous system reported to OPCS. Otherwise, there has been no significant change in the incidence of the more serious types of malformation. The incidence rate for all reported malformations increased between 1968 and 1976 from 16·8 in each thousand live and still births to 21·0 in each thousand; but this increase was due to a widening of the range of conditions reported rather than to a greater incidence of defects.

Birth injury
266   A reduction in the incidence of death from birth injury is shown by a comparison of one of the studies of the 1958 cohort and a similar study of all births in one week in 1970 carried out jointly by the Royal College of Obstetricians and Gynaecologists and the National Birthday Trust Fund.[27] 13·6 perinatal deaths from birth injury were recorded for each 1,000 births in the 1958 study, and 8·2 in that relating to 1970. There are no accurate figures for the incidence of birth injury causing serious and lasting handicap in survivors, but it may be reasonable to suppose that this has been declining also.

Congenital defects which might have been prevented
267   Estimates of the extent to which congenital defects including birth injuries might have been prevented have been made by Dr Renwick, whose report is annexed to Volume One. He estimated that in the 30 years from 1945, some 12,500 babies were born with defects which might have been prevented before or during birth, given the current state of knowledge – an incidence of 0·5 per thousand births. Other estimates have been in the range 0·1 to 0·5 per 1,000 births. The major causes were rubella and other infections, and birth injury. Identifiable drug induced defects represented only a small proportion.

268   In most cases of infection it would be impossible to establish fault. If infections are excluded, together with other cases which are unlikely to recur,

the remaining birth defects for which someone might possibly be held to be at fault might number about 100 a year. Most of these would arise from birth injury.

269   If on average there were as many as 50 defects a year (other than those resulting from birth injury) which might be attributable to negligence on the part of a drug manufacturer or anyone else, these would represent only 0·25 per cent of an estimated total of some 20,000 birth defects in the United Kingdom each year.

Disabled children

270   Estimates of numbers of disabled children depend on how disability is defined. With a wide definition, including the educationally subnormal and the emotionally disturbed or maladjusted, the number could be several hundred thousand.

271   With a narrow definition limited to children under 16 living at home who were severely disabled to a degree similar to that which now determines entitlement to help from the Family Fund, the estimated numbers would be those in Table 54.

Table 54   Numbers of severely disabled children

United Kingdom: Estimates in
round numbers for 1965–1969   Numbers

Congenital defect	90,000
Injury	1,000 to 2,000
Disease	8,000 to 9,000
Total	100,000

Estimated by the Commission from data prepared by
the University of York.

272   The estimates are based on investigations of the children in the 1958 cohort at ages 7 and 11 supplemented by an analysis of the records of the County Borough of York.[28] The cohort data related to samples of the child population in 1965 and 1969. The number of children under 16 is not much different now from the average of the figures for those two years, and no adjustment has been made to bring the estimate up-to-date. In the costings in Chapter 30, allowance has been made for future changes in numbers of severely disabled children of the same extent as the changes in the total number of children, on the assumption that the incidence of severe disability is unlikely to alter substantially.

The Family Fund
273   The Family Fund was established by the Government in 1973, and provides assistance to families in which there is a child under 16 who is very

severely disabled physically or mentally. It meets needs which are outside the scope of other services. It is administered by the Joseph Rowntree Memorial Trust.

274 The following paragraphs contain notes prepared by the Trust with the help of their medical advisers of the kinds of disability likely to qualify for help from the Fund.

275 The requirement which must be fulfilled to qualify for help from the Family Fund is that the disability must be very severe. The following examples are given for general guidance and the circumstances of each case are considered on their merits.

Nature of disability	*Factors which would make the disability severe*
Absence or functional loss of limbs:	Two or more limbs involved.
Arthrogryposis:	Severe deformity.
Asthma:	Severe involvement of lungs seriously limiting the child's activities, physical, social and educational.
Cerebral palsy:	Severe disorder of movement.
Cystic fibrosis:	Severe involvement of lungs seriously limiting the child's activities, physical, social and educational.
Double incontinence in a child 5 years or over:	Double incontinence, as contrasted with enuresis and encopresis means the total absence of control of bladder and bowel through organic defect.
Epilepsy:	Frequent fits not controlled by drugs.
Hyperkinetic syndrome:	Very severe over-activity.
Impairment of hearing:	Severe impairment or complete loss.
Impairment of vision:	Severe impairment or complete loss.
Infantile spinal muscular atrophy: (Werdnig Hoffman disease)	Severe muscular weakness.
Mental subnormality:	Intelligence quotient less than 50. (Less than 35 for mongols.)
Mongolism (Down's Syndrome): (see additional note)	Additional disabilities and special problems of care.
Multiple malformations:	Severe malformations none of which itself constituted a severe disability might together do so.
Muscular dystrophy:	Severe disorder of movement.
Osteogenesis imperfecta:	Severe deformity.
Spina bifida:	Paralysis of lower limbs with incontinence of urine or faeces.

Factors to be considered in deciding if disability is very severe:

i   Degree of disability, especially low intelligence, limitation of mobility, abnormal behaviour, impairment of vision and hearing, severe problems of communication.

ii   Combined effects of disabilities occurring together.

iii Needs for night attendance, frequent visits to clinics and hospital, special diets, and modifications to home.

ADDITIONAL NOTE ON MONGOLISM (DOWN'S SYNDROME)

276   The Trustees, on the advice of their professional advisers, take the view that the diagnosis of mongolism should not automatically place a child in the category of 'very severely disabled'. In order to qualify for help from the Family Fund, there will have to be a clearly recognised additional disability which is not usually present in mongolism (for example, deafness, grossly hyperactive behaviour, or a malformation of the heart).

CHAPTER 11

Occupiers' liability

277 From the personal injury survey, it is estimated that about 100,000 injuries in 1973 occurred on the public highway, and 90,000 elsewhere on other persons' premises, in circumstances suggesting that they might have been due to an act or omission of the highway authority or the owner of the premises. There was some overlap between public highway and motor or commuting injuries and some of the other injuries were on employers' premises, representing an overlap with work injuries.

278 These injuries led to payments of tort compensation in close on 11,000 cases, representing a somewhat lower proportion than for all personal injuries which might have been attributable to the act or omission of another. The compensation payments cannot be accurately sub-divided between public highway and other cases, but the small number of cases recorded in the survey suggested that tort compensation was more commonly obtained for injuries on the public highway than on other premises. About 1 per cent of the cases led to a court hearing – much the same proportion as for all personal injuries.

279 The average payment in 1973, converted to the January 1977 price level, was about £500, half the average figure for all tort payments for personal injury or death.

280 No analysis of all occupiers' liability cases is available, but information is collected about one or two special groups, for example trespassers on the railways, for whom some figures are given in Chapter 8.

CHAPTER 12

Criminal injuries

281 About 720 people a year died in the United Kingdom as the result of criminal acts in the years 1973 to 1975, and about 55,000 were injured in 1973.

282 The estimate of number of injuries is based on the personal injury survey, not on the statistics of crimes of violence against the person reported to the police. The latter are incomplete since they do not cover non-indictable assaults, and since not all indictable assaults are reported to the police; on the other hand, the statistics include some assaults which would not have resulted in 4 or more days' incapacity. The Scottish figures are more limited in coverage than those for England and Wales.

283 The figures for England and Wales provide an indication of trends, showing an increase at a rate of about 11 per cent a year from 1966 to 1976.

Tort compensation

284 Tort claims in respect of criminal injury are rare, but not entirely unknown. The personal injury survey found six people who had considered making a claim. One of them had succeeded in obtaining compensation.

Criminal injuries compensation

285 Apart from social security, the main source of recompense is from criminal injuries compensation. In Great Britain, a compensation scheme administered by the Criminal Injuries Compensation Board came into operation on 1 August 1964. In Northern Ireland, a statutory scheme has been in operation since 1969; compensation awards there have hitherto been made by the county court, but for injuries since August 1977 awards are being made by the Secretary of State.

286 Awards are normally limited to cases where the circumstances of the injury have been the subject of criminal proceedings, or have been reported to the police without delay. The injury must be one for which compensation of not less than £150 would be awarded. Injuries inflicted by other members of the same family do not qualify. In Northern Ireland, claims for mental disturbance arising from crimes of violence are admitted only if at least £1,000 would be awarded.

287 In Great Britain, the number of applications to the Board has increased year by year since the scheme started; in Northern Ireland, there was a drop

in the most recent year – the financial year 1976/77. In that year, there were nearly 14,000 awards of compensation in Great Britain, and over 3,600 in Northern Ireland. Details are given in Table 55.

Table 55 Growth of criminal injuries compensation

	Applications	Claims disposed of	Awards	Total value of payments
Great Britain		Numbers		£'000
1964/65	554	130	114	33·4
1965/66	2,452	1,375	1,164	402·7
1966/67	3,312	2,717	2,404	914·2
1967/68	5,316	3,869	3,490	1,293·8
1968/69	6,437	5,985	5,060	1,673·0
1969/70	7,247	6,817	5,614	1,992·4
1970/71	7,419	5,893	4,901	2,090·0
1971/72	9,886	9,449	8,102	3,300·9
1972/73	10,926	9,387	8,322	3,449·5
1973/74	12,215	10,564	9,024	4,043·0
1974/75	14,227	12,506	10,708	5,059·4
1975/76	16,690	13,599	11,500	6,476·7
1976/77	20,400	16,393	13,951	9,677·4
Northern Ireland				
1968/69	6	..	..	2·4
1969/70	1,297	..	..	131·9
1970/71	1,024	..	..	443·5
1971/72	2,811	..	..	724·5
1972/73	5,640	..	..	2,173·5
1973/74	4,025	8,120[1]	..	3,886·4
1974/75	4,324	3,590	..	6,022·6
1975/76	7,673	5,027	4,580	7,937·8
1976/77	6,948	4,122	3,643	6,300·3

1 Total for period 1968–69 to 1973–74.

Sources: Criminal Injuries Compensation Board.
　　　　　Northern Ireland Office.

288　About 85 per cent of the claims disposed of in a year in Great Britain now result in the payment of compensation, and a slightly higher proportion in Northern Ireland. In 1976/77, the average payment was about £700 in Great Britain and about £1,700 in Northern Ireland.

CHAPTER 13
Injuries caused by animals

289 Information about injuries involving animals is far from complete.

Wild animals

290 Injuries caused by wild animals were too few to show up in the personal injury survey, unless a number of insect bites sufficiently serious to have led to four or more days' incapacity were to be so classified.

Domestic and farm animals

291 The personal injury survey gives an estimate of about 25,000 injuries in 1973 which may have been caused by domestic or farm animals. Dogs were the animals mainly concerned.

Farm animals

292 The Health and Safety Executive have taken over from the Ministry of Agriculture, Fisheries and Food responsibility for compiling statistics of injuries on farms in England and Wales, among which injuries caused by animals are distinguished. The figures are mainly based on claims for social security benefit made by farmers and farmworkers, and include only a few accidents to others which are of particular types which are required to be reported.

293 In 1974, there were 3 deaths on farms caused by animals, two by bulls and the third through crushing by cows. Cattle were also responsible for most of the recorded injuries, as is shown in Table 56.

Table 56 Farm accidents involving animals

England and Wales: 1974

		Injuries to:			
	Total	Self employed	Managers/ Foremen	Em- ployees	Others
Injuries caused by:					
Bulls	39	1	2	35	1
Other cattle	409	2	7	398	2
Other animals	126	2	1	123	–
Total	574	5	10	556	3

Source: Ministry of Agriculture, Fisheries and Food.

Dogs

294 Statistics for Great Britain published by the Department of Transport[29] show that in about 0·7 per cent of road accidents there was a dog on the road, and in about 0·6 per cent of cases another animal. If the proportion for dogs can be applied to the estimate of 349,000 injuries a year involving motor vehicles, one obtains an estimate of 2,400 for the annual number of motor vehicle injuries involving dogs. The corresponding estimate for other animals is just over 2,000, covering injuries involving all kinds of animals – domestic, wild, farm, and horses other than those being ridden (which are classed as non-motor vehicles).

295 The report by the Department of Prices and Consumer Protection[21] on the first six months of its surveillance of home accidents in England and Wales shows that just over 0·5 per cent involved dogs, including injuries resulting from people falling over them. Application of this percentage to a figure of 820,000 injuries a year in private homes gives an estimate of 4,400 for the number of home accidents involving dogs.

296 The Post Office have supplied figures for the years 1972 to 1974 of the numbers of postmen bitten by dogs. The annual average was 173, representing an incidence of 1·6 per 1,000 postmen.

Horses

297 Injuries involving horses were not separately identified in the personal injury survey. They are known to have represented most of some 30,000 sporting injuries involving a form of transport. If occurring on the road, they were classified under motor vehicles if a motor vehicle was involved, but otherwise among the 50,000 injuries involving non-motor vehicles. The total number of injuries involving horses but not motor vehicles, on the road or elsewhere, is likely to be not less than 20,000 or 30,000 a year.

298 That horse riding involves a degree of risk was confirmed by the British Horse Society, who said that in 1973 90 riders had been killed in traffic accidents; many of these would have involved motor vehicles.

299 This figure looks high in relation to the Department of Transport's statistics of road injuries reported to the police. These include casualties involving horse riders under 'other non-motor vehicles'. In recent years, about 350 casualties a year have been recorded under this heading, including no more than 10 people killed. The figures do not include accidents involving horses while being led (which are included as pedestrian casualties), nor are all injuries to riders reported, especially in cases not involving a motor vehicle.

Tort compensation

300 Injuries caused by farm animals are mainly to employees, and could be the subject of claims under employers' liability. Other injuries involving animals are not for the most part attributable to the act or omission of another person. Tort claims in respect of them were too few to be distinguished in any of the available statistics.

PART III

Surveys carried out for the Commission

CHAPTER 14

Personal injury survey: general description

301   The personal injury survey was carried out in order to fill some of the gaps in the existing statistical information about injuries. It was initiated in 1973, and interviews were carried out in 1974. Most of the work was done by the Office of Population Censuses and Surveys, but some of the work relating to work illnesses was sub-contracted to a private survey organisation, Social and Community Planning Research.

302   Questions were included about numbers and categories of injury, the circumstances in which people had been injured and the consequences of injury. In particular, information was sought about financial consequences – losses of income, expenses incurred, and compensation obtained, including the history to date of any claim in tort.

Scope of the survey

303   It was not possible to limit the survey to certain classes of injury, and to exclude others. Though most home accidents were outside the terms of reference, some were within them as being attributable, for example, to a defective product. The remit covered some injuries treated by general practitioners as well as in hospital, and some injuries to housewives, children or the retired as well as to the working population. The field to be covered was wider than that covered by any existing set of administrative records, which could not therefore be used as a basis for sampling. Nor was it practicable, because of the range of questions, to add them to one of the continuing surveys carried out for the Government, such as the general household survey. The only way of covering the whole field was to approach a random sample of households and seek to identify those of their members who had been injured in a given period.

304   It was not possible to limit the survey to injuries within the terms of reference since it was not always practicable in the course of an interview to determine whether a particular injury was within them or not. In subsequent editing, an attempt was made to distinguish between injuries possibly or certainly within the terms of reference and those certainly outside them; but most of the analysis relates to all the injuries that were covered.

305   The injuries covered were those which had required a visit to hospital or to a doctor, and which were of a degree of severity similar to that which gives entitlement to social security benefit. Since the survey related to injuries of all kinds, the criterion of severity for inclusion was not the social security criterion of four or more days' incapacity for work, but the wider and less

precise one of four or more days' incapacity for activity of any kind normally undertaken. Analysis of the results for those at work at the time when they were injured showed that use of the latter criterion led to the inclusion of about 23 per cent more cases than the former. In the estimates of aggregate numbers given earlier in this volume, and also in the first volume of the report, adjustment has been made to the more restricted basis of four or more days' incapacity for work, or an equivalent degree of severity. But in the report on the survey contained in this and the following chapters, the injuries included are those satisfying the wider criterion.

306   Since the Social Survey Division of the Office of Population Censuses and Surveys does not operate in Northern Ireland, and in order to limit expense, the survey was carried out only in Great Britain.

Conduct of the survey

307   The survey was carried out in two phases. The first interview, most often with the housewife, sought to identify any members of the household who might qualify for a more detailed interview at the second phase, carried out some months later.

308   The main category identified consisted of people injured during 1973, for whom 3,302 satisfactory interviews were obtained. Other groups included 589 people injured from 1966 to 1972 who had attempted to make tort claims; 3 relatives of people who had died from injuries sustained in 1973; 299 people who from 1970 to 1973 had contracted illnesses which they believed arose from their work; and 2,693 people under 24 at the beginning of 1974 who had been born with defects.

Role of the survey

309   The survey supplemented existing partial sources of information by providing for the first time information about the whole range of injuries. The survey data were in some respects less reliable than the existing information about particular kinds of injury, but the survey had the merit of covering the whole field in a consistent way, and without leaving any gaps. Information was obtained about injuries to people not in the working population about which little had previously been known.

310   Many of the results of value were obtained by analysing in a variety of ways the information which had been collected about injuries of different kinds to different groups in the population. The actual numbers of injuries were less useful, partly because they were derived from a sample, but also because those initially interviewed did not report all the injuries to members of their households which were within the scope of the survey. How this deficiency was identified, and how it arose, are explained in Chapter 21.

311   Despite this drawback, the survey was used, with an approximate allowance for under-recording and in conjunction with other data, in building up the general picture of the pattern of injuries given in Chapter 2 of this volume.

There was, however, no basis for making adjustments for under-recording to the detailed figures given in the following chapters, and these are given without adjustment, and unaccompanied by any corresponding estimates of national aggregates.

Sources of further information

312 The questionnaires used in the survey have not been reproduced here because of their length. Copies are available from:

The Social Survey Division
Office of Population Censuses and Surveys
St Catherine's House
10 Kingsway
London WC2B 6JP.

313 Arrangements have been made for the main body of survey material to be deposited in the survey archive of the Social Science Research Council at the University of Essex, in a form which does not allow individuals to be identified. It includes the magnetic tapes on which the data are recorded and related documentation, including copies of the detailed tabulations so far prepared. Any application for the use of this material should be made to:

Social Science Research Council
Survey Archive
University of Essex
Wivenhoe Park
Colchester, Essex CO4 3SQ.

CHAPTER 15

Personal injury survey: analysis of injuries and of the injured

Classification of injuries

314   Injuries were classified in relation to the five categories of the terms of reference, which for convenience are reproduced here:

Injury suffered by any person

a   in the course of employment;

b   through the use of a motor vehicle or other means of transport;

c   through the manufacture, supply or use of goods or services;

d   on premises belonging to or occupied by another; or

e   otherwise through the act or omission of another where compensation under the present law is recoverable only on proof of fault or under the rules of strict liability.

315   The groups of injury distinguished in the survey started with five main classes corresponding to these categories. A sixth class included injuries outside the terms of reference, but which were covered by the survey. Each of the main classes was sub-divided, so that altogether 25 different sub-groups of injury were identified.

316   The survey class corresponding to the first category of the terms of reference was defined broadly so as to include injuries at the place of work outside working hours and injuries on the way to or from work, as well as injuries arising in the course of work or during working hours. The second class too was widely defined to include any injury caused in some way by a means of transport, even if it was not in use as such at the time, for instance, during repairs. The third class included injuries which might have been caused by defects or hazards in goods or services; the fourth, injuries suffered by persons entering on other persons' premises (including highways) and which might have been caused by defects or hazards in the premises. The fifth class included injuries which might have been caused in other ways by the act or omission of another person. Injuries could be included in more than one of these five classes.

317   The sixth residual class of injuries outside the terms of reference included, among other injuries, most injuries in the home and many injuries which happened to occur on someone else's premises but were not attributable to any defect or hazard in the premises.

318   The cases shown in the first five main classes of injury, numbering about two thirds of the total, were taken as being potentially within the remit, even though only a minority of them had led to tort claims. They included, for

example, all injuries to children under any kind of formal supervision, although in most of these cases no fault could be attributed to the supervisor.

Table 57 Classes of injury

Great Britain: 1973

	Number recorded	Percentage of total
Injuries possibly due to the act or omission of another		
Work injuries	1,112	33·7
At work	951	28·8
At work place outside working hours	32	1·0
On way to or from work	129	3·9
Transport	523	15·8
Motor vehicles		
Moving road vehicles	321	9·7
Stationary	76	2·3
Other moving vehicles		
Non-motor vehicles on the road	58	1·8
Non-road vehicles	18	0·5
Sports transport	36	1·1
Other	14	0·4
Possible fault in goods or services	78	2·4
Possible fault in goods	25	0·8
Possible fault in services	43	1·3
Possible fault in goods and services	10	0·3
Possible fault in other persons' premises	207	6·3
On public highway	108	3·3
On other premises owned or occupied by another	99	3·0
Possibly caused in other ways by the act or omission of another	602	18·2
Criminal violence	62	1·9
Children under school supervision	231	7·0
Children under other formal supervision	20	0·6
Children playing together or fighting	72	2·2
During sports or games	86	2·6
Domestic or farm animal	29	0·9
Other	102	3·1
Total	2,206[1]	66·8

Table 57—*continued*

	Number recorded	Percentage of total
Injuries not due to the act or omission of another		
At home	639	19·4
In other private homes	79	2·4
During sports or games where no other person involved	60	1·8
Other	318	9·6
Total	1,096	33·2
All injuries	3,302	100·0

1 Excluding duplication. The total number of 2,206 is consequently less than the sum of the numbers shown against the previous headings (2,522), in which 272 injuries are counted twice and 22 three times.

319   Apart from the last class of injury which, by definition, excludes any injuries covered elsewhere, the main classes are not mutually exclusive. It is theoretically possible for a case to appear under all five main heads although none appeared under more than three. Within each main class, however, the sub-groups are mutually exclusive.

320   The relationships between the numbers recorded under the different headings are affected by the fact that some kinds of injuries, in particular injuries at work, were more fully reported than others.

321   The work injuries shown include injuries to the self employed as well as to employees. They include also some injuries leading to less than four days off work, though to four or more days' incapacity for some other activity normally undertaken.

322   Transport injuries were classified according to whether or not they involved a motor vehicle, whether the vehicle was moving or stationary, and whether they took place on or off the road. The following notes describe how they were grouped:

i   The largest sub-group consisted of injuries caused by motor vehicles moving on the road, together with those caused by cars, motor cycles and commercial vehicles moving in such places as car parks and private driveways, to which similar insurance arrangements apply.

ii   There was quite a large group of injuries involving stationary motor vehicles. It included injuries caused by the opening or closing of vehicle doors, or by falls from or in vehicles, injuries to children playing in vehicles, and injuries during the repair of vehicles or during loading and unloading. Nearly half the injuries in this group occurred at work.

iii Non-motor injuries on the road involved pedal cycles, and occasionally horses.

iv The small group of injuries caused by non-road vehicles in motion concerned such vehicles as agricultural tractors when not on the road, industrial trucks and mobile cranes, as well as any air, sea or rail injuries.

v The other specific sub-group distinguished consisted of injuries involving vehicles used off the road for purposes of sport. Most of them involved horses, but there were also a few involving scrambler motor cycles.

323 The number of injuries recorded as possibly due to faulty services was greater than the number possibly due to faulty goods. Injuries caused by drugs and medical injuries were included here.

324 The injuries classified as possibly due to some defect in premises included those attributable to defects in the public highway, which accounted for more than half the numbers in this group.

325 Forty per cent of the other injuries classed as possibly caused by the act or omission of another were to children at school or under other formal supervision. There were also appreciable numbers of injuries to children playing together or fighting, and to people engaged in sporting activities involving others besides themselves.

326 Of the injuries not due to the act or omission of another, the majority took place in private homes. Home injuries in total represented 27 per cent of all the injuries reported, of which 22 per cent were clearly outside the terms of reference, and 5 per cent might have been within them.

327 In the analyses of the survey results, injuries have sometimes been grouped in other ways.

Overlap between classes of injury

328 In some of the tables, there is double counting of injuries falling within more than one class; if so this is made clear.

329 Table 58 gives details of the overlapping, and Table 59 brings together the figures relating to the major area of overlap, namely between work and transport injuries. The overlap between injuries at work and motor vehicle injuries consisted mainly of injuries to those employed as drivers or working on vehicles. Many but by no means all commuting injuries involved motor vehicles.

330 In Table 60, and in some later tables, duplication has been eliminated by assigning injuries only to the class which appears first. Under this system of classification, work takes priority over all other classes of injury, and transport over the rest. When the overlap with work injuries is eliminated, injuries caused by moving or stationary motor vehicles numbered 255; with the addition of 75 cases also classified as commuting and 67 other work cases shown in Table 59, the total becomes 397 as in Table 57.

Table 58 Overlap between classes of injury

i All injuries in Great Britain: 1973

	Numbers of injuries recorded									
	At work	At work place outside working hours	Commuting	Motor, moving	Motor, stationary	Other transport	Goods or services	Public highway	Other premises	Others possibly due to the act or omission of another
Under 1 or 2 headings[1]										
At work	**820**			25	33	23	9	2	9	20
At work place outside working hours		**25**		1		1				5
Commuting			**34**	62	4	3	2	10	1	2
Motor, moving	25	1	62	**187**			5	10	1	16
Motor, stationary	33		4		**31**			1		4
Other transport	23	1	3			**77**	2	3		12
Goods or services	9		2	5		2	**55**			1
Public highway	2		10	10	1	3		**73**		2
Other premises	9			1					**84**	4
Others possibly due to the act or omission of another	20	5	2	16	4	12	1	2	4	**526**
Sub-totals	941	32	117	307	73	121	74	100	99	592
Under 3 headings[2]	10		12	14	3	5	4	8		10
Totals	951	32	129	321	76	126	78	108	99	602

1 Injuries classified under only one heading appear in main diagonal; those under two headings appear twice off the main diagonal (in relevant rows and columns).

2 22 injuries, details of which are given in part ii of this table.

Table 58 Overlap between classes of injury

ii Injuries classified to three headings   Numbers of injuries recorded

	Third heading Goods or services	Third heading Public highway	Other	Total
First two headings				
At work/motor, moving	3	1	1	5
At work/motor, stationary		1	2	3
At work/other transport	1		1	2
Commuting/motor, moving		4	5	9
Commuting/other transport		2	1	3
Totals	4	8	10	22

Table 59 Overlap between work and transport injuries

Great Britain: 1973   Numbers of injuries recorded

	Total injuries	Of which recorded also as: Motor, moving	Of which recorded also as: Motor, stationary	Of which recorded also as: Other transport
Injuries:				
At work	951	30	36	25
At work place outside working hours	32	1	–	1
Commuting	129	71	4	6

Sex, age and economic status

331   An analysis of the data recorded in the survey by sex, age and economic status is shown in Table 61. This and subsequent tables cover injuries whether or not due to the act or omission of another. In Table 61 duplication has been eliminated. The patterns shown here for Great Britain differ from those shown by the estimated aggregate figures for the United Kingdom shown in Chapter 2, in which corrections were made for the fact that some classes of injury were more fully reported than others (for example, work injuries better than others, and injuries to women better than injuries to men).

332   A more detailed analysis of the incidence of injury by sex and age recorded in the survey is given in Table 62, injuries at work and motor injuries being distinguished. The incidence rates are expressed as the numbers of injuries to be expected in 1973 for each 1,000 people in the relevant sex and age group.

Table 60 Classes of injury with duplication eliminated

Great Britain: 1973 Numbers of injuries recorded[1]

At work	Arising from work or during working hours	951
At work place outside working hours	At place of work outside working hours	32
Commuting	On way to or from work	129
Motor, moving	Moving motor vehicles on the road, moving cars and commercial vehicles off the road	219
Motor, stationary	Stationary motor vehicles	36
Other transport	Non-motor and non-road vehicles and other transport injuries (including air, sea and rail)	94
Goods or services	Possible fault in goods and/or services (including medical services)	56
Public highway	Possible defects in public highway	75
Other premises	Possible defects in premises owned or occupied by another	88
Others due to the act or omission of another	Possibly caused in other ways by the act or omission of another	526
Total possibly due to the act or omission of another		2,206
Injuries not due to the act or omission of another		1,096
All injuries		3,302

1 Injuries are counted only in the first class in which they appear.

Table 61 Injuries by sex, age and economic status

Great Britain: 1973

i All injuries Numbers of injuries recorded[1]

	Both sexes				Males				Females			
	Total	0–14	15 to 59/64	60/65+	Total	0–14	15–64	65+	Total	0–14	15–59	60+
Employees	1,747	–	1,675	72	1,230	–	1,211	19	517	–	464	53
Self employed	126	–	118	8	103	–	99	4	23	–	19	4
Unemployed	20	–	19	1	14	–	14	–	6	–	5	1
Children and students[2]	902	774	128	–	541	446	95	–	361	328	33	–
Others not at work	507	–	179	328	65	–	15	50	442	–	164	278
Total	3,302	774	2,119	409	1,953	446	1,434	73	1,349	328	685	336

ii At work

	Both sexes				Males				Females			
	Total	0–14	15 to 59/64	60/65+	Total	0–14	15–64	65+	Total	0–14	15–59	60+
Employees	874	–	848	26	699	–	688	11	175	–	160	15
Self employed	71	–	69	2	65	–	63	2	6	–	6	–
Children and students[2]	6	3	3	–	5	2	3	–	1	1	–	–
Total	951	3	920	28	769	2	754	13	182	1	166	15

Table 61—*continued*

iii   Motor (i.e. moving plus stationary, not work)

	Both sexes 15 to				Males				Females			
	Total	0–14	59/64	60/65+	Total	0–14	15–64	65+	Total	0–14	15–59	60+
Employees	188	–	183	5	125	–	125	–	63	–	58	5
Self employed	12	–	10	2	11	–	9	2	1	–	1	–
Unemployed	4	–	4	–	4	–	4	–	–	–	–	–
Children and students[2]	72	59	13	–	41	32	9	–	31	27	4	–
Others not at work	54	–	16	38	9	–	3	6	45	–	13	32
Total	330	59	226	45	190	32	150	8	140	27	76	37

iv   Other injuries

	Both sexes 15 to				Males				Females			
	Total	0–14	59/64	60/65+	Total	0–14	15–64	65+	Total	0–14	15–59	60+
Employees	685	–	644	41	406	–	398	8	279	–	246	33
Self employed	43	–	39	4	27	–	27	–	16	–	12	4
Unemployed	16	–	15	1	10	–	10	–	6	–	5	1
Children and students[2]	824	712	112	–	495	412	83	–	329	300	29	–
Others not at work	453	–	163	290	56	–	12	44	397	–	151	246
Total	2,021	712	973	336	994	412	530	52	1,027	300	443	284

1 Duplication eliminated.
2 Children under 15, and students in full-time education.

333   This analysis is affected by the incomplete reporting of injuries. The incidence rates shown are all too low, those for males to a greater extent than for females, so that the true differences between the sexes up to age 60 are greater than those which appear.

334   It is possible none the less to draw the following conclusions:

i   The incidence of injury is greater for males than for females at all ages up to 60. For men at work, the incidence is several times as great; allowing for the numbers of men who are at work being 50 per cent greater than those of women it is clear that men have an appreciably higher risk of accident, not surprisingly given that they do most of the more dangerous jobs.

ii   Injury rates reach a peak at 10–14 for girls and 15–19 for boys but then decline. The highest accident rates are found among males in their later teens.

iii   Road injuries represent a minority of the total numbers. Even among boys in the 15–19 age group, they account for no more than 20 per cent of all injuries as defined in the survey.

iv   For men the decline in injury rates in early adult life tends to continue, with a sharp drop at retirement age, whereas injury rates for women after age 30 are higher than for women in their twenties. From about age 60, women have a greater rate of injury than men. Injuries to people over 60 largely occur in private homes but include also many injuries resulting from falls in the street.

Table 62   Incidence of injuries by sex and age

Great Britain: 1973   Incidence rates per 1,000 people[1]

	Both sexes			Males			Females		
	Total	At work	Motor[2]	Total	At work	Motor[2]	Total	At work	Motor[2]
0–4	17·6	0	1·6	22·5	0	1·2	12·8	0	1·7
5–9	32·0	0	2·6	38·3	0	3·4	25·4	0	1·6
10–14	49·2	0·4	3·6	51·5	0·5	3·6	47·2	0·2	3·4
15–19	54·8	15·3	10·6	80·7	24·2	16·0	27·6	5·4	4·4
20–24	43·9	20·2	7·0	69·2	33·6	10·2	19·7	4·1	4·1
25–29	42·5	18·9	4·5	66·0	35·0	7·2	20·8	3·6	1·6
30–34	43·7	18·3	5·2	61·9	31·1	7·5	26·4	5·5	2·3
35–39	38·4	21·5	4·9	51·9	33·0	6·8	25·3	6·6	2·3
40–44	31·7	18·1	3·8	37·9	26·1	3·0	25·4	9·7	4·0
45–49	31·9	15·3	3·3	34·8	20·7	4·6	29·0	9·5	1·3
50–54	34·0	13·6	4·9	35·6	20·3	5·6	32·5	7·1	3·4
55–59	33·9	15·3	4·6	36·1	25·9	4·8	31·6	5·4	3·7
60–64	31·8	10·0	3·7	31·7	17·2	4·1	32·0	3·0	2·7
65–69	25·3	3·7	3·1	14·6	4·6	2·8	34·6	2·3	3·0
70–74	25·7	0·3	3·3	15·5	0·7	2·1	32·9	0	3·9
75–79	29·9	0·9	3·2	15·9	2·7	0	37·6	0	5·0
80 and over	39·2	0	3·3	24·1	0	1·9	45·8	0	4·0
All ages	35·5	10·2	4·3	43·4	17·1	5·6	28·2	5·2	3·0

1 Based on the whole sample of 3,302 injured people, excluding 3 where age was not given.
2 Including injuries while at work.

335   Table 63 gives an analysis of the incidence of injury by employment status and sex.

336   Those at work are more subject to injury than those who are not, no doubt because they generally lead more active lives. Male employees have a much higher risk of injury than the male self employed, partly because of different employment patterns. The corresponding comparison for females is not of significance as the number of self employed women was small.

Socio-economic groups

337   Table 64 sets out the distribution of households in which someone had been injured during 1973 according to the socio-economic group of the head of the household, together with the most nearly comparable distribution for all

heads of household in Great Britain derived from the general household survey for 1971.

Table 63   Incidence of injuries by employment status and sex

Great Britain: 1973   Incidence rates per 1,000 people[1]

	Both sexes			Males			Females		
	Total	At work	Motor[2]	Total	At work	Motor[2]	Total	At work	Motor[2]
Employees	47·6	23·8	5·5	54·9	31·2	7·8	36·1	12·2	4·9
Self employed	36·2	20·3	5·5	35·6	22·6	6·4	39·0	10·9	1·6
Others	27·1	0·1	2·5	31·5	0·2	3·0	24·6	–	2·3
Total	35·5	10·2	4·3	43·4	17·1	5·6	28·2	5·2	3·0

1 Based on the whole sample of 3,302 injured people, excluding 5 for whom information was not given.
2 Including injuries while at work.

Table 64   Analysis by socio-economic group of head of household

Great Britain   Percentages

	Households with a member injured and where head of household at work[1]	All households in Great Britain where head of household below pensionable age[2]
Professional	4·4	4·9
Employers and managers	13·9	15·9
Intermediate and junior non-manual	15·3	19·6
Skilled manual	45·2	37·3
Semi-skilled manual and personal service	16·7	17·1
Unskilled manual	4·5	5·1
Totals	100·0	100·0

1 Personal injury survey, 1973.
2 General household survey, 1971.

338   For all groups except skilled manual workers the figures show rather lower percentages in the first column relating to households containing someone who had been injured. The results may well have been affected, however, by

97

different reporting rates among the different groups. Caution should therefore be exercised in drawing any firm conclusions from this table.

Geographical differences

339   The geographical variation in the incidence of injuries is shown in Table 65, with work injuries distinguished from others.

Table 65   Incidence of injuries by region

Great Britain: 1973   Incidence rates per 1,000 people[1]

	Total	At work	Other
Region			
Northern	41·3	13·7	27·6
Yorkshire and Humberside	38·7	14·3	24·4
North Western	40·0	10·8	29·2
East Midlands	39·8	14·0	25·8
West Midlands	33·8	9·0	24·8
East Anglia	31·1	7·7	23·4
South Western	34·2	7·5	26·7
Wales	38·5	12·0	26·5
Greater London	33·0	9·4	23·6
South Eastern	33·0	7·7	25·3
Scotland	31·0	9·7	21·3
Great Britain	35·5	10·2	25·3

1 Based on the whole sample of 3,302 injuries.

340   Regional differences do not appear to be large. Higher than average rates of work injury were recorded in the Northern region, Yorkshire, the East Midlands and in Wales. The incidence of work injury was well below the average in the South East apart from London, in East Anglia, and in the South West. There is some association between the incidence of work injury and the presence of heavy industry, although not a very strong one. No clear pattern appears in the figures for injuries other than work.

341   In Scotland, the incidence of work injury did not differ much from that in England and Wales. The incidence of injuries of other kinds appears to have been somewhat lower.

Heads of household

342   Of the 3,302 injuries during 1973 which were recorded, 1,400 were to heads of household and 1,902 to others. Most of the heads of household were men, but 283 were women, of whom 38 had children. The reported incidence

of injury to heads of households was relatively high, mainly because they were much more likely to be injured at work than others.

343   Table 66 shows the pattern of dependants of injured men who were heads of household and for whom this information was given.

Table 66   Dependants of injured men who were heads of household

Great Britain: 1973

	Numbers recorded	Percentages
Working wife and:		
No children	239	22
1 child	98	9
2 children	122	11
3 children or more	56	5
Non-working wife and:		
No children	137	12
1 child	106	10
2 children	163	15
3 children or more	94	9
No wife and no children	76	7
No wife and 1 or more children	3	–
Totals	1,094[1]	100

1 Excluding 23 injured heads of household who did not supply this information.

Housewives

344    $4\frac{1}{2}$ per cent of all injuries recorded in 1973 – 151 cases – were to housewives, defined for the purpose of this survey as married women under 60 not at work. 69 per cent of injured housewives had no grounds for making a tort claim. The pattern of their injuries is compared in Table 67 with the pattern for all injuries other than those connected with work. The recorded annual incidence of injury to housewives was relatively low – 15·4 per 1,000, compared with 35·5 per 1,000 for the whole sample.

Industry

345   The incidence of injuries at work recorded by the survey in the industry groups distinguished in the Standard Industrial Classification is shown in Table 68.

Table 67   Injuries to housewives compared with all injuries not connected with work

Great Britain: 1973

	Housewives		All injuries not connected with work	
	Numbers recorded	Percentages of total	Numbers recorded	Percentages of total
Motor	13	8·6	255	11·6
Other transport	–	–	94	4·3
Goods or services	8	5·3	63	2·9
Public highway	15	9·9	88	4·0
Other premises	3	2·0	90	4·1
Others possibly due to the act or omission of another	11	7·3	565	25·8
Not due to the act or omission of another	104	68·9	1,096	50·0
Totals[1]	151	100·0	2,190	100·0

1 After double counting has been eliminated.

Fatal injuries in 1973

346   Interviews with dependants were achieved in three of the five cases of fatal injury identified. These three cases had a number of features in common. In each case the injury occurred as a result of an accident at work and the victim was a young married male manual worker with young children. All three victims had life insurance cover and payments of £750, £400 and £2,000 were made. In all three cases an attempt was made by the widow to claim damages and in two cases settlements were made out of court, with payments of £14,000 and £20,000. In the third case, the claim was dropped, largely because there was some doubt about the outcome since the injured man had been in part responsible for the accident.

Table 68   Incidence of injuries at work by industry

Great Britain: 1973

	Numbers of injuries recorded	Incidence rates per 1,000 workers
Agriculture, forestry and fishing	44	32·8
Mining and quarrying	62	96·7
Food, drink and tobacco	39	35·0
Coal and petroleum products	2	18·5
Chemical and allied industries	20	35·9
Metal manufacture	40	35·9
Mechanical engineering	59	44·2
Instrument engineering	1	4·1
Electrical engineering	28	19·4
Shipbuilding and marine engineering	9	34·1
Vehicles	49	32·5
Metal goods not elsewhere specified	30	34·6
Textiles	17	16·5
Leather, leather goods and fur	2	35·7
Clothing and footwear	12	16·8
Bricks, pottery, glass, cement, etc.	21	61·2
Timber, furniture, etc.	17	42·7
Paper, printing and publishing	17	17·4
Other manufacturing industries	18	38·2
Construction	130	42·0
Gas, electricity and water	12	20·4
Transport and communication	66	26·3
Distributive trades	86	17·9
Insurance, banking, finance and business services	4	2·3
Professional and scientific services	62	12·3
Miscellaneous services	65	17·4
Public administration and defence	34	13·4
All injuries at work	946[1]	23·6

1 Excluding 5 cases where the industry was not given.

CHAPTER 16

Personal injury survey : severity of injury

347   The degree of severity of injuries was indicated in one way or another by several items of information collected in the personal injury survey: the duration of incapacity, the type and duration of medical treatment, the nature of the injury, and whether it had permanent after-effects. None provided a wholly satisfactory measure of severity. Injuries grouped together according to one or other criterion could encompass a wide range of conditions. The least unsatisfactory measure was duration of incapacity, although even this was influenced by the injured person's activities and by his own reaction, both physical and psychological, to injury.

348   All the measures and the analyses based on them are affected by the fact that serious injuries were more fully reported than slight ones. Percentages of the total number of injuries represented by incapacity of more than six months may be two or three times the true figures. Comparison between classes of injury, however, will be distorted only if the bias is different for the various classes compared.

Durations of incapacity

349   Periods of absence from work and from school or college were the most clearly defined durations, though even here recollection might not be fully accurate. A less precise measure of duration was used for injuries not leading to absence from work, school or college, namely incapacity for any normal activity, including housework, school activities, sport and play. By definition this duration could not be less than duration of absence from work, school or college and it could be much longer. Since the survey included injuries if they had led to four or more days of incapacity of any kind, it follows that some injuries to those at work were included even where there was less than four days' absence from work (and similarly for those in full time education).

350   It was not possible to express durations of incapacity according to these different criteria in terms of any common measure. There was no simple relationship between, for example, incapacity for work and incapacity for any normal activity. The question on incapacity for any normal activity was variously answered; some said there was no incapacity when they had managed to function effectively in spite of an inconvenience such as an arm in plaster; others claimed to be incapacitated by trivial injuries.

351 Differences between measures of duration are illustrated in Table 69, which compares the patterns of duration for particular groups of injured. Duration of incapacity for any normal activity is compared with length of absence from work, school or college. The table shows how incapacity for any normal activity can outlast absences from work, school or college; and the preponderance of short periods of absence from work and, even more, from school or college. The high proportion of short absences among children and students may not necessarily indicate that injuries to children were generally less severe than injuries to adults, though this might have been a contributory factor. It might be that a child with minor injuries was more likely to have been treated by a doctor and thus to have qualified for inclusion in the survey, than an adult with similar injuries. In the same way minor injuries to workers, who might have visited a doctor simply in order to obtain a medical certificate, might have been more often included than minor injuries to non-workers. Other possible reasons for the high proportion of short absences among children are that they stay away more readily than adults for minor injuries, or that they have greater power of recuperation.

Table 69 Duration of incapacity by type of incapacity

Injuries to employed persons and to children and students in full-time education
Great Britain: 1973

	Work	Incapacity for School or college	Any normal activity
	Numbers of injuries recorded		
Total numbers	1,873	774	2,647
Not analysed[1]	353	378	
Incapacity of 4 days or more	1,520	396	2,647
	Percentages		
4 days–2 weeks	29·2	57·3	21·2
Over 2 weeks–1 month	24·4	19·9	23·2
Over 1 month–6 months	41·2	21·7	37·4
Over 6 months	5·2	1·0	18·2
Total	100·0	100·0	100·0

1 Incapacitated for less than 4 days (for particular activity) together with those injured while on holiday or absent from work, and a few providing unsatisfactory information.

Incapacity for work

352 Varying durations of incapacity for different classes of injury are best shown by concentrating on those in employment at the time of injury, a group comprising more than half of all injuries recorded in 1973. The corresponding

indicator of duration is then the most clearly defined of the measures, length of absence from work. If one case in which no answer was given is excluded, the survey produced 1,872 cases of injuries to the employed where there were at least four days of incapacity for any normal activity. 352 of the injured workers were, for various reasons, not away from work for four days or more. From these figures an indicator of the relationship between the broader and narrower measures of duration can be derived. The number of cases (1,872) on the broader measure is 23 per cent greater than the number (1,520) on the narrower measure.

353   Table 70 analyses the 1,520 cases of absence from work of four or more days. Injuries not involving work or transport tended to be less severe, and transport injuries were those most likely to lead to long periods of incapacity.

Table 70   Duration of incapacity for work, by class of injury

Injuries to employed persons in Great Britain: 1973

	Total	At work	Transport	Other
	Numbers of injuries recorded			
Total numbers[1]	1,873	945[2]	231	697
Not analysed[3]	353	132	41	180
Incapacity of 4 days or more	1,520	813	190	517
	Percentages			
4 days–2 weeks	29·2	26·2	28·9	34·1
Over 2 weeks–1 month	24·4	24·7	20·0	25·5
Over 1 month–6 months	41·2	43·5	42·1	37·1
Over 6 months	5·2	5·5	8·9	3·3
Total	100·0	100·0	100·0	100·0

1 Duplication eliminated.
2 Excluding 6 students injured while in employment.
3 Incapacitated for less than 4 days, injured while on holiday or absent from work, and one case where information not provided.

354   The frequency of lengthy absences from work was greater for males than for females, and greater for older than for younger people injured. (Table 71.)

Medical treatment

355   The under-reporting of the less memorable injuries, especially of those not requiring any hospital treatment, is shown by Table 72. The more recent the injuries in 1973, the larger was the proportion of cases reported which had been treated outside hospital and the smaller the proportion of in-patient cases. It may be assumed that since some bias remains even in the last quarter,

104

the true proportion of injuries not requiring hospital treatment is somewhere over 20 per cent. Most of the injured, some two thirds, were treated in out-patient departments, and no more than 13 per cent became in-patients.

Table 71   Duration of incapacity for work, by sex and age

Injuries to employed persons in Great Britain: 1973

	Males			Females		
	15–29	30–44	45+	15–29	30–44	45+
	Numbers of injuries recorded					
Total numbers	553	413	367	137	156	247
Not analysed[1]	109	78	52	32	37	45
Incapacity of 4 days or more	444	335	315	105	119	202
	Percentages					
4 days–2 weeks	39·4	25·1	20·6	43·8	31·1	18·3
Over 2 weeks–1 month	23·9	26·6	20·3	21·9	29·4	26·7
Over 1 month–6 months	33·3	45·1	48·9	32·4	36·1	47·5
Over 6 months	3·4	3·3	10·2	1·9	3·4	7·4
Total	100·0	100·0	100·0	100·0	100·0	100·0

1 Incapacity for less than 4 days, injured while on holiday or absent from work, and one case where information not provided.

Table 72   Type of medical treatment

All injuries in Great Britain: 1973

	All injuries in 1973	Injuries during:			
		1st Qtr	2nd Qtr	3rd Qtr	4th Qtr
Numbers of injuries recorded	3,302	662	730	951	959
		Percentages			
Type of treatment:					
Hospital in-patient[1]	17·3	19·6	20·3	17·4	13·5
Hospital out-patient[2]	66·5	65·4	66·3	67·1	66·7
Not in hospital	16·2	15·0	13·4	15·6	19·8
Total	100·0	100·0	100·0	100·0	100·0

1 Whether or not also treated as out-patient or outside hospital.
2 Whether or not also treated outside hospital.

356 Duration of medical treatment is a further indicator of the proportion of severe injuries. The analyses of Tables 73 and 74 give results distinguishing some of the smaller classes of injury. Comparison with Table 70 for those who had work injuries indicates how medical treatment outlasted incapacity.

Table 73   Duration of medical treatment for work and transport injuries

Great Britain: 1973

	All injuries in 1973	At work	Commut- ing and work related	Moving motor vehicles	Other transport
Numbers of injuries recorded[1]	3,302	951	161	321	202
			Percentages		
Medical treatment of:					
Less than 4 days	7·1	4·6	6·2	7·5	5·9
4 days–2 weeks	20·3	20·0	15·5	17·8	22·8
Over 2 weeks–1 month	19·0	19·7	16·8	10·9	18·8
Over 1 month–6 months	28·7	25·3	32·3	24·9	30·2
Over 6 months	23·7	29·0	28·6	38·6	21·3
Not given	1·2	1·4	0·6	0·3	1·0
Total	100·0	100·0	100·0	100·0	100·0

1 Duplication not eliminated from figures for the four classes of injury.

357   On this criterion, injuries at work appear to be marginally more severe than injuries in general. The frequency of prolonged medical treatment, lasting for at least six months, tends to be highest for injuries from criminal violence, for those sustained from moving motor vehicles and for those arising from defective goods and services.

Nature of injuries

358 Table 75 gives an analysis by nature of injury, classified according to the nature of injury codes of the International Classification of Diseases (ICD). The residual category at the end includes a few conditions added to the ICD for the purpose of the survey, which are described in Chapter 21. Two classes of injury, at work and transport (other than when working), are distinguished; all other injuries are lumped together in a third class. An injured person who had suffered multiple injuries would appear under more than one head. Multiple entries were particularly frequent for transport injuries. Lacerations, contusions,

and superficial injury, separately or together arose more frequently in transport cases than in other classes of injury.

Table 74 Duration of medical treatment for other injuries

Great Britain: 1973

| | Possible fault in goods or services | Premises | Possibly due to the act or omission of another | | | Not due to the act or omission of another |
			Children[1]	Criminal violence	Other	
Numbers of injuries recorded[2]	78	207	323	62	217	1,096
Medical treatment of:			Percentages			
Less than 4 days	3·8	4·3	11·8	9·7	8·3	7·7
4 days – 2 weeks	21·8	21·7	22·0	16·1	22·6	20·2
Over 2 weeks – 1 month	7·7	17·4	22·0	17·7	20·3	19·9
Over 1 month – 6 months	26·9	34·3	30·3	24·2	27·6	30·7
Over 6 months	39·7	21·7	13·6	32·3	19·4	19·9
Not given	–	0·5	0·3	–	1·8	1·6
Total	100·0	100·0	100·0	100·0	100·0	100·0

1 Children under supervision and children playing or fighting.
2 Duplication not eliminated.

Permanent effects

359 In 29 per cent of all recorded injuries, it was reported at interview that the injury had, or might have, resulted in permanent damage. Because of the bias in the sample towards more severe injuries, this probably overstates the true proportion, which is likely to be less than one quarter. Table 76 shows the reported proportions for all injuries, for those injured at work and for three other classes with above average proportions. The figures are consistent with other information and, in particular, with the proportions of injuries involving medical treatment of over six months (also shown in the table). It was again found that severity was related to age; the proportion of permanent or possibly permanent damage increased with the age of the person injured.

Table 75   Nature of injury, by class of injury

Great Britain: 1973

	ICD Code (N codes)	All injuries in 1973	At work	Transport	Other
Numbers of injuries recorded[1]		3,302	951	432	1,919
Nature of injury:[2]		Percentages			
Fracture:					
skull/face	800–804	2·4	1·2	6·1	2·2
trunk	805–809	3·5	3·2	8·4	2·6
upper limb	810–819	16·4	10·7	14·2	19·7
lower limb	820–828	10·3	8·4	11·2	11·0
Dislocation without fracture	830–839	5·7	6·9	5·4	5·2
Sprain/strain	840–848	23·8	28·2	25·2	21·3
Internal injury[3]	850–869	5·7	2·7	20·7	3·9
Laceration/open wound	870–907	25·7	25·8	43·4	21·5
Superficial injury	910–918	9·8	6·4	22·4	8·6
Contusion etc.	920–929	19·4	15·8	43·1	16·0
Foreign body[4]	930–939	1·4	2·9	0·2	0·9
Burns	940–949	3·1	2·9	1·2	3·6
Adverse effects[5]	960–999	5·4	4·1	4·9	5·4
Other conditions		8·1	9·0	7·7	7·8

1 Duplication eliminated.
2 Injuries may be classified under more than one head; totals of percentages exceed 100.
3 Intra-cranial, chest, abdomen, pelvis.
4 Effect of foreign body entering through orifice.
5 Poisonings, medical injuries, and effects of other external causes.

Table 76   Permanent or possibly permanent effects

Great Britain: 1973

	All injuries in 1973	At work	Moving motor vehicle	Possible fault in goods or services	Criminal violence
Numbers of injuries recorded[1]	3,302	951	321	78	62
Percentages of injuries with:					
Permanent effects[2]	29	34	40	41	37
Medical treatment of over 6 months[3]	24	29	39	40	32

1 Duplication not eliminated.
2 Injuries reported as leading to permanent or possibly permanent damage.
3 From Tables 73 and 74.

CHAPTER 17

Personal injury survey: financial consequences of injury

360 Detailed information was recorded at interview about losses and receipts which arose as a direct result of injury. On the one hand, there were losses of earnings arising from absence from work, together with expenses of various kinds, and losses of income by family members taking care of injured persons. On the other hand, there were many types of receipts to be taken into account. They included the relevant social security benefits, and allowances and receipts from such sources as private insurance, trade unions and friendly societies. Benefits in kind, such as treatment under the National Health Service, were not included in the present analysis. The balance between losses and receipts is shown in Tables 80 and 81.

361 The amounts of earnings lost, of other financial losses and of compensation received were not always exactly remembered 8 to 24 months after the injury. The tables given here should therefore be taken as showing the broad pattern of losses and receipts rather than as indicating exact relationships between their component parts.

362 By the time of interview, the full financial consequences were not always known. Only about half the tort claims had been settled. Since these could not be taken as representative of the totality, receipts of tort compensation are shown only in a footnote. On the other side of the account, 62 persons were still suffering financial loss at the time of interview. In order not to leave these more serious cases out of account, figures are included of their aggregate values up to the date of interview. No attempt was made to estimate the capital value of losses and receipts continuing after that date. Such an estimate would depend not only on the age pattern and the expectation of life, but on prospective earnings if work was resumed later, as quite often happens. (The analysis of long term incapacity in Chapter 2 shows that only a small proportion of those incapacitated remain permanently unable to do any work at all.)

Loss of earnings

363 The main loss is that arising directly from absence from work, though some injured workers would not have been incapacitated for work, but for some other activity. For the employed, the gross loss of earnings was taken as the normal take home pay at the rate of earnings on the job at the time of injury. From this was deducted any sick pay received from the employer. For the self employed, the injured person's own estimate of loss of earnings was taken.

364 Employers' sick pay was reported as having been received by about half the employees injured. Where there was sick pay it could be in full or in part, and for the whole or only part of the period up to return to work. How much was obtained varied greatly between types of occupation, as shown in Table 77.

Table 77 Sick pay, by socio-economic group

Great Britain: Injuries to employees in 1973

	Professional and managerial	Other non-manual	Manual		
			Skilled	Semi-skilled[2]	Un-skilled
Numbers of injuries[1]	81	271	636	402	119
		Percentages			
Full or part sick pay throughout	77	72	45	42	43
Sick pay part of time	9	6	4	5	2
No sick pay	11	21	50	52	53
Not recorded	4	1	1	1	2
Total	100	100	100	100	100

1 Injuries to employees involving absence from work, excluding 7 cases not classified by socio-economic group.
2 Including personal services and agriculture.

365 Frequently employers made up sickness benefit under the national insurance scheme to full pay. Where this was reported, Table 77 shows the amount as part sick pay. There must, however, be cases of this kind unrecorded and so left under the full pay heading. Against this, since sickness benefit does not attract tax whereas sick pay is taxed as earned income, there is a small gain which is here ignored.

366 Table 78 gives distributions of loss of earnings, both gross before and net after deduction of sick pay, for all injuries to employees leading to absence from work and to self employed persons reporting loss of earnings. Since there is no sick pay for the self employed, their losses appear equally in the gross and net distributions.

Other losses

367 Altogether 85 per cent of injured employees had returned to their former job by the date of interview. The remaining cases comprised not only those with continuing absence from work, but also some injured persons who needed to change jobs and in some cases to change occupations. Where this resulted,

111

as it usually did, in reduced pay, the loss was taken as reported up to the date of interview. The average figure for all those reporting reduced pay was £207. Where reduction of pay was temporary, the loss was on average little more than £100; the amounts were greater for reductions continuing up to the interview, over £500 in one third of such injuries.

Table 78   Loss of earnings, before and after deduction of sick pay[1]

Great Britain: Injuries to employees and self employed in 1973[2]

Loss	Gross loss	Net loss
£[3]	Percentages	
No loss	–	19·0
Less than 10	4·4	6·1
10 – 19	7·7	7·9
20 – 49	20·3	18·2
50 – 99	20·3	15·8
100–199	17·4	13·1
200–499	19·3	13·8
500–999	5·2	3·7
Over 1,000	2·5	2·2
Not recorded	3·0	0·5
Total	100·0	100·0
Average	£189	£144

1 Amounts up to time of interview.
2 Injuries (1,592 in total) involving absence from work for employees, or loss of earnings for self employed.
3 At 1973 prices.

368   Some injured persons had additional losses, from reduction or elimination of income from sources other than the main employment. These could be second jobs or casual earnings. The amount of these losses, as estimated by the informant, was on average £107.

369   A main item of expenses in some cases was loss of income incurred by family members needing to look after the injured person. Some of the injured in need of such care were themselves employees; more usually, they were children or other non-workers and the main loss was of this indirect kind. The loss was £56 on average over all cases where family members were reported as losing earnings.

370   Expenses necessarily connected with the treatment of an injury arose in more than half of all injuries. On average they came to only £6, but this might be a small under-statement since some minor expenses might have been overlooked

at interview. A great variety of expenses was reported. The most frequent were travelling expenses, prescription charges and medical or surgical items; others ranged from domestic help to extra laundry and special foods.

Receipts

371   Table 79 summarises information on social security benefits and other receipts of compensation. The figures shown relate to all 1973 injuries. Details provided at interview were checked, to the limited extent possible, for accuracy and internal consistency. There remained some under-reporting: not all small receipts could have been remembered, and as explained above, there were almost certainly some cases recorded as having full sick pay when in fact sickness benefit was made up to full pay.

Table 79   Receipts by type

Great Britain: All injuries in 1973

	Proportion of those injured receiving benefit[1]	Average amount received[2]
	Percentages	£
Sickness/injury and related benefits	32·3	108
Attendance allowance	0·1	..
Unemployment benefit	0·3	129
Supplementary benefit	0·6	47
Rent/rates rebates	1·0	41
Criminal injuries compensation	0·5	406
Private insurance	7·0	39
Other receipts[3]	5·1	17

1 Out of 3,302 injured persons; some received more than one benefit.
2 Up to date of interview; at 1973 prices.
3 From trade unions, friendly societies and charities.

372   Sickness benefit, injury benefit (for industrial injuries) and related benefits represented by far the most important receipts, in respect both of numbers and amounts. Partly because of under-recording, they were reported as having been received by only two thirds of workers injured in 1973 who were absent from work for four or more days. Those who failed to qualify included those with insufficient or no contributions, including many self employed. Married women employees who had opted out of the general national insurance scheme were eligible for injury benefit if injured at work, but not for sickness benefit if injured elsewhere. Some injured workers may not have realised that they were eligible for particular benefits.

373   Three injured non-workers received attendance allowance, which in 1973 was the only state benefit available to non-workers.

113

374   There were a few reported claims, all small, for supplementary benefits and for rent or rates rebates. Claims for criminal injuries compensation were also few but generally quite large. Unemployment benefit, being paid only to those fit for work, did not usually arise for injured employees. In a few cases, 10 in all, amongst those needing to change job or occupation because of injury, the recorded absence from work included a short period looking for work; the unemployment benefit was then regarded as having been paid as a result of the injury.

375   Some 10 per cent of the injured reported relevant private insurance, either general accident policies or specific cover against loss of income or private medical expenses. Claims were made by about 70 per cent of these injured persons; most were met in full and fairly promptly, over two thirds within a month of the claim. The amounts reported were small, rarely exceeding £100. The self employed were more likely to have received money from private insurance than were other groups.

376   In 5 per cent of the injuries there were other sources of relief, mainly from trade unions but also from schemes operated by friendly societies or from charities. The amounts received averaged less than £20.

Balance of losses and receipts

377   Table 80 sets out the balance of losses and receipts in aggregate for all 1973 injuries, excluding only a few cases of incomplete information. Similar estimates are given in Table 81 for some broad categories of injury; it distinguishes injuries where financial loss was still being incurred at the time of interview, and those which had been the subject of a tort claim, either settled or still being pursued.

378   Of those without continuing losses or tort claims, the group who did best in terms of the proportion of losses covered by receipts of compensation were employees injured at work; 60 per cent of their losses were made good. Employees injured elsewhere than at work recovered nearly half their losses.

379   The self employed fared less well. They reported larger average losses than employees, with less than one third of them covered by receipts. The self employed did not receive injury benefit for injuries at work, or employers' sick pay. Since their loss of earnings usually had to be estimated, there may have been a tendency to exaggerate.

380   In contrast with the figures for workers, those for non-workers showed little in the way of financial losses, and still less by way of receipts. Appreciable losses occurred only in the form of loss of income by a member of the family.

381   As was to be expected, net losses were largest for injuries with losses continuing up to the date of interview. The extent of the net losses depended both on the large gross losses incurred and on the relatively small offsets. Offsets tended to be relatively smaller because entitlement to some benefits – earnings related benefit, and in most cases employers' sick pay – would have ceased by the time of interview. Consequently less than 40 per cent of the gross losses had been recovered.

Table 80   Losses and receipts[1]

All injuries in Great Britain in 1973

	Numbers[2]	Average[3]	Aggregate value[4]
		£	£'000
Losses			
Gross earnings losses while away from work	1,614	189	305·6
Sick pay	837	88	73·5
Net earnings losses	1,614	144	232·1
Reduced pay[5]	120	207	24·8
Other income[6]	95	107	10·2
Other people's income[7]	247	56	13·8
Expenses	1,899	6	10·7
Total losses	3,296		291·6
Receipts			
Sickness/injury benefit and related benefits	1,065	108	114·5
Unemployment benefit	10	129	1·3
Supplementary benefit	20	47	0·9
Rent/rates rebates	32	41	1·3
Criminal injuries compensation	17	406	6·9
Private insurance	232	39	9·0
Other receipts[8]	153	17	2·5
Total receipts	3,296		136·5[9]
Net loss	3,296		155·1

1 Losses and receipts to date of interview at 1973 prices.
2 All injuries (3,302 in total) less 6 cases with incomplete information.
3 Obtained from cases with amounts recorded.
4 Estimated by summation over classes of injury; average for each class from recorded information taken as applying to cases without information.
5 Loss arising from lower pay obtained on return to work.
6 Mainly in respect of second job.
7 Income lost by other family members.
8 From trade unions, friendly societies and charities.
9 In addition, settled tort claims provided £30,300.

Table 81   Losses and receipts by certain classes of injury

Great Britain: Injuries in 1973

i No continuing losses and no tort claim

	Injuries to employees			Injuries to others	
	At work	Transport[1]	Other	Self employed	Non-workers
Numbers	722	153	646	117	1,367
	£'000 at 1973 prices				
Losses					
Gross earnings losses while away from work	98·2	21·4	57·0	13·8	0·8[2]
Sick pay	28·3	8·0	21·1	–	–
Net earnings losses	69·9	13·4	35·9	13·8	0·8
Reduced pay	2·9	0·7	1·9	0·8	–
Other income	2·5	0·7	2·6	0·2	0·5
Other people's income	0·9	0·6	1·9	0·3	7·7
Expenses	1·5	0·6	1·4	0·5	3·9
Receipts					
Sickness/injury benefit and related benefits	42·8	5·8	15·9	2·7	0·3
Unemployment benefit	0·6	–	0·1	–	–
Supplementary benefit	0·1	–	0·1	0·4	0·2
Rent/rates rebates	0·1	–	0·2	–	–
Criminal injuries compensation	1·7	–	1·4	0·4	0·3
Private insurance	1·2	0·4	2·5	1·2	0·8
Other receipts	0·7	0·2	0·6	–	0·1
Totals					
Losses	77·7	16·0	43·7	15·6	12·9
Receipts	47·2	6·4	20·7	4·7	1·7
Net losses	30·5	9·6	23·0	10·9	11·2
Averages	£	£	£	£	£
Losses	108	104	68	134	9
Receipts	65	42	32	41	1
Net losses	42	62	36	93	8

1 Excluding injuries while at work.
2 Lost earnings of students injured while they had a part time job.

ii With continuing losses or tort claims

	Injuries with continuing losses[3]	Injuries with tort claims	
		Settled	Outstanding
Numbers	62	122	107
	£'000 at 1973 prices[4]		
Losses			
Gross earnings losses while away from work	54·4	23·6	36·4
Sick pay	5·4	4·3	6·6
Net earnings losses	49·0	19·4	29·8
Reduced pay	15·9	0·9	1·8
Other income	1·9	0·9	0·9
Other people's income	1·4	0·2	0·8
Expenses	1·2	0·5	1·0
Receipts			
Sickness/injury benefit and related benefits	21·7	8·6	16·6
Unemployment benefit	0·5	0·1	–
Supplementary benefit	–	0·1	0·1
Rent/rates rebates	0·7	0·2	0·1
Criminal injuries compensation	2·8	0·4	–
Private insurance	0·6	0·2	2·1
Other receipts	0·3	0·1	0·5
Totals			
Losses	69·4	21·9	34·4
Receipts	26·6	9·7[5]	19·4
Net losses	42·8	12·2	15·0
Averages	£	£	£
Losses	1,120	180	321
Receipts	430	80	181
Net losses	691	100	140

3 Including 17 with outstanding tort claims.
4 Losses and receipts up to date of interview.
5 In addition, tort receipts totalled £30,300.

382   Average losses and receipts were relatively large also for injuries which were the subject of tort claims, reflecting the fact that the injuries for which tort claims are made tend to be rather more serious than other injuries. Most

tort claims are made by those who are working, and the balance between receipts and payments – excluding tort compensation – was similar to that for employees, receipts covering something like half the losses.

383   In those cases which had been settled, the tort compensation received exceeded the estimated losses. This result may be explained by two factors. First, most of the tort compensation would have been for non-pecuniary rather than for pecuniary loss. Secondly, the claims settled by the time of interview would have tended to be the smaller ones, for which there may have been some tendency towards over-compensation.

CHAPTER 18

Personal injury survey: tort claims

384 A number of questions were asked in the survey about how injuries had occurred, and about attempts to claim damages.

Who caused the injury

385 Those interviewed were asked whether the injury had been caused by another person 'by something they did or failed to do', and also whether it had been in any way the injured person's own fault. A third of the injured thought that someone else might have caused their injury, at least in part. Details are given in Table 82.

386 The answers indicated the injured person's opinion rather than the objective facts but clearly, if he did not blame anyone, there would rarely be a question of a tort claim. Not all of the injuries classified in the survey as possibly due to the act or omission of another were regarded by the informant as having been 'caused' by someone else. Informants sometimes equated cause with moral blame, and were reluctant, for instance, to say that a child had caused the injury.

387 On the other hand, there were a number of cases where the informant felt that someone was to blame, but where there appeared to be no possibility of liability. Most of these injuries involved children, in circumstances where either it was not clear what happened, but the informant felt that he knew who was to blame, or where the accident appeared on the facts to have happened purely by chance, though the informant attributed blame to someone. An example of the latter is a case where a child was inadvertently scalded during a quarrel between the parents; the mother felt that the father was to blame, though there seemed to be no grounds for a claim.

388 Table 83 shows the kinds of people or organisations said to have caused or possibly caused the injury.

Attempts to claim damages

389 Only 11 per cent of the injured took any steps towards making a claim for tort compensation, even to the extent of discussing the possibility with someone else. The reasons given for not taking action by those who thought that someone might be held responsible for their injury are shown in Table 84. Some people gave more than one reason. Reasons commonly given by those

119

who took no action were that they were not seriously injured, they did not know how to go about making a claim, they had no proof of fault, the person responsible was close to them, or it would have been too much trouble.

Table 82 Opinions about who was at fault

Great Britain: All injuries in 1973[1]   Percentages

	All injuries	At work	Transport[2]	Other
Caused by another, not fault of injured person	23	24	43	19
Caused by another and fault of injured person	10	9	12	10
Fault of injured person alone	38	30	30	44
No one's fault	28	37	15	27
All injuries	100	100	100	100

1 Excluding 9 where no opinion expressed.
2 Excluding transport injuries while at work.

Table 83 Person or organisation causing injury

Great Britain: Injuries in 1973

Number of people or organisations said to have caused or possibly caused injury	
	1,121

Description	Percentages
Employer/fellow employee[1]	23
Driver of vehicle[2]	
Injured person passenger	3
Injured person pedestrian or in other vehicle	15
Local authority[3]	7
Manufacturer/supplier of goods/services	7
Assailant (not in same household)	6
Someone participating in sport	10
Doctor/nurse/medical authority	2
Member of family/friend[4]	17
Others	10
Total	100

1 Excluding injuries involving vehicles on the public highway.
2 Excluding injuries involving vehicles at place of work.
3 Mainly public highway cases.
4 Other than those described above.

Table 84 Reasons for not making a claim

Great Britain: Injuries in 1973   Percentages

Not seriously injured	22
Did not know how to claim/that they could claim	19
It was just an accident	11
Too much trouble/did not want to make a fuss/too upset	11
It would have meant claiming against a member of the family/friend	10
Felt that it was partly own fault	9
Did not lose any/much money/not off work	8
Did not know who was responsible/identity of wrongdoer	8
Could not prove anyone at fault/no witnesses/no evidence	6
Did not think about it/glad to be alive/more concerned about injuries	5
Thought it would cost too much/might lose money	4
Others	13
Total	126[1]

1 In some cases more than one reason was given.

390   Where advice was sought, it was most often sought from a solicitor or trade union or both. Others discussed the matter with family and friends, employers, citizens' advice bureaux, doctors or insurance companies. The proportion consulting a solicitor was highest for injuries caused by moving motor vehicles. A trade union was consulted much more frequently in the case of injuries arising out of work than for other injuries, and would often act on behalf of the injured person in claiming for a work injury.

Outcome of claim

391   Informants were asked about the progress of their claim. It was not always possible to establish in detail what steps had been taken. Some informants who had put their claim in the hands of a solicitor or trade union may not have been kept fully informed of what was happening.

392   Table 85 shows the proportion of cases settled, dropped or still being pursued, distinguishing those where a solicitor had been consulted.

393   About a third of the claims attempted were still outstanding at the time of the interview, 8 to 24 months after the injury occurred.

394   Only 6 per cent of claims were said to have proceeded as far as the issuing of a writ and less than 2 per cent to have reached court. The latter figure is based on only six injuries, three of which were to members of one family injured in the same car accident.

Table 85 Outcome of claim by action taken

Great Britain: Attempted claims in 1973

	All attempted claims	Action taken		
		Solicitor not consulted	Solicitor consulted	
			No letter sent	Letter sent
Numbers of attempted claims	358[1]	124	62	168
Outcome of claim	Percentages			
Payment agreed	34·1	24·2	16·1	48·8
Claim dropped	31·3	60·5	40·3	7·1
Still pursuing claim	34·6	15·3	43·5	44·0
Total	100·0	100·0	100·0	100·0

1 Including 4 cases where action taken not known, but excluding 6 cases where outcome not known.

395 Table 86 shows the outcome of the claim by class of injury. Claims involving moving motor vehicles were most likely to have been settled by the time of the interview; claims other than employers' liability or motor claims were most likely to have been dropped.

Table 86 Outcome of claim by class of injury

Great Britain: Attempted claims in 1973

	All injuries	At work	Motor vehicle[1]	Other
Numbers of attempted claims	364	178	127	75
Outcome not given	6	3	2	1
Numbers of claims where outcome known	358	175	125	74
Outcome of claim	Percentages			
Payment agreed	34·1	32·0	42·4	23·0
Claim dropped	31·3	28·6	18·4	58·1
Still pursuing claim	34·6	39·4	39·2	18·9
Total	100·0	100·0	100·0	100·0

1 Including claims for injuries while at work.

Estimates for claims resulting in payments

396 In order to give some measure of the proportion of injuries which result in payment of tort compensation estimates have been made of the proportion of claims outstanding at the time of interview which might have eventually

succeeded, at least in part. The estimate is based on data derived from the insurance survey described in Chapter 22.

397   Table 87 gives the proportions of injuries estimated on this basis which would result in tort compensation being paid, by class of injury. Injuries caused by motor vehicles sustained while the injured person was at work are included against both the work and motor vehicle headings. Compensation would have been obtained in an estimated 6½ per cent of all injuries, including those clearly not attributable to anyone other than the injured person. The proportion obtaining compensation would have been highest for those injured by motor vehicles.

Table 87   Proportions of injuries where tort compensation obtained

Great Britain: Injuries in 1973

	Number of injuries	Estimated number of payments[1]	Estimated percentage of injuries where payment made
Class of injury			
At work	951	99	10½
Motor vehicle[2]	397	99	25
Other injuries possibly due to the act or omission of another	924	27	3
All injuries possibly due to the act or omission of another[3]	2,206	215	10
Injuries not due to the act or omission of another	1,096	–	–
All injuries	3,302	215	6½

1 Numbers estimated by assuming that payments were made in respect of the following percentages of claims outstanding at time of interview: at work 60 per cent, motor vehicle 90 per cent, other injuries 70 per cent.
2 Including 66 injuries while at work, estimated to have led to 10 payments.
3 Excluding duplication.

398   Table 88 gives a further analysis of the proportions obtaining tort compensation. It shows that workers are more likely to obtain compensation than non-workers, and men more likely than women. Children under the age of 15 stand a particularly poor chance. The lower proportion of injured adult non-workers obtaining compensation seems to be because the circumstances of their injuries are less likely to support a claim. The lower proportion in respect of children occurs whatever the circumstances of the injury; compensation is rarely obtained even for injuries caused by a motor vehicle.

399   The estimated proportion of injuries resulting in the payment of tort compensation steadily increases with the severity of injury as measured by

duration of incapacity. This conclusion is based on an analysis limited to those in work at the time they were injured, for whom a consistent measure of severity was given by length of absence from work.

Table 88 Further analysis of proportions of injuries
where tort compensation obtained[1]

Great Britain: Injuries in 1973	Percentages
All injuries	$6\frac{1}{2}$
Demographic group	
Working men	10
Working women	8
Other men	5
Other women	4
Children under 15	1
Duration of incapacity for work[2]	
4 days – 1 month	6
Over 1 month – 2 months	12
Over 2 months – 3 months	13
Over 3 months – 6 months	20
Over 6 months	31

1 Estimated as in Table 87.
2 Injuries to people in employment.

400   Most of the injuries covered by the survey were relatively slight, providing little incentive to claim, which partly explains why tort compensation was obtained in no more than an estimated 6·5 per cent of all injuries. For the more serious injuries, the proportion estimated to have been compensated through tort was appreciably greater, reaching 31 per cent for those off work for six months or more.

The process of settlement

401   Where a settlement had been reached, informants were asked why they had accepted the offer instead of trying to obtain more. Most had acted on the advice of a solicitor or trade union. Half considered the amount was fair, or at least as much as they could hope to get. Others said they had settled because they wanted to forget about the matter, or because they were afraid to spend more money on pressing their case, or because if they went further they might end with nothing at all.

402   In just over a third of cases in which a settlement had been reached, interim offers had been made and rejected before the final settlement. Usually there had been only one previous offer. Occasionally there had been two or three.

403   Those who had dropped their claim were asked the reasons. Some had been advised by their solicitor or someone else to do so, or had realised they could not prove their case; others had become discouraged or were afraid of the cost of further action, or did not know what further steps they could take.

How compensation was used

404   Table 89 shows how payments of tort compensation had been spent by those who had been injured both in 1973 and in the period from 1966 to 1972. Some people had devoted the money to more than one purpose. Most people spent their money on current expenses; only a minority in either group invested any. It may be relevant that payments reported were generally not large, the average for those injured in 1973 being £249. The proportion of those receiving compensation for injuries in 1973 who invested any of their money may possibly under-estimate the true proportion, since claims settled by the time of interview would tend to be smaller than average. On the other hand, as small claims tend to be forgotten with the passage of time, the proportion of those injured during 1966–72 who invested any money may overstate the true proportion.

Table 89   Use made of lump sums[1]

Great Britain		Percentages
	Injuries in 1973	Injuries in 1966–72
Replacement of damaged property	13·9	6·5
Payment of debts/general living expenses	51·5	37·3
Luxuries/having a holiday	32·7	39·0
Investing some/all	5·0	9·3
Banking some/all	11·9	13·1
Other uses:		
Paying off part/all of mortgage		4·0
	5·0	
Remainder		6·8

1 Reported by those who had already spent or decided how to spend their money

Opinions of the legal system

405   About 30 per cent of those who had consulted a solicitor about claiming for injuries in 1973 were satisfied, and where a settlement had been reached by the time of the interview the proportion was about 40 per cent. Some 50 per cent were not altogether satisfied. The remainder gave no opinion. Those who were not satisfied were asked why; their reasons are shown in Table 90.

Table 90 Reasons for dissatisfaction with the legal system

Great Britain: Injuries in 1973

Number not altogether satisfied	120
Reason for dissatisfaction	Percentages
Too expensive	13
Takes too long	34
Legal advisers do not give good service	21
Difficulties of pursuing claim	19
The system is not adequate to the individual case	14
The system is hard to understand	23
Other reasons	6
Total	130[1]

1 In some cases more than one reason was given.

406 Causes of dissatisfaction are brought out more vividly in the words of individual victims. The following is a selection of comments made by people injured in the years from 1966 to 1972 who had attempted to claim, for the most part unsuccessfully. They inevitably present a one-sided view, since comments were not sought from those who were satisfied.

Ignorance and fear of the law

407 Unfamiliarity with the law and lack of confidence in lawyers are illustrated by the following quotations:

i The ordinary working man doesn't know the half of the law and some lawyers aren't too keen on telling you. People don't actually know what they can claim, for example, what the loss of an eye is worth. You're in the dark really and at the mercy of the lawyer.

ii People are frightened by the law, I know I am. I live an honest life but courts and the law frighten me. There is a lack of communication between different levels of people.

iii The law doesn't look after the people at all, particularly the under-privileged. Solicitors aren't interested. It's altogether hopeless. It's all right for those union members – they have it all done for them. I had to trust this posh solicitor and where did it get me? £80! Taking advantage of a poor old woman!

iv I thought to lose my finger was a big thing – I thought I'd get some money to pay for when I was off work. I went to a solicitor. He said that as I was self employed it wasn't much good. He said he was going to check up and let me know and write back, but he never did.

v   I think for the average manual worker claiming must be a hard job. Solicitors are – or try to appear – too busy. They are unhelpful if not actually awkward. Ordinary people don't know what to do or how to go about it.

Delay

408   The following comments reflect the frustration and worry resulting from prolonged uncertainty:

vi   I felt worn out by all this trouble taking two years. After all, at my age I could have been dead before it was settled. I found it a worry not knowing if I was going to win my case or not. I kept thinking about the legal costs and where I would get the money from if I failed.

vii This has all taken so long and nothing has been done yet. I've got financial difficulties and been worried to death about the mortgage payments. I've a big family and my pigs have to be fed. It's all been a nightmare for me.

Premature settlement

409   But there were complaints too from those who had settled prematurely:

viii At that time I didn't know how much I was going to suffer. They should make provision for later in life. At that particular moment the money seemed enough, but who knows if I'll be handicapped all my life.

ix I signed the papers before I was personally fit to sign them. Otherwise I would have claimed for the loss of my legs as well, but I signed the papers before my legs were amputated and I can't make another claim.

Expense

410   There was a widespread feeling that poor people were at a disadvantage:

x   There still exists a law for the rich and a law for the poor. If you've got the money to fight you can pay the really top people and then you will win, but otherwise you haven't got the same chance.

xi   I was only allowed so much from legal aid and I couldn't afford to go any further with it.

xii You're pushed into a corner having to accept a settlement rather than having the chance to go to court because of the threat of being awarded a lower figure and thereby having to meet your costs.

Difficulties of pursuing a claim

411   A number of those injured complained of the trouble involved, for example, in finding witnesses:

xiii The person I was claiming against was taken to court and found guilty on the charge of dangerous driving, but I had to bear all the inconvenience and cost.

xiv The solicitor said we should go back and see the state of the road and measure the holes and see if we could get any witnesses and bring back photographs. I had a broken arm and my husband was at work so he couldn't do it. It didn't seem worth it.

xv You see really I'd no claim because the witness didn't write or speak English, and he was frightened to death of losing his job.

xvi The whole process is diabolical. I don't see why you should have to fight so hard, especially when you are the innocent party. It's disgusting and degrading to have to be examined by the other side.

CHAPTER 19

Personal injury survey: work illnesses

412   Work illnesses were the subject of a separate follow-up survey with its own questionnaire. The survey covered a few self employed as well as employees.

413   In this survey, work illnesses were given a wide interpretation. Many more illnesses were included than would qualify for industrial injuries benefits, either under the present system or under the alternative arrangements proposed in Volume One. The present system provides benefits for prescribed diseases arising in prescribed occupations in which the disease is known to be prevalent. The alternative arrangements would add diseases shown to be probably due to the individual's work, and to be a particular risk of that occupation.

414   There are two respects in which the cover of the survey was wider. First, the illnesses recorded in the survey consisted of those which the respondent – usually the sick person himself – believed to be connected in any way with his work. Secondly, they included illnesses where conditions at work were only one causal factor among others or where they had aggravated an existing illness, as well as those where they were believed to be the sole cause of illness.

Basis of the analysis

415   The sample was made up of two parts: all illnesses initially said to have originated in 1973 and 10 out of every 19 cases where the onset of illness had been given as 1970, 1971 or 1972. 299 valid returns were obtained. 172 of them were in the first part of the sample and 127 in the second. To make the results representative of the whole period 1970–73, the numbers recorded in the second part of the sample were multiplied by 1·9, and added to those derived from the first part. The analysis is based on the adjusted total of 413, that is to say $172+(127\times1\cdot9)$.

Incidence of work illness

416   A comparison was made of the distribution of the adjusted total of 413 work illnesses among different groups in the population with the corresponding distribution of all employees found in the general household survey for 1973 (Table 91). Men, particularly those in skilled manual jobs, were more likely to contract work-related illnesses than women. In the employed population, there were three men for every two women, but six men reported work illnesses for every two women. The disproportion in incidence between the sexes was, however,

less for work illnesses than for work injuries. Among women, the highest incidence of work illnesses was in semi-skilled manual jobs. Non-manual employees, both men and women, had a low incidence of work-related illness.

Table 91   Work illness by socio-economic group

Great Britain: 1973

	Reported work illnesses		All employees[1]	
	Men	Women	Men	Women
Adjusted numbers	310	103		
	Percentages		Percentages	
Professional workers and managers	12	5	19	5
Other non-manual workers	7	30	18	49
Manual workers				
Skilled	56	8	41	9
Semi-skilled[2]	19	48	17	28
Unskilled	6	8	5	9
Total	100	100	100	100

1 From general household survey.
2 Including personal services and agriculture.

Relation of work to illness

417   Assessments by informants of the relation between illness and work were inevitably subjective. The results obtained depended on the response to questions on the informants' views and beliefs about what was often a complicated set of contributing factors.

418   A broad distinction was made between illnesses probably linked to work and those where the link was doubtful. An illness was classified as probably linked to work when work was said to be its only cause, or to have made a major contribution to its development. Cases where the link was doubtful included those where work had been a minor factor among others, or where conditions of work had aggravated a constitutional illness. Of the total of 413, 290 were classified as probably linked to work, and 123 as doubtful.

419   There was a fair measure of correspondence between the views of informants on the relation of work to illness, classified in this way, and those of their doctors as reported. Cases where doctors' views were reported represented more than half the total. A comparison between informants' and doctors' reported views is given in Table 92.

Table 92   Reported views on work as a cause of illness

Great Britain: 1973   Adjusted numbers of informants

	Informant's opinion	
	Probable link[2]	Doubtful link[3]
Doctor's opinion[1]		
Work cause of illness	147	20
Work possible cause	25	27
Work not a cause	2	2
Not recorded	116	74
Total	290	123

1 As reported by informants.
2 Including 45 cases where injury benefit received.
3 Including 3 cases where injury benefit received.

420   The total of 413 included 48 cases of diseases prescribed under the industrial injuries scheme for which injury benefit had been received; surprisingly 3 of them were not reported as being probably linked to work. There were 245 cases classified as probably linked to work which were not covered by the industrial injuries scheme (though in many of them sickness benefit would have been received). The survey therefore suggests that illnesses believed to have arisen at work and not at present prescribed may be of the order of five times as numerous as those which are.

421   The survey provides no guidance as to which illnesses if any might deserve to be brought within the industrial injuries scheme. But it does indicate the existence of a widespread belief that many illnesses which are not prescribed can be attributed to working conditions. The nature of these illnesses is considered in the next section.

Nature of work illnesses

422   The classification of reported illnesses into the eight categories of Table 93 is somewhat rough. It is based on interpretations of descriptions supplied by informants, in some cases supported by reports of a doctor's diagnosis.

423   Respiratory diseases form the largest single category. Of the serious diseases of this kind which are prescribed under the industrial injuries scheme, such as pneumoconiosis, there were only two cases reported in the survey. The bulk of the diseases in this category were believed to be probably linked with work and as arising largely from manual jobs involving exposure to dust, fumes, or damp. Many of them were described as bronchitis.

424   The two next largest categories are those in which the main prescribed diseases fall. Half of the reported cases of dermatitis and similar skin disorders were prescribed and most of the others were probably linked with work, e.g. in

the chemical and petroleum industries. Diseases of the musculo-skeletal system cover a wide range including traumatic inflammation of the tendons (hand or forearm), arthritis and back strain. Apart from the prescribed diseases, many were reported as probably linked with work involving physical activity.

Table 93 Nature of work illnesses

Great Britain: 1973

	Total		Injury benefit received	Other cases			
				Probable link		Doubtful link	
	Adjusted number	%	Adjusted number	Adjusted number	%	Adjusted number	%
Respiratory	97	23	2	69	28	26	22
Circulatory	55	13	–	24	10	31	26
Nervous system or sense organs	37	9	–	29	12	8	7
Mental	57	14	–	41	17	16	13
Skin and sub-cutaneous tissues	60	15	30	25	10	5	4
Musculo-skeletal and connective tissue	81	20	14	43	17	24	20
Digestive system	11	3	2	4	2	5	4
Other	15	4	–	10	4	5	4
Total	413	100	48	245	100	120	100

425 Circulatory diseases and mental disorders can arise from working long hours or under mental strain and were frequently reported. There were particular difficulties here since mental disorder is not easily attributed to a specific job. These diseases and disorders had a high incidence among non-manual workers.

426 Diseases of the nervous system, sense organs and digestive system were reported less frequently. They were attributed to a variety of poor working conditions, for example noise, or to the need to work irregular hours. Like mental disorders, they were conditions found more often among younger than among older workers.

Possibility of prevention

427 Informants were asked whether, in their view, employers could have done anything to prevent the conditions causing work illnesses. There is again a considerable subjective element in the results, but even so, it is perhaps significant that no more than a third thought employers could have taken action to improve working conditions. The proportion varied, as was to be expected, with the

extent to which informants linked work with illness. Of those in receipt of industrial injury benefit, nearly half believed employers could have prevented harmful conditions; the proportion was 35 per cent of those whose illness was probably due to work, and 18 per cent of those where the link was doubtful.

Absence from work

428   The proportions of work illnesses reported as requiring no time off work, and as involving lengthy spells of absence, shown in Table 94, were both relatively large. The proportion extending over six months was probably inflated by the bias in the survey towards the more serious cases. No time off was taken in the majority of cases of diseases of the nervous system or of the sense organs. On the other hand, there were many absences of over six months in cases of respiratory and circulatory diseases.

Table 94 Duration of absence from work by nature of work illness

Great Britain: 1973   Percentages

	Total	Absence from work				
		None	1 month or under	Over 1 month– 6 months	Over 6 months	Not applicable[1]
Respiratory	100	14	26	32	24	4
Circulatory	100	4	12	25	52	7
Nervous system or sense organs	100	61	23	5	5	5
Mental	100	12	26	45	17	–
Skin and sub-cutaneous tissue	100	23	28	46	3	–
Musculo-skeletal and connective tissue	100	17	32	40	7	4
Digestive system	100	–	27	64	9	–
Other	100	13	13	40	33	–
Total	100	18	25	35	18	4

1 Informants not working at time of illness or no information supplied.

Change of job

429   One half of all informants reported some change in the nature or conditions of employment because of their illness. 13 per cent stopped work, and 37 per cent changed to a different job, mostly with the same employer. The proportion of those with changed jobs was higher, nearly two thirds, among informants in receipt of benefit for prescribed diseases.

Financial consequences of illness

430   The assessment of the financial consequences of work-related illness, like the corresponding assessment for injuries, was uncertain, the more so since the date of onset was not always exactly known. A further cause of uncertainty was that in this part of the survey respondents were asked to compare incomes from all sources at the time of interview with what they would have been if there had been no illness.

431   The survey shows that if those unable to make this comparison are treated as having experienced some loss, informants were divided roughly between 60 per cent with no financial loss and 40 per cent with some loss. The absence of loss may have been due to no time being taken off work or to pay being fully made up. Where there were losses, the extent varied considerably. In 37 cases out of 413, losses were estimated at 90 per cent or more.

432   Where there was loss of income, by far the largest component was loss of pay while away from work. Some 6 per cent of all informants, however, said they had lost earnings, all small amounts under £200, from such sources as second jobs of a part time nature. An equal number reported lost income by someone else in the household, generally a wife or husband.

433   Other losses attributed to work illness were expenses incurred in the treatment of the illness. Two thirds of all informants reported some expenses, although these were generally quite small. The main expenses were prescription charges and travel costs. Other expenses reported, each by a few informants, included payments for surgical appliances and other medical or dental items, for domestic help, and for extra heating.

434   The extent to which loss was eliminated or reduced by sick pay from the employer is indicated in Table 95. Illnesses deemed to be related to work sometimes involved no period away from work. Of those who needed to take time off, a little under one half got no sick pay from their employer and a little

Table 95   Sick pay during work illness
Great Britain: 1973

	Adjusted numbers	Percentages
Full or part sick pay	161	39
No sick pay	153	37
Not applicable:		
No time off	75	18
Self employed	12	3
Other[1]	12	3
Total	413	100

1 Not working at time of illness or no information supplied.

over one half received such pay, either in full or in part, whether for all or for part of the period of absence. These proportions are much the same as those recorded in the survey for work injuries.

435   The other main source of financial help during illness consisted of benefits from central and local government schemes. The corresponding amounts were not given with sufficient precision to be analysed. Some 55 per cent of all informants with work illnesses received benefit of one kind or another; some obtained more than one type of benefit. Twelve per cent received industrial injury benefit. Sickness benefit, followed by invalidity benefit when absence exceeded six months, was received by nearly all the others in receipt of some benefit. Unemployment benefit, supplementary benefit, and rent or rates rebates were received mainly in cases of lengthy absence from work.

436   Other offsets to losses were not numerous. Only 7 per cent of all informants with work-related illness said that they had private medical insurance. Of these, only about one in four made claims in respect of the illnesses reported. Half were successful and half not. Of somewhat more significance were those – 5 per cent of the total – who received special payments from their employers. These were mostly lump sums, varying from under £10 to over £1,000, usually made on the early retirement of the employee.

Tort claims

437   Of the adjusted total of 413 cases, only 26, or 6 per cent, led to claims for tort compensation. Twelve of these were in respect of diseases prescribed under the industrial injuries scheme. Another 12 were in respect of illnesses probably linked to work. The outcome, as far as known at the time of interview, is shown in Table 96. Only two claims had by then succeeded, each with damages under £800. As many as 14 claims had been given up.

Table 96   Tort claims for work illness

Great Britain: 1973   Adjusted numbers of informants

	Total	Injury benefit received	Other cases	
			Probable link	Doubtful link
Number of tort claims attempted	26	12	12	2
Payment agreed	2	1	1	–
Claim dropped	14	7	5	2
Still in progress	10	4	6	–

438   Reasons for not making tort claims for work illnesses were similar to those given by people who had been injured, for example, that the illness was not

regarded as the employer's fault or was trivial. Additional reasons given in respect of illnesses were that work had not been a major cause, or that the link between work and illness could not be established.

Views on compensation

439   About one in three informants had nothing to say when asked for their views on the compensation system as a whole. Of the others, those who were critical outnumbered by two to one those who were satisfied. Some thought that procedures were difficult to understand or too protracted. Others regarded the compensation as inadequate. Most employees, however, felt that employers treated them well. On the other hand, the self employed regarded the compensation system as ill-suited to their problems.

440   Views on the industrial injuries scheme were sought from those who had claimed injury benefit, whether successfully or not. The answers, summarised in Table 97, indicate some dissatisfaction with the scheme. This was expressed more or less strongly by about one quarter of those obtaining benefit and by about half of those not successful. The reasons were generally that the benefit received was inadequate or that rejection of the claim was unjustified.

Table 97   Views on industrial injuries scheme for work illnesses

Great Britain: 1973	Adjusted numbers of informants who claimed benefit	
	Successful claims	Unsuccessful claims
Completely satisfied	21	–
Fairly satisfied	14	5
Not very satisfied	5	1
Not at all satisfied	6	7
Don't know	2	2
Total numbers	48	15

CHAPTER 20

Personal injury survey : birth defects

441 Information about people living at home who had suffered from defects present at birth was obtained in the first phase of the survey. Many of the defects were no longer present at the time of interview, and it was evident, in particular by comparing answers to the questions about birth defects with answers to other questions, that birth defects had not always been remembered and reported.

442 Because of the problem of accurate recollection, and since some information about birth defects was available from the other sources quoted in Chapter 10, it was not thought worthwhile to carry out a follow-up study of birth defects. The data obtained in the first phase of the survey could not be used to provide a measure of the incidence of birth defects, but an analysis was made of the types of defect identified, whose results are given below.

Scope of the analysis

443 The questions relating to birth defects had been phrased in general terms, and the data required sifting before they could be analysed. Some cases were excluded, for instance where there was insufficient evidence that the condition described was congenital in origin, or where, although the condition was unusual, it did not amount to a defect. On the other hand, cases were included in the analysis where answers to a question elsewhere in the survey about medical treatment during 1972 and 1973 revealed the existence of defects clearly antenatal in origin which had not been acknowledged as such.

444 The sample analysed was limited to those born from 1950 onwards, that is, aged under 24 at the beginning of 1974. Older people were excluded as being especially unlikely to remember defects corrected early in life, and since their experience related to an earlier stage in the recognition and treatment of congenital defects.

445 In all 2,693 cases were analysed. Of the total, 2,295 cases were clearly birth defects; a further 398 cases were regarded as possible defects and included in the analysis.

Nature of birth defects identified

446 Table 98 shows the nature of the defects described. A list of the conditions included under the headings in Tables 98 and 99 is given in paragraph 451. Multiple conditions were assigned to the main or most severe condition present.

137

447 The most commonly reported defects were those affecting the senses (mainly minor defects of sight) and a wide variety of conditions of the joints or bones. Most defects were more commonly found in males than females. The overall ratio, at 1·32:1, was rather higher than has been found in some other studies.

Table 98 Birth defects by nature of defect and sex

Great Britain: Persons under 24 in January 1974   Numbers in sample

	Total	Male	Female
Joints or bones	469	229	240
Circulatory system	217	114	103
Respiratory system	41	23	18
Central nervous system	115	72	43
Genito-urinary system	127	111	16
Digestive system/alimentary tract	327	216	111
Senses	611	332	279
Endocrine/metabolic/nutritional	44	24	20
Skin	181	93	88
Mental/learning	157	97	60
Other hereditary	58	34	24
Other congenital defect	284	158	126
Birth injury	41	21	20
Condition possibly attributable to medical negligence[1]	21	10	11
Total	2,693	1,534	1,159

1 Before or shortly after birth.

448 An analysis by age and nature of defect is given in Table 99. In general, the number of cases reported declines with increasing age. There are, however, exceptions. These are mainly among defects of the senses and learning difficulties, which may often not become apparent until the child attends school.

449 The overall decline in the number of reported cases with increasing age may be attributed mainly to forgetfulness on the part of the informant. Some defects present at birth would have been corrected by the time of interview, some would have cleared up spontaneously, and others, though still present, might no longer be regarded as defects. All of these would tend to be forgotten as time passed. As a result, the older the person at the time of interview the less the likelihood that the defect would be remembered. Of those born with serious defects, some might have died from them, or no longer be cared for in private homes by the time of the interview. Again there would in consequence be a decline with increasing age in the numbers reported.

Table 99   Birth defects by nature of defect and age

Great Britain: Persons under 24 in January 1974   Numbers in sample

	0–4	5–9	Ages 10–14	15–19	20–23
Joints or bones	178	136	75	46	34
Circulatory system	74	65	34	30	14
Respiratory system	20	8	5	2	6
Central nervous system	30	41	22	17	5
Genito-urinary system	44	33	40	4	6
Digestive system/alimentary tract	126	99	57	27	18
Senses	198	202	131	57	23
Endocrine/metabolic/nutritional	17	11	9	2	5
Skin	72	40	31	24	14
Mental/learning	24	56	48	23	6
Other hereditary	13	16	17	8	5
Other congenital defect	110	72	49	33	20
Birth injury	22	7	5	6	1
Conditions possibly attributable to medical negligence[1]	6	6	5	2	2
Total	934	792	528	281	159
Incidence per 1,000 in age group	112·6	86·9	64·3	43·5	31·7

1 Before or shortly after birth.

450   In nearly 60 per cent of the cases some residual effects were reported, although these included some which were quite trivial and others such as short sight which could be corrected with suitable devices. Hereditary conditions and mental or learning difficulties were most likely to have continuing effects.

Classification of defects

451   Following is a list of the conditions included under each of the headings used in the tables.

Joints and bones

conditions of toes
club foot/talipes
flat feet/fallen arches/high arches
bowed legs/knock knees/pigeon toes
reduction deformity not
classified elsewhere
dislocated hip
clicky hip
absence of part of lower limb or hip

condition of finger
absence of part of upper limb/shoulder
curvature of spine
hole/indentation at base of spine
torticollis/deformity between spine
and shoulder tip
other conditions of joints and bones
not listed above

Circulatory system

hole in heart
heart murmur
defective valve

blue baby
other conditions of heart or circulatory
system

Respiratory system

condition of lung
condition of nose
condition of larynx

condition of trachea
other respiratory conditions

Central nervous system

spina bifida
hydrocephalus
cerebral palsy

epilepsy
paralysis
other conditions of central nervous
system

Genito-urinary system

duplex kidney/solitary kidney
kidney disease
condition of ureter/bladder

phimosis
undescended testicle
other genital conditions

Digestive system/alimentary tract

cleft palate
hare lip
tongue tied
oesophageal obstruction/stricture

pyloric stenosis
condition of stomach/intestine/bile duct
hernia
condition of rectum/anus

Senses

total or partial blindness
squint/lazy eye/cast/turn
glaucoma
short/long sight
colour blindness
droopy eyelid
blocked tear duct

other eye conditions
total or partial deafness
deaf and dumb
perforated eardrum
other ear conditions
other conditions of senses

Endocrine/metabolic/nutritional

diabetes
coeliac disease
thyroid deficiency/hyperactivity/goitre

phenylketonuria
other endocrine/metabolic/nutritional
conditions

Skin

eczema
birth mark/nevus

other skin conditions

Mental/learning

mental retardation/handicap
speech impediment or other defect

dyslexia
other mental/learning disorders

Familial/hereditary

Down's syndrome
cystic fibrosis
haemophilia

muscular dystrophy
other hereditary conditions

Other congenital defects

condition of the blood (excluding
hereditary conditions)
neoplasm
prematurity
jaundice

brain damage/injury
condition attributed to
lack of oxygen at birth
convulsions/fits
inadequately described conditions

Birth injury

injury due to forceps delivery/
instrumental intervention
fracture or dislocation attributed to
birth injury
haematoma of head attributed to birth
injury

condition attributed to protracted
labour
other conditions attributed to birth
injury

*Conditions possibly attributable to
medical negligence*

maternal condition

retrolental fibroplasia

thyroid deficiency with resulting mental
retardation
other unspecified glandular defects or
conditions

CHAPTER 21

Personal injury survey: methodology

Period covered

452 The main requirement at the outset was to identify members of a sample of the population who had been injured during a given period. Ideally the period in question would have been short, ending not long before the date of the first interview. To allow for seasonal variations, initial interviews would have been carried out on a continuous plan over a period of twelve months. Where the effects of the injury continued beyond the time of the first interview, further interviews would have been conducted later at intervals.

453 Such arrangements would have entailed a large number of interviews, both to identify an adequate sample of people who had been injured shortly before the initial approach, and to follow some of them up over a lengthy period. They were unacceptable on grounds of cost, and because of the delay before results could have been obtained.

454 Instead, a compromise was adopted. It was decided that the main objective should be to identify at a first interview people who had been injured at any time during 1973 – the previous complete calendar year – and to follow them up with a single interview some months later. This made it possible to limit the size of the initial sample and allowed for coverage of at least medium term consequences of injury. The use of a twelve month period eliminated seasonal variations. To find out something about longer term consequences of injury, it was decided to try also to identify certain groups of people who had been injured in earlier years – in particular those who had attempted to claim damages. These arrangements meant that the survey required informants to recall what had happened months, and in some cases years, earlier.

Selection of the sample

455 The basic sample consisted of members of private households living at addresses selected from the electoral registers, and took the form of a two stage stratified sample.

456 The first stage of the sampling procedure was to select 100 parliamentary constituencies from a sampling frame of 617 constituencies in Great Britain, which were stratified by region, and between urban and other areas. In order to limit expense, six constituencies in the Highlands and Islands of Scotland

142

with a sparse and widely scattered population were omitted from the sampling frame.

457   The second stage was to select every 73rd page from the electoral registers for the constituencies chosen. Interviewers visited all households on the selected pages. The households were therefore closely grouped. This method of sampling too was designed to limit the expense of interviewing at the cost of some increase in sampling error.

458   The sample necessarily excluded people living in institutions, and those living at addresses where no elector appeared on the register. People who had been members of the sampled households during the period covered by the survey, but had left them before fieldwork took place, for example through death or emigration, were also excluded. It is estimated that people excluded by the method of sampling would account for no more at most than 5 per cent of the total population.

459   Very little information was available beforehand about the incidence of injuries other than those resulting from work accidents and road accidents, but in the light of what information there was it was judged that an initial contact with approximately 35,000 households would yield sufficient numbers for the purposes of the survey.

460   Since it was not known how many people with injuries of different kinds would be identified, decisions about the exact size and composition of the samples to be selected for detailed interviews were left until the basic information had been gathered and analysed. Fieldwork was accordingly carried out in two phases: first in the households which made up the basic sample of the population, and later wherever possible with the injured individuals selected for follow-up interviews.

Initial interviews

461   Because of the dearth of other information about many kinds of injuries, results were wanted as early as possible. The pilot survey was therefore of limited scope.

462   The initial fieldwork was carried out during March, April and May 1974, and an interview was attempted with a member of each household at each address. In most households only one person was interviewed – most often the housewife, sometimes the head of household, and occasionally another responsible adult.

463   The main objectives at this stage were to identify injured persons who might be interviewed at length later, and to collect demographic information – such as age and sex – about all members of all households contacted, so that the incidence of injury among different demographic groups could be calculated. Some information about the nature and circumstances of the injuries was collected, partly because it was needed for the selection of those to be followed up later, and partly in order to provide some early information.

464   The six groups it was sought to identify are described in the following paragraphs.

People injured during 1973
465   Injuries during 1973 to be taken into account were defined, not only by the date of the injury, but by its severity, and by rules determining whether or not borderline cases should be included.

466   So that injuries in 1973 might not be missed because of uncertainty about the date when they had been incurred, and to ensure adequate numbers, respondents were asked about injuries sustained since the beginning of 1972. The number of people injured during 1973 who were identified proved to be sufficient, and the follow-up interviews were limited to them.

467   The criteria of severity were chosen so as to be as close as possible to the criteria of eligibility for state sickness or industrial injuries benefits. The injuries included were restricted to those which had been treated in hospital or by a doctor, and which had led to at least four days' incapacity for work or for other normal activities, such as housework. These criteria were not based on an objective assessment of the medical severity of the injury. Whether or not an injury is incapacitating will depend upon what the injured person normally does and the kind of person he or she is as well as upon the injury itself. Whether or not it is treated by a doctor may depend upon other factors as well as these. For example, a worker is likely to see a doctor for a relatively trivial injury if he needs a medical certificate, and mothers may be more inclined to have their children's injuries treated by a doctor than their own. The sample is not, therefore, representative of injuries of a given degree of severity but rather of injuries, actually treated by a doctor or in hospital, which were regarded by the informant as leading to some degree of incapacity for four days or more.

468   Some borderline conditions presented difficulty. Complaints such as sprains and strains, skin complaints, allergies and mental or emotional reactions to trauma could not easily be categorised, and might be left out if informants were simply asked about 'injuries'. The interviewer therefore started by asking about all occasions on which members of the household had visited a hospital or seen a doctor since the beginning of 1972, continuing with questions about the nature of the complaint and the length of incapacity it caused. Cases which might deserve to be followed up were identified in the course of a careful examination of all the replies received, and rules for dealing with borderline cases were developed. For example, a sprain or a skin complaint was accepted as an injury if it was attributed to a specific external cause or series of events. Although interviewers were instructed to probe for what the doctor said about the cause, the criteria were inevitably subjective. The conditions eventually accepted as injuries correspond broadly with those listed in the International Classification of Diseases under the heading 'Accidents, poisonings and violence', but with the addition of certain conditions classified under other headings if these were attributed to an external cause. The main examples were

traumatic arthritis or rheumatism, dermatitis or other skin complaints, hernia, and psychological reaction to trauma. Allergies were excluded because of the difficulty found in determining whether or not they arose from a specific external cause.

469   In many cases, the information given at the first interview was inadequate. Whenever there was any doubt – about the nature of the condition, the date of the accident or the duration of incapacity – the case was selected for a second interview.

People suffering in 1973 from disease attributed to their work

470   At the initial interview, informants were asked about any kind of ill-health which any member of the household had suffered since the beginning of 1972 which was believed to result from his work. (Subsequently, only illnesses present in 1973 were analysed.) Questions followed about the nature of the illness and the duration of incapacity. No attempt was made at the initial stage to judge the validity of the claim that the illness was due to work, although colds caught from colleagues were excluded. Complaints were classified as 'work illnesses' rather than 'work injuries' if they were said to be due to work and did not satisfy the criteria adopted for identifying injuries. Doubtful cases were included among those to be followed up.

People injured from 1966 to 1972 who had attempted to recover damages

471   The intention was to include among those to be interviewed in detail later anyone who, following a past injury, had taken any step, however half-heartedly, towards claiming damages in tort, since it was of interest to know why claims had been dropped in the early stages. 'Making an attempt to claim', therefore, included talking the possibility over with someone, even if nothing further was done.

472   Some informants confused other kinds of compensation, such as personal insurance or industrial injury benefit, with tort compensation. They were excluded if it was quite clear that no attempt had been made to recover damages, but as with other questions doubtful cases were included among those to be followed up.

473   Analysis by the year of injury showed a steady decline in the number of attempted claims reported as one went back in time. Some decline of this sort was inevitable because of the exclusion from the sample of people who had died since they were injured or who were no longer in the population sampled – because they had emigrated, entered institutions, or for some other reason. The numbers declined more sharply before 1965, indicating increased failure to remember events so far back, and it was decided that follow-up interviews should be restricted to people injured in 1966 or later.

People injured before 1973 who were still suffering after-effects

474   It had been hoped that investigation of those whose injuries had left persisting after-effects would throw light on the longer term effects of serious

injury. Examination of the responses at the first phase showed, however, that this question had been variously interpreted. Some people reported apparently trivial after-effects, while others said that there had been no after-effects, even when the injury had resulted, for example, in amputation. It was not thought worth while to carry out further work on this group.

People with defects present at birth
475 Informants were asked whether or not anyone in the household had had anything wrong with them at birth – either physical or mental – including anything that was only discovered later. In spite of the wide interpretation of the question which was encouraged, it became clear that there was considerable under-reporting, at least of minor defects. Medical treatment was often reported during 1972 or 1973 for conditions which might have been or almost certainly were birth defects, although these were not reported in answer to the direct question about birth defects.

476 Because of expected difficulties in obtaining reliable information, in particular about the financial consequences of birth defects, over the long periods of time involved, and since some information was available from other sources, it was decided not to follow up this group. A detailed analysis was made, however, of the types of defect reported in the initial interview about people born with defects in 1950 or later, and the results are given in the previous chapter.

Dependants of people who had died as a result of injuries in 1973
477 It is not possible, in a survey of a sample of households, to identify household members who have died, since in many cases the households to which they belonged no longer exist. An attempt was made, however, to identify households in which some member or members had been financially dependent on the victim of a recent fatal accident. Only five such cases were found for accidents in 1973 and follow-up interviews were achieved in three cases.

People injured more than once
478 A number of people were found who had been injured on more than one occasion during the periods covered by the survey. However, the analysis was made in terms of injuries rather than of people, on the ground that each injury is usually a separate occasion for compensation.

Follow-up interviews
479 Particulars are given in Table 100 of the numbers of interviews which were completed with the different classes of people who had been identified, and of the numbers eligible for inclusion in the analysis.

Injuries
480 The same questionnaire was used for those injured during 1973, those injured from 1966 to 1972 who had attempted to claim damages, and the dependants of people who had died following injury in 1973. For these cate-

gories, the follow-up interviews were carried out between September and December 1974, the fieldwork being interrupted in order to avoid the period immediately preceding the general election in October. Interviews were attempted for all cases of injury during 1973, including the five fatal cases, and, in order to limit expense, for half the 1966–72 cases.

481 Interviews were generally with the injured person, if aged sixteen or over; exceptionally, where he was not available, a suitable proxy was interviewed. If the injured person was a child under sixteen, the interview was with a parent or other adult member of the household, although the child might be consulted for details.

482 The main areas covered by the interview were the circumstances of the accident, the nature of the injuries and any permanent effects resulting from them, medical treatment, effects on work and other activities, financial losses resulting from the injury, and types of compensation received, including state benefits. There was also a detailed section dealing with attempts to recover damages in tort.

483 Some cases proved to be ineligible for inclusion in the analysis, either when the details were checked with the people concerned, or when the completed questionnaires were edited. A high proportion of the alleged claims for damages arising from 1966 to 1972 proved to be ineligible, largely because the claim turned out to have been for state benefits or private insurance and not for tort compensation.

484 The categories of injury in the cases where detailed interviews were completed were compared with the categories in cases lost from the sample because of non-contact or refusal, and little difference in pattern was found. It is reasonable to conclude that non-response at the second phase did not affect the findings significantly.

485 Incidence rates expressed as the numbers of injuries to be expected in a year among 1,000 people in a particular category have been calculated with reference to the numbers of people in the households from which information was obtained at the initial interviews. They consequently take account of any differences in composition between these households and the whole population.

Work illnesses

486 Cases of illness attributed to work were the subject of a separate follow-up inquiry, with a specially designed questionnaire. The fieldwork was carried out between 4 March and 2 April 1975. The work on the survey was divided between the Office of Population Censuses and Surveys and a private survey organisation, Social and Community Planning Research; the former organisation carried out the sample design, fieldwork, costing and editing, and the latter directed the project and was responsible for drafting the questionnaire and for analysing the results.

Table 100 Numbers of interviews

Great Britain   Numbers

First interviews	
Addresses	
Calls made	40,748
Contact made	34,575
Households	
Contact made	36,074
Completed interviews	35,556
Second interviews	
Injuries during 1973	
Interviews:	
Attempted	4,233[1]
No contact or refusal	348
Ineligible	583
Eligible	3,302
Work illnesses	
Interviews:	
Attempted	497[2]
No contact or refusal	60
Ineligible	138
Eligible	299
Injuries from 1966 to 1972 where an attempt was made to claim damages	
Interviews:	
Attempted	1,053[3]
No contact or refusal	80
Ineligible	384
Eligible	589
Deaths in 1973 following injury	
Interviews:	
Attempted	5[1]
Eligible	3

1 All cases identified.
2 All cases believed to have begun in 1973, and 10 in 19 of those believed to have begun from 1970 to 1972.
3 Half the cases identified.

487   A major problem with this part of the survey was to determine the date of onset of illness, which had to be done if any attempt was to be made to ascertain the annual incidence of illnesses thought to be due to work. There was inevitably much vagueness about when long lasting illnesses had begun, and as with injuries, the sample for follow-up was restricted to the more recent cases. The omission of most cases of long term illnesses such as pneumoconiosis was considered acceptable since in general such illnesses were already well documented.

488   At the initial interview, a question was asked about when the sufferer first had medical treatment; but a better guide in identifying the most recently developed cases was provided by questions about whether the person concerned was suffering from thc illness during 1972 and during 1973. Those selected for follow-up interview were all those where work illnesses were said to be present in 1973 but not in 1972, together with 10 in 19 of those suffering from the illness in 1973, with a stated date of onset in 1970, 1971 or 1972, or with no date given. This proportion was chosen with a view to selecting about 500 cases for a second interview.

489   At this second interview, the sufferer himself was asked when he had first consulted a doctor, and the answers given often differed from those recorded at the initial interview. It was necessary to discard 90 cases because the date of onset proved to be earlier than 1970. A further 48 were rejected for other reasons, the main one being that the illness was not after all thought to have arisen at work.

Accuracy

Sampling errors

490   Data derived from a sample may not be exactly representative of the whole field from which thc sample is drawn. The standard error of sampling is a measure of the amount by which a value derived from a particular sample is likely to differ from the true value. If a statistic derived from a sample of adequate size – say a percentage, p – has a standard error of e, there is a 95 per cent probability that the range from p–2e to p+2e includes the true value.

491   In the personal injury survey, sampling errors were generally less important than reporting errors. The information given below provides a broad indication of their probable magnitude in relation to percentages estimated from the main part of the survey relating to injuries in 1973.

492   The calculations were complicated, and the sampling errors increased, since the personal injury survey used a two stage sample; first, a stratified sample of 100 constituencies out of 617, and secondly a sample, initially of 1 household in 73, within each constituency. A description of the procedure for calculating sampling errors for a survey of this character has been given in one of the reports on the general household survey carried out each year for the Central Statistical Office.[30]

493   Table 101 sets out estimated standard errors in the personal injury survey for a selection of percentages. They incorporate an approximate allowance for the effect of the sample design.

494   The standard error depends on the size of the calculated percentage, and on the number of injuries on which it was based. For percentages derived from the whole sample of injuries in 1973, this number was 3,302. The standard error is the same for 90 per cent as for 10 per cent (though of course proportionately smaller in relation to 90 per cent than to 10 per cent); more generally, it is the same for (100–p) as for p, where p is any percentage.

Table 101   Standard errors of sampling for percentages

	Percentages				
	10 or 90	20 or 80	30 or 70	40 or 60	50
Number of injuries on which percentage based					
100	3·5	4·6	5·3	5·6	5·8
200	2·4	3·3	3·7	4·0	4·1
500	1·5	2·1	2·4	2·5	2·6
1,000	1·1	1·4	1·7	1·8	1·8
3,302	0·6	0·8	0·9	1·0	1·0

495   The following are two examples of the use of this table.

i The percentage of all injuries which arose in the course of work was 28·8 per cent. From the bottom line of the table the standard error was 0·9. So, leaving reporting errors out of account, there was a 95 per cent probability that the figure was between 27·0 per cent and 30·6 per cent.

ii Of 151 injuries to housewives, 31·1 per cent were treated as being within the terms of reference and 68·9 per cent were outside them. Interpolating in the column headed 30 or 70, the standard error would have been about 4·5 per cent. So disregarding reporting errors, there was a 95 per cent probability that the percentages were in the ranges 22·1 to 40·1, and 59·9 to 77·9 respectively.

Incomplete recording of injuries
496   Subsequent analysis, and comparisons with such other data as are available, have shown that not all injuries within the scope of the survey were reported at the initial interviews.

497   The analysis consisted of a comparison of the numbers of injuries recorded as having occurred at different times during 1973. It showed that fewer injuries were recorded early in the year than during similar periods later in the year, and closer to the date of interview. The differences were greater than could easily be explained by other, for example, seasonal factors.

498 Other data with which comparison was made included social security statistics, the hospital in-patient enquiry, the survey of insurance claims, and the analysis of cases dealt with by the courts. Exact comparisons were hardly ever possible because of differences of definition, and in almost every case extensive adjustments had to be made to the data before comparison could be made. Individual comparisons were consequently not reliable or conclusive, but taken together they pointed to a substantial deficiency in the estimates based on the survey.

499 The problem of identifying certain individuals within a sample of households has been met in other surveys, though usually in the form of identifying people possessing particular characteristics at the time of interview. This has proved difficult enough. In the personal injury survey, the difficulty was greater, since what was to be identified was an injury sustained some months or even years earlier, often to someone other than the person initially interviewed. Subsequent editing led to the elimination of cases wrongly included in the first place, but not to the recovery of cases wrongly omitted.

500 The evidence indicates that serious injuries were more fully reported than slight ones. Injuries to women appear to have been more fully reported than injuries to men – probably because most of the respondents at the first interviews were housewives; and injuries at work more fully reported than injuries elsewhere, probably because the initial interview, with a view to identifying work illnesses, included specific questions about incapacity associated with work. However, injuries leading to tort claims appear to have been reported to much the same extent as others.

501 Households where interviews were completed during the first phase of the survey represented 1 in 575 of all households. Consequently aggregate numbers of injuries in 1973 are estimated in the first place by multiplying the numbers recorded in the survey by a factor of 575. To allow also for under-recording, a larger adjustment is needed. To arrive at estimates for injuries in the United Kingdom leading to four or more days' incapacity for work or the equivalent, survey numbers need on average to be multiplied by 924; the appropriate factor was larger for some categories of injuries, and smaller for others.

Accuracy of reporting

502 Much of the subject matter of the survey proved difficult for those interviewed. The difficulties were aggravated by the time factor. For injuries during 1973, the interval between the injury and the detailed follow-up interview was at least eight months and could be as long as two years. Inaccuracy in the reporting of details was therefore to be expected. The fact that the interview covered a number of technical or difficult areas which many informants did not understand well was another source of inaccuracy.

503 The section of the questionnaire dealing with the circumstances of the injury was not difficult and it is believed that the information given here was usually reliable. Cases in which the basic facts might have been in doubt included those involving children when no adult was present. Although it was

relatively easy to establish when, where and in what circumstances an injury occurred, information about the cause and who, if anyone, was responsible, was based almost entirely on the subjective opinion of one of the people involved and should be treated with caution.

504   Information about the type of injury and any permanent effects is probably reasonably accurate.

505   Answers to the questions about length of incapacity are probably approximations in many cases, especially when the period of incapacity was short. The questions about incapacity for housework and other normal activities may have been interpreted differently by different informants. Whereas length of time off work or school was a matter of fact, how long it had been difficult to do housework or other normal activities could not be measured consistently.

506   As in other surveys, there were problems in obtaining financial information, especially where the questions asked for specific amounts of money. Inaccuracies were most likely when the amounts were small – for example, the amounts spent on prescription charges or other expenses.

507   The questions about tort claims were difficult both because informants did not understand the technicalities of the law and because sometimes they did not know exactly what had happened. For example, of the small group of people who said that their cases had gone to court, several were almost certainly confusing an action for damages with a prosecution brought by the police, and others probably reported that they had 'taken the case to court' simply because they had consulted a solicitor. Many informants were unable to answer questions about whether or not a solicitor's letter had been sent to the defendant, a writ served or the case set down for hearing in court. Even the question of whether or not the case had been handled by a solicitor was complicated by the fact that work accident cases may have been dealt with by a trade union, and the informant may have been unaware that the union employed a solicitor.

CHAPTER 22

Insurance claims

508 A survey of insurance claims disposed of in November 1973 was carried out by the British Insurance Association (BIA), with the participation of Lloyd's underwriters as well as of insurance companies which were members of the BIA. The results of the survey were presented as evidence in September 1974.

509 It is estimated that claims on insurers represent about 88 per cent of the total number and about 94 per cent of the total value of all personal injury claims in tort. The great majority of other claims were made on organisations carrying their own risk (Chapter 23). Apart from these there are claims on medical defence societies and other professional organisations, and claims against unidentified drivers, which are dealt with by the Motor Insurers' Bureau.

510 Particulars were collected in the survey of all personal injury claims arising in the United Kingdom for which insurers' files had been closed in the four weeks from 5 to 30 November 1973. They were analysed in a number of ways, among others by type of claim, size of payment, heads of damages, the stage at which claims were settled, and the period from injury or claim to settlement. The analysis covered claims disposed of by settlement, rejected claims which the claimant had abandoned, and claims decided by the courts. Claims in cases of death were distinguished from those relating to injury, and claims in Northern Ireland from those in Great Britain. Claims under employers' liability in respect of industrial illness were included. Some of the analyses were limited to the data for Great Britain. In addition information was collected about large personal injury claims involving payments of over £25,000 disposed of during the whole of 1973.

Claims and payments

511 8,275 claims disposed of in November 1973 were analysed. Of these, 7,123 or 86 per cent resulted in some payment being made. The payments of over £25,000 in 1973 which were analysed numbered 64.

512 Payments usually included the reimbursement to the claimant of his legal or other expenses. Separate particulars were obtained of these, which are summarised later in this chapter. The main analysis, however, relates to payments made by way of compensation, excluding any expenses repaid to the claimant.

513 The values of payments reported may be taken as relating approximately to the level of prices in November 1973. The average amount of compensation paid, at this price level, was £572, equivalent to about £1,000 at the price level of January 1977.

514 The number of claims in relation to the size of population was slightly greater in Northern Ireland than in the rest of the United Kingdom. A higher proportion of claims resulted in payment, and the average sum paid was greater (Table 102).

Table 102 Claims and average payments by place of origin

United Kingdom: November 1973

	Number of claims	Number in which payment made	Average amount of compensation
Great Britain	7,957	6,817	£566
Northern Ireland	318	306	£699
United Kingdom	8,275	7,123	£572

515 Just over 2 per cent of claims and 11 per cent of the total amount paid related to fatal injuries (Table 103).

Table 103 Fatal and non-fatal claims

United Kingdom: November 1973

	Number of claims	Number in which payment made	Compensation paid Total	Average amount
			£	£
Fatal	181	157	439,551	2,800
Non-fatal	8,094	6,966	3,633,764	522
Total	8,275	7,123	4,073,315	572

Stage at which settled

516 Eighty six per cent of claims were settled without the issue of a writ. Only 3 per cent were set down for trial, and only 1 per cent reached the courts (Table 104). Average compensation payments, in cases where they were made, were greater for the claims which proceeded to the later stages, reflecting the fact that insurers are less ready to settle larger claims, and claimants have more incentive to pursue them.

154

Table 104 Stage at which claim settled

United Kingdom: November 1973

	Number of claims		Average payment where made
	Number	Percentage of total number	
Stage at which settled			£
Without issue of a writ	7,117	86·0	400
After writ, before case set down	878	10·6	1,423
After setting down, before trial	185	2·2	2,087
In court, including at door of court	95	1·1	1,604
All claims	8,275	100·0	572

Types of claim

517 The greatest number of claims was made under employers' liability, but the greatest number of payments related to motor claims (Table 105).

Table 105 Claims and payments by type of claim

United Kingdom: November 1973

	Number of claims	Payments of compensation		
		Number	Number of payments as percentage of number of claims	Average amount
			%	£
Employers' liability				
Injury	3,920	3,052	78	539
Disease	99	56	57	1,202
Motor vehicle	3,241	3,159	97	672
Products and services	78	61	78	270
Occupiers' liability	439	389	89	287
Other	498	406	82	271
Total	8,275	7,123	86	572

518 More than 70 per cent of insurance claims for fatal injuries involved a motor vehicle (Table 106).

155

Table 106   Fatal and non-fatal claims by type of claim
United Kingdom: November 1973   Numbers

	Fatal	Non-fatal
Employers' liability		
Injury	30	3,890
Disease	5	94
Motor vehicle	130	3,111
Products and services	–	78
Occupiers' liability	7	432
Other	9	489
Total	181	8,094

Analysis by heads of damages

519   Insurers were asked to distinguish in non-fatal cases between special and general damages, and to sub-divide general damages between compensation for future loss of earnings, for other future pecuniary losses, and for non-pecuniary loss. Special damages are ascertained pecuniary losses up to the date of settlement or trial. Future pecuniary losses arise from future loss of earnings and continuing additional expenses incurred in consequence of injury. Compensation for non-pecuniary loss includes compensation for pain and suffering, for functional disability, and for loss of ability to enjoy life.

520   The sub-division of general damages was not made for all claims, and the analysis shown in Table 107 is partly based on estimation. It shows that about two thirds of the total amount paid in tort compensation was for non-pecuniary loss, that not quite a quarter represented known losses already incurred, and that only about 10 per cent was for pecuniary losses after the date of settlement or trial. The smallness of the last proportion reflects in part the length of time taken to settle.

Table 107   Analysis by heads of damages
Great Britain: November 1973

	Percentage of total amount paid
Special damages	23·9
General damages	76·1
Future earnings loss	8·3
Other pecuniary loss	1·6
Non-pecuniary loss	66·2
Total	100·0

521   For small claims, the predominant element was compensation for non-pecuniary loss. For payments above £2,500 the proportion of payments represented by non-pecuniary loss fell, until for payments over £25,000 it was less than half (Table 108).

Table 108   Heads of damages by size of payment

Great Britain: November 1973

	Special damages	General Damages		
		All	Non-pecuniary loss	Pecuniary loss
Size of payment £	Percentages of total payments in size range			
1– 50	21	79	78	1
51– 100	32	68	67	1
101– 250	36	64	63	1
251– 500	33	67	66	1
501– 1,000	28	72	70	2
1,001– 2,500	22	78	73	5
2,501– 5,000	17	83	70	13
5,001–10,000	14	86	56	30
Over 10,000	11	89	54	35
Over 25,000[1]	7	93	48	45

1 From large claims enquiry for 1973.

522   Table 109 shows the distributions of the numbers and amounts of compensation payments by size of payments. Nearly half the payments in November 1973 were of less than £200, and only 1 per cent exceeded £5,000, although these accounted for 23 per cent of the total amount paid out. The distribution was a skew one, and the median payment, just over £200, was well below the average value of £572.

Legal and other fees

523   Information was collected in the survey about legal and other fees reimbursed to claimants, and about fees paid by insurers on their own account. Information about insurers' own administrative and other costs in respect of personal liability business was collected, not in this survey, but in a separate survey of revenue and expenditure, which was used in making the estimates of the cost of the present system of compensation given in Chapter 29.

Table 109   Distribution of compensation payments by size

United Kingdom: November 1973

	Percentage of total number of payments	Percentage of total amount paid
Size of payment £		
1– 100	28·6	2·8
101– 200	19·7	5·5
201– 500	28·0	16·6
501– 1,000	12·1	15·6
1,001– 2,000	6·9	17·8
2,001– 5,000	3·3	18·7
5,001–10,000	0·9	10·8
Over 10,000	0·4	12·1
All payments	100·0	100·0

524   Most claims involved the repayment of fees to claimants, but less than half involved the payment of fees by insurers (Table 110). No doubt insurance companies rely largely on their own staff whereas claimants have to pay for corresponding advice.

Table 110   Proportion of claims in which fees were paid

United Kingdom: November 1973

	Total number	Proportion involving		
		Claimants' fees	Insurers' fees	Any fees
		Percentages		
Employers' liability	4,019	72	41	77
Motor vehicle	3,241	89	45	92
Other	1,015	56	29	63
All claims	8,275	76	41	81

525   For claims in respect of employers' liability and motor vehicles, which make up the vast majority, claimants' fees were greater than insurers' fees (Table 111). Again this was because insurance companies could rely on their own staff for advice.

Table 111   Average fees

United Kingdom: November 1973   £

	Claims involving		
	Claimants' fees	Insurers' fees	Any fees
Employers' liability	92	80	128
Motor vehicle	86	54	110
Other	82	104	121
All claims	89	71	119

526   All the fees paid amounted to 20 per cent of compensation payments. About 85 per cent of all fees were legal fees; the remainder represented fees paid to medical and other experts.

Reasons for litigation

527   Table 112 analyses the reasons for litigation in the 14 per cent of cases which led to the issue of a writ. Disputes about liability and about quantum appear to have been about equally frequent.

Table 112   Reasons for litigation

United Kingdom: November 1973

	Percentage of total number of claims
Dispute over	
Liability	26
Quantum	24
Liability and quantum	27
Apportionment of liability	4
Payment of interest	3
Other	17
All claims where writs issued	100

Period from injury to disposal of claim

528   Just under a half of all claims were disposed of within a year of the injury or death, and 80 per cent within two years (Table 113). This analysis omits claims relating to industrial disease, which tend to take longer than other personal injury claims.

Table 113   Distribution of claims by time from injury to disposal[1]

Great Britain: claims disposed of in November 1973   Percentages

Period (*months*)	Percentage of claims disposed of within period		Cumulative percentage of claims disposed of by end of period	
	By number	By amount	By number	By amount
0–3	4·6	0·6	4·6	0·6
over 3–6	12·6	4·0	17·2	4·6
over 6–9	16·6	8·2	33·7	12·8
over 9–12	15·1	11·0	48·8	23·8
over 12–24	31·6	35·4	80·4	59·2
over 24–36	12·4	21·8	92·7	81·0
over 36–48	4·9	12·4	97·7	93·3
over 48–60	1·5	3·1	99·1	96·4
over 60	0·9	3·6		
All claims	100·0	100·0	100·0	100·0

1 Excluding claims in respect of industrial diseases.

529   The average time taken to submit a claim was 5 months in the case of fatal accidents and 3 months for non-fatal accidents.

Period from claim to disposal

530   The median period from claim to disposal for all claims was $9\frac{1}{2}$ months, although it was less for claims where compensation was obtained and considerably longer for unsuccessful claims. Almost all claims disposed of within the first year were settled with payment, mostly for relatively small sums. The proportion of claims resulting in some payment fell as the time from claim to disposal increased, but the average sum paid rose (Table 114).

531   Another way of looking at the relationship between delay and size of payment is to consider what proportion of payments in each size range took more than a certain time to settle. Taking the arbitrary period of two years from the date of claim, Table 115 shows that, although only one tenth of all payments were not made within this period, the proportion rose with increasing size of payment, so that for payments of more than £25,000 the proportion was nearly three quarters.

Table 114   Distribution of claims by time from claim to disposal

Great Britain: claims disposed of in November 1973

	Percentage of claims by number	Payments of compensation	
		Number of payments as percentage of number of claims	Average payment
Period (months)	%	%	£
0–3	9·9	98	133
over 3–6	19·7	98	224
over 6–9	18·2	96	318
over 9–12	13·1	93	524
over 12–24	26·4	71	852
over 24–36	8·7	66	1,482
over 36–48	2·7	70	2,199
over 48–60	0·8	73	1,802
over 60	0·4	70	4,330
All claims	100·0	86	566

Table 115   Percentage of payments which had not been settled within two years of date of claim, by size

United Kingdom: claims disposed of in November 1973

	Percentage of payments not settled within 2 years
Size of payment £	
1–500	5
501–1,000	15
1,001–5,000	33
5,001–10,000	58
10,001–25,000	54
more than 25,000[1]	73
All payments	10

1 From large claims enquiry for 1973.

Reasons for delay

532   Table 116 gives an analysis of the stated reasons for delay in respect of the 90 per cent of claims which took more than three months from the date of

the claim to disposal. The commonest reasons for delay were medical prognosis and disputes over liability, quantum, or both liability and quantum. For all claims, disputes over liability were the more frequent, but if unsuccessful claims are excluded, disputes about quantum (including those where liability was also in dispute) predominated. Claims involving disputes about liability took longest to settle.

Table 116   Analysis by reasons for delay[1]

Great Britain: claims disposed of in November 1973

	Percentage of all claims[1]	Median period from claim to disposal (months)
Reason for delay		
Medical prognosis	19·5	9·8
Liability dispute	21·2	16·4
Quantum dispute	13·5	9·3
Liability and quantum dispute	13·1	12·3
Delay by claimant	15·6	9·8
Other	17·1	7·9
Total	100·0	9·5

1 Where period from claim to disposal was greater than three months.

Degrees of liability accepted

533   An appreciable proportion of claims – more than a quarter of the total numbers – were settled on the basis of partial and not full liability. Percentages settled on the basis of full, partial or no liability are given for the different types of claim in Table 117.

534   Most, but not all, claims settled without liability being admitted did not involve any payment to the claimants. Conversely, there was a small number of claims (about 1 per cent of the total) where some degree of liability was recorded but no payment was made. The British Insurance Association thought that these may have been claims where there was the possibility of some liability on the part of the defendant, but the claim was not pressed.

Motor vehicle claimants

535   A special analysis was made of motor vehicle claimants (Table 118). For the majority of claims which related to policies covering private cars (about 78 per cent of the total numbers) the analysis distinguished between passengers in the insured car, drivers or passengers in other vehicles, and other people.

Table 117 Degrees of liability admitted by type of claim

Great Britain: November 1973   Percentage of total number of claims of each type

| | Degree of liability | | | |
	Full	Partial	None	All
Employers' liability				
Injury	49	29	22	100
Disease	33	22	45	100
Motor vehicle	75	22	3	100
Products and services	67	11	22	100
Other	60	26	14	100
All claims	60	26	14	100

Table 118 Analysis of motor claims

Great Britain: November 1973

		Percentage of total number of motor vehicle claims	
Private cars	*Claimant*		
	All claimants	78·1	
	Passenger in insured car		12·2
	Another car		
	Driver		19·7
	Passenger		14·8
	Motor cycle		
	Rider		11·0
	Passenger		1·3
	Motor vehicle other than car or motor cycle		
	Driver		0·8
	Passenger		1·6
	Other person[1]		16·7
Motor cycles	All claimants	2·6	
Other motor vehicles	All claimants	19·3	
All motor vehicles	All claimants	100·0	

1 Includes pedestrians, cyclists, horse riders and any first party claims by drivers of insured vehicles.

Coverage of the survey

536   The claims finally disposed of in the four weeks in November 1973 to which the survey related are believed to have been representative of the generality of claims on insurers. On the other hand they represented not quite 4 per cent of all claims handled by insurers in a year as against the 8 per cent which might have been expected in a 4 week period. The period chosen was one when fewer than average claims were disposed of; some insurers did not contribute to the survey; and of those who did, some did not analyse all the claims disposed of in the period concerned.

CHAPTER 23

Claims on organisations carrying their own risk

537 A number of large organisations, mainly in the public sector, themselves accept responsibility for payment of any claims against them for damages for personal injury. Such organisations are mainly to be found among nationalised industries, public transport undertakings, large private sector employers, government departments, health authorities, police forces and port authorities. Some, including government departments and health authorities, are required by law to bear their own risk; others choose to do so. Some organisations cover only part of their own risk, taking out insurance for payments beyond a certain limit.

538 A survey of organisations known to carry their own risk of liability, or thought likely to do so, was carried out by the secretariat. Questionnaires were issued in September 1974, asking for the numbers of claims and the amounts of payments on them in the United Kingdom in 1972 and 1973. It was thought that most respondents would be unable to provide an analysis of claims in the same detail as that in the survey of insurance claims described in the previous chapter.

539 Information about payments on claims was obtained from 78 organisations, estimated to account for about 85 per cent by number and 93 per cent by value of all claims met by organisations that carry their own risk of liability. Estimates were made of the number and amounts of claims not reported, and also of the proportion of the payments made which represented the recovery by the claimant of legal and other fees he had paid out as distinct from the compensation he obtained.

540 Table 119 indicates the proportions of all claims and payments which were dealt with by organisations carrying their own risk. They are estimated to have accounted for nearly 12 per cent of the 250,000 claims made annually, and to have provided just over 6 per cent of the total amount of tort compensation.

Expenses
541 Organisations carrying their own risk reported relevant expenses they had themselves met; the total expenses of all such organisations in 1973 are estimated to have amounted to £1·3 million. Claimants' fees in 1973 were estimated at £1·1 million. The two components of expenses taken together represented about one third of the total amount of compensation payments

165

made by organisations carrying their own risk – a smaller proportion than that estimated elsewhere for insurance companies when their internal as well as their external expenses are taken into account.

Table 119 Claims and payments dealt with

United Kingdom: 1973

	Total	Met by organisations carrying their own risk	Met by insurers and others[1]
Numbers of claims (thousands)	250	29	221
Numbers of payments (thousands)	215	24	191
Payments of compensation (£ million)	114	7	107

1 Motor Insurers' Bureau and mutual indemnity associations.

Types of claim

542 Table 120 analyses numbers of claims and numbers and value of payments by type of claim, distinguishing compensation payments from the total payments including claimants' fees.

Table 120 Analysis by types of claim

United Kingdom

		Numbers of claims	Numbers of payments	Total payments including fees	Payments of compensation
		Numbers[1]		£ thousand[1]	
Employers' liability	1972	12,430	10,070	5,640	4,890
	1973	11,660	9,720	6,480	5,610
Road	1972	15,800	13,000	1,090	980
	1973	14,920	12,240	1,060	950
Other transport	1972	1,130	1,110	300	250
	1973	1,110	1,100	310	260
All other	1972	1,310	860	540	460
	1973	1,370	900	520	430
Totals	1972	30,680	25,050	7,580	6,570
	1973	29,070	23,960	8,360	7,250

1 Rounded to the nearest 10 or £10,000.

543 Employers' liability represented about three quarters of the total amount of compensation by organisations carrying their own risk, but claims were of diverse kinds and were not concentrated in this field. A large number of small claims dealt with by bus companies explains why over half the total number of claims, although only about 15 per cent of the total amount of compensation, appear against the road heading. The average amount of compensation paid for road injury in 1973 was only about £70.

Types of organisation

544 Table 121 contains a similar analysis by type of organisation. It shows that about 70 per cent of tort compensation outside the field of insurance was provided by nationalised industries.

Table 121 Analysis by type of organisation
United Kingdom

			Estimates for all organisations carrying their own risk[1]			
		Numbers of organisations reporting	Numbers of claims	Numbers of payments	Total payments including fees	Payments of compensation
					£ thousand	
Government	1972	16	960	460	440	380
departments	1973	16	1,050	530	520	450
Local authorities	1972	3	1,520	1,310	180	150
	1973	3	1,620	1,390	180	160
Nationalised	1972	7	9,800	8,310	5,310	4,590
industries[2]	1973	7	8,810	7,640	5,930	5,120
Transport	1972	12	16,840	13,970	1,060	950
undertakings[3]	1973	12	16,030	13,330	1,180	1,050
Other public	1972	23	920	630	440	380
organisations[4]	1973	23	810	610	390	340
Large private	1972	17	630	370	150	130
organisations	1973	17	750	460	160	140
Totals	1972	78	30,680	25,050	7,580	6,570
	1973	78	29,070	23,960	8,360	7,250

1 Rounded to the nearest 10 or £10,000.   3 Bus companies and London Transport.
2 Includes British Airways and British Rail.   4 Includes port, health and police authorities.

Conduct of the survey

545 Questionnaires were sent to 369 organisations employing large numbers of people and known or thought likely to carry their own risks. They were

first asked whether they insured against liability of different kinds for providing compensation for personal injury. If they did and carried no risk themselves, no further information was asked for.

546   Complete returns were provided by all the major organisations carrying their own risk.

547   The remaining questions covered the following, information being requested for 1972 and 1973 (or proximate accounting years):

The number of claims of different types and their outcome
Payments made
Expenses incurred, including legal costs
Severity of injury
The stage reached before settlement or judgment
The number of employees

Most organisations were unable to respond to the questions on severity of injury or stage reached before settlement or judgment, and the partial information received was not analysed.

Methods of estimation

548   Since it was evident that estimates for organisations not contributing to the survey would make no more than a minor contribution to the totals, only limited investigations were made to provide a basis for them. No returns were lacking from government departments, or from local authorities known to carry their own risks. (Most local authorities were covered by insurance.) For two missing nationalised industries, both fairly small, estimates were based on published employment figures. For the remaining categories, estimates of aggregates were made by multiplying the reported figures by the ratio of the total number of organisations known to be carrying their own risk to the number reporting. The possible resulting error is greatest in respect of transport undertakings, for which one quarter of the total amount paid out in compensation was estimated.

549   The payments reported were the total amounts paid out including legal and other fees recovered by claimants. The payments figures were split between compensation and claimants' fees on the assumption that for each type of claim the fees would represent the same proportion of the total payments as for the most nearly equivalent category in the survey of insurance claims described in the previous chapter.

Further information

550   Further information about this survey may be obtained from:

The Lord Chancellor's Office,
Statistics Unit,
67 Tufton Street,
London SW1P 3RG.

CHAPTER 24

Claims in the courts

551 Analyses were made of claims for compensation for personal injury which were set down for hearing in England and Wales and in Northern Ireland, or for which writs were issued in Scotland. In each case, the analyses covered cases disposed of in 1974. The cases analysed represented between 3 and 4 per cent of all personal injury claims in the United Kingdom. The remainder had been settled or abandoned at earlier stages. The numbers are given in Table 122.

Table 122 Numbers analysed

1974   Numbers

	Writs issued	Cases set down	Cases receiving full trial
England and Wales		7,733	1,870
Northern Ireland		1,415	238
Scotland	552	204[1]	95
United Kingdom		9,352	2,203

1 Proof arranged.

552 The analyses were carried out by the Lord Chancellor's Office, the Northern Ireland Office and the Northern Ireland Supreme Court of Judicature, and the Scottish Home and Health Department.

553 The systems of personal injury litigation in England and Wales and in Northern Ireland are basically the same, the major difference being that in England and Wales the case is usually decided by a judge alone, whereas juries (which in civil proceedings consist of seven persons) are normally used in Northern Ireland. In Scotland, as in England and Wales, cases are usually heard without a jury, but there are other differences, and it is not feasible to combine the information from the three separate jurisdictions to produce a full analysis for the United Kingdom. The next section summarises information which can be brought together for the United Kingdom, and is followed by three sections giving details for England and Wales, Northern Ireland and Scotland separately.

169

United Kingdom

554 Personal injury claims make up only a small proportion of civil cases in the courts of the United Kingdom; the majority relate to debt or matrimonial disputes. Personal injury cases heard in the Queen's Bench Division of the High Court in England and Wales and in the High Court in Northern Ireland, however, represent the majority of cases in these jurisdictions.

555 Few of the cases analysed received a full trial. In England and Wales cases set down were most commonly settled some time before the hearing, whereas in Northern Ireland a higher proportion were settled immediately before the hearing was due (see Tables 124 and 132). In Scotland most cases were recorded as being settled without going to proof (trial).

556 Throughout the United Kingdom the majority of personal injury claims concerned employers' liability or transport.

557 The outcome of the case was known in England and Wales and in Northern Ireland if the case received a full trial or if the terms of a settlement were made known to the court. These cases amounted to only 40 per cent of cases set down in England and Wales, but to 72 per cent in Northern Ireland. Where the outcome was known, the plaintiff was successful in three quarters of cases in England and Wales and in over 90 per cent in Northern Ireland. In Scotland, the exact outcome was not known for most of the settled cases, but it appears that some compensation was obtained in over 80 per cent of cases where writs had been issued.

558 The median award was highest in Northern Ireland and lowest in Scotland (Table 123).

Table 123   Median awards

1974

	£
England and Wales	1,155
Northern Ireland	1,420
Scotland	875

559 The time taken from injury to issuing a writ was considerably longer in Scotland than in England and Wales, although time intervals at later stages were comparable. The difference may arise because of the necessity in Scotland to specify the amount claimed, giving Scottish lawyers an additional reason for waiting for a claimant's medical condition to stabilise before pursuing a claim.

560 At the time the enquiries were carried out, claims in the county courts in England and Wales were limited to £750 and in Northern Ireland to £300. Claims for more than these amounts were dealt with in the High Court. No monetary limits exist in respect of ordinary actions in the sheriff courts in Scotland, but in practice the larger claims come before the Court of Session.

England and Wales

561 In England and Wales nearly 60 per cent of the cases set down were withdrawn before hearing, a settlement having been agreed in most cases. Just under a quarter reached judgment. A smaller proportion of cases reached judgment in the High Court in London than elsewhere (Table 124).

Table 124 Method of disposal of claims

England and Wales: 1974

	High Court		County courts	All courts	Percentage of total number of claims set down
	London	District Registries			
	Numbers of claims				%
Withdrawn before hearing	1,499	1,436	1,631	4,566	59·0
Settled at door of court (without notice)	109	318	38	465	6·0
Settled in court without hearing	98	185	208	491	6·3
Settled during hearing	78	105	158	341	4·4
Judgment after full hearing	380	789	701	1,870	24·2
All claims set down	2,164	2,833	2,736	7,733	100·0

Table 125 Nature of claims

England and Wales: 1974

	High Court		County courts	All courts	Percentage of total number of claims set down
	London	District Registries			
	Numbers of claims				%
Employers' liability	1,058	1,643	1,413	4,114	53·2
Transport	954	1,041	961	2,956	38·2
Goods and services	3	7	12	22	0·3
Medical negligence	19	20	5	44	0·6
Occupiers' liability	86	68	99	253	3·3
Other personal injuries	44	54	246	344	4·4
All claims set down	2,164	2,833	2,736	7,733	100·0

562 Transport and employers' liability claims made up over 90 per cent of cases set down for hearing (Table 125).

563 A fifth of plaintiffs received legal aid, although the proportion varied considerably between categories (Table 126). Defendants obtained legal aid in less than 1 per cent of cases.

Table 126 Provision of legal aid to plaintiffs

England and Wales: 1974

	Number of plaintiffs with legal aid	All claims	Percentage with legal aid
	Numbers		%
Employers' liability	687	4,114	17
Transport	594	2,956	20
Goods and services	11	22	50
Medical negligence	23	44	52
Occupiers' liability	89	253	35
Other personal injuries	116	344	34
All claims set down	1,520	7,733	20

564 The plaintiff obtained compensation in about three quarters of the cases where the outcome was known, which exclude cases withdrawn before the hearing. Figures are given in Table 127. However, it was not necessarily only the plaintiff who was injured. Particularly in cases involving a collision between vehicles the defendant might also have been injured, and might have made a counter-claim against the plaintiff. Of the small number of cases involving judgment for both parties, most were transport claims, and some may have been of this kind. Others may have involved a number of defendants, not all of whom were found to be at fault.

Table 127 Outcome of case

England and Wales: 1974   Numbers of claims

In favour of plaintiff	2,295
In favour of defendant	747
Judgment for both plaintiff and defendant	30
Outcome not known	4,661
All claims set down	7,733

565 Awards in respect of transport and employment claims tended to be higher, with median awards of £1,670 and £1,375 respectively, compared with £465 for other types of claim. Table 128 gives a distribution of awards by size for 2,313 cases where the amount was known to the court.

Table 128 Size of awards

England and Wales: 1974

	All awards known	Up to £200	£201 to £1,000	£1,001 to £5,000	£5,001 to £25,000	£25,001 to £125,000	Over £125,000	Median award
	Numbers of awards							£
Employers' liability	1,129	130	399	379	200	21	–	1,375
Transport	947	164	270	235	225	52	1	1,670
Goods and services	6	2	1	2	–	1	–	..
Medical negligence	5	1	1	2	1	–	–	..
Occupiers' liability	82	16	31	25	10	–	–	710
Other personal injuries	144	65	51	18	9	1	–	290
Totals	2,313	378	753	661	445	75	1	1,155

Table 129 Average interval between injury and disposal of claim

England and Wales: 1974   Months

	High Court		County courts	All courts
	London	District Registries		
Employers' liability	45	43	25	38
Transport	41	35	17	33
Goods and services	80	56	17	40
Medical negligence	60	57	44	57
Occupiers' liability	47	43	21	37
Other personal injuries	46	50	17	27
All claims set down	43	41	21	36

566 The average time interval between the injury and the disposal of the claim for cases set down for trial was three years. About 10 per cent of claims were disposed of in less than a year; nearly a quarter took more than four years. Cases in the county courts were disposed of more quickly than those in the High Court. On average, claims involving medical negligence took longer than others. Details are given in Table 129.

567 The average interval between injury and disposal was made up in the way shown in Table 130.

Table 130   Average interval at each stage
England and Wales: 1974   Months

Average interval	
From injury to writ	16
From writ to setting down	13
From setting down to disposal	7

568 The majority of cases which received a full hearing were completed in a day. Cases in the county courts were completed more quickly than those in the High Court (Table 131).

Table 131   Hearing times of full trials
England and Wales: 1974

	High Court		County courts	All courts	
	London	District Registries		Number	Percentage of total number
Duration of hearing		Numbers of cases			%
Not more than 2 hours	55	125	227	407	21·8
Over 2 hours–1 day	156	436	451	1,043	55·8
Over 1 day–2 days	110	164	21	295	15·8
Over 2 days–1 week	53	59	2	114	6·1
More than 1 week	6	5	–	11	0·6
Totals	380	789	701	1,870	100·0

Northern Ireland

569 Just over half the cases set down in the courts in Northern Ireland were settled immediately before the hearing was due. A third of cases in the county courts received a full trial compared with only about 10 per cent in the High Court. Details are given in Table 132.

174

Table 132   Method of disposal of claims

Northern Ireland: 1974

	High Court	County courts	All courts	Percentage of total number of claims
	Numbers of claims			%
Withdrawn before hearing	254	114	368	26·0
Settled at door of court or in court without hearing	623	111	734	51·9
Settled during hearing	30	45	75	5·3
Judgment after full hearing	108	130	238	16·8
All claims set down	1,015	400	1,415	100·0

570   An analysis of claims in the county courts by nature of claim shows a smaller proportion of employers' liability claims than in England and Wales but a larger proportion classified to the residual heading for other personal injuries (Table 133). A full analysis was not made for cases in the High Court. A sample analysis indicated that the proportions of transport and employers' liability cases were similar to those in the courts in England and Wales – about 40 per cent and 50 per cent respectively.

Table 133   Nature of claims in the county courts

Northern Ireland: 1974

	Number of claims	Percentage of total number of claims
Employers' liability	99	24·8
Transport	178	44·5
Goods or services	22	5·5
Medical negligence	–	–
Occupiers' liability	20	5·0
Other personal injuries	81	20·3
All claims set down in the county court	400	100·0

571   Ten per cent of plaintiffs in the county courts received legal aid. Details are not available for the High Court.

572   The plaintiff was successful in over 90 per cent of cases in the High Court where the outcome was known (Table 134).

Table 134   Outcome of cases in the High Court

Northern Ireland: 1974   Numbers of claims.

In favour of plaintiff	713
In favour of defendant	44
Judgment for both plaintiff and defendant	4
Withdrawn before hearing	254
All claims set down in the High Court	1,015

573   Information is not available specifically about the outcome of cases in the county courts but only about awards made, from which it appears that a rather smaller proportion of plaintiffs were successful than in the High Court (Table 135).

Table 135   Outcome of cases in the county courts

Northern Ireland: 1974   Numbers of claims

Payment made	209
No payment made	47
No information	144
All claims set down in the county courts	400

574   Table 136 gives an analysis of High Court awards by size, but without any analysis by type of claim.

Table 136   Size of awards in the High Court

Northern Ireland: 1974   Numbers of awards

All awards known	Up to £300	£301– £750	£751– £5,000	£5,001– £25,000	£25,001– £125,000	Over £125,000
719	23	169	401	118	7	1

575   In 1974, claims in the Northern Ireland county courts were normally limited in personal injury cases to amounts of up to £300, although it is possible that a few awards were for larger amounts. Most awards were less than £150. Table 137 gives an analysis of 209 awards whose amount was known.

Table 137   Size of awards in county courts

Northern Ireland: 1974   Numbers of awards

	All awards known	Up to £200	£201–£750
Employers' liability	43	36	7
Transport	96	73	23
Goods and services	8	6	2
Medical negligence	–	–	–
Occupiers' liability	8	6	2
Other personal injuries	54	49	5
Totals	209	170	39

576   Table 138 combines the data about size of awards for the High Court and the county courts. The median award in all courts in Northern Ireland in 1974 was £1,420.

Table 138   Size of awards in all courts

Northern Ireland: 1974

All awards known	Up to £750	£751 to £5,000	Over £5,000	Median award
	Numbers of awards			£
928	401	401	126	1,420

577   No information is available about the time from injury to issuing a writ in Northern Ireland. The average interval from the issue of a writ to setting down for trial in the High Court was between 12 and 18 months, and from setting down to disposal slightly over 2 years. Cases in the county courts were dealt with more quickly; the average time between setting down and disposal was just under 2 months.

Scotland

578   Details of the method of disposal of Scottish cases are given in Table 139. Only 17 per cent of the cases in which a writ had been issued received judgment after full proof (trial).

Table 139   Method of disposal of claims

Scotland: 1974

	Court of Session	Sheriff courts	All courts	Percentage of total number of claims
	Numbers of claims			%
Full proof held	26	69	95	17·2
Settled without full proof	286	130	416	75·4
Otherwise disposed of	11	30	41	7·4
All claims where writs issued	323	229	552	100·0

579   Cases involving employers' liability were the most numerous in Scotland, as in England and Wales (Table 140).

Table 140   Nature of claims

Scotland: 1974

	Court of Session	Sheriff courts	All courts	Percentage of total number of claims
	Numbers of claims			%
Employers' liability	186	120	306	55·4
Transport	111	75	186	33·7
Goods and services	1	5	6	1·1
Medical negligence	1	1	2	0·4
Occupiers' liability	8	14	22	4·0
Other personal injuries	16	14	30	5·4
All claims where writs issued	323	229	552	100·0

580   Nearly a quarter of pursuers (plaintiffs) received legal aid (Table 141). Defenders (defendants) obtained legal aid in less than 1 per cent of cases.

581   The pursuer was successful in rather fewer than half the cases where a full proof was held (Table 142).

Table 141 Provision of legal aid

Scotland: 1974

	Number of pursuers with legal aid	All claims	Percentage with legal aid
	Numbers of claims		%
Employers' liability	75	306	25
Transport	44	186	24
Goods and services	4	6	67
Medical negligence	1	2	50
Occupiers' liability	3	22	14
Other personal injuries	8	30	27
All claims where writs issued	135	552	24

Table 142 Outcome of cases where full proof held

Scotland: 1974   Numbers of claims

Judgment after proof	
For pursuer	44
For defender	50
For both	1
Total	95

Table 143 Outcome of cases disposed of without full proof

Scotland: 1974   Numbers of claims

Settled without full proof	
For pursuer	175
Recorded as 'joint minutes' or 'tender and acceptance' with no further information	240
For both parties	1
Otherwise disposed of	
Dismissed or withdrawn	29
Full amount for pursuer[1]	12
Total	457

1 Cases where defender failed to appear in court.

582   Some information is available about cases disposed of without a full proof (Table 143). The great majority involved some payment to the pursuer. 38 per cent were clearly settled in favour of the pursuer, and a further 53 per cent were either settled for the pursuer ('tender and acceptance') or technically for the defender ('joint minutes') but usually involving the payment of an agreed amount of damages, on receipt of which the pursuer would drop the case.

583   Table 144 gives the distribution by size of awards in 231 Scottish cases where the amount was known. The median award in 1974 for all categories of claim was £875. Awards in respect of employment and motor vehicle claims tended to be higher than for others.

Table 144   Size of awards

Scotland: 1974

	All awards known	£1 to £200	£201 to £1,000	£1,001 to £5,000	£5,001 to £25,000	Over £25,000	Median awards
			Numbers of awards				£
Employers' liability	110	8	47	45	9	1	1,000
Transport	93	8	41	33	11	–	950
Goods and services	3	2	1	–	–	–	..
Medical negligence	1	–	1	–	–	–	..
Occupiers' liability	9	3	4	1	1	–	} 475
Other personal injuries	15	3	10	2	–	–	}
Totals	231	24	104	81	21	1	875

584   Since in Scotland the amount claimed has to be specified, it is possible to compare amounts obtained with those claimed. On average, a smaller proportion of claims was awarded in the Court of Session than in the sheriff courts, where claims tended to be smaller (Table 145).

Table 145   Average proportion of claim obtained

Scotland: 1974   Percentages

	Court of Session	Sheriff courts
Motor vehicle	36	62
Employers' liability	34	52
Other personal injuries	35	46
All claims where award known	35	47

585   Table 146 contains an analysis of average intervals between an injury and the disposal of a resulting claim, based on records of 204 cases where proof was arranged. The data are comparable with those for England and Wales given in Table 129 above.

586   Claims in the sheriff courts were settled more quickly than those in the Court of Session. In all courts, only 5 per cent of claims were disposed of less than a year after the date of injury, and a third took over four years. Claims involving employers' liability took longer than motor vehicle claims. Other types of claim were too few for separate analysis.

Table 146   Average interval between injury and disposal of claim, for cases where proof arranged

Scotland: 1974   Months

	Court of Session	Sheriff courts	All courts
Employers' liability	54	39	48
Transport	42	29	37
Other personal injuries	57	35	40
All claims where proof arranged	50	36	44

587   Table 147 shows how the average interval of 44 months was made up. On average over two years elapsed between the date of the injury and the issue of a writ.

Table 147   Average interval at each stage

Scotland: 1974   Months

Average interval	
From injury to writ	26
From writ to fixing proof	12
From fixing of proof to disposal	6

588   The lengths of court hearings in Scotland are analysed in Table 148. More than a third of cases which received a full hearing took longer than a day.

Coverage of the surveys

589   As all the analyses are based on court records for the whole of 1974, the information can be taken to be reliable and complete.

Table 148 Hearing times where full proof held

Scotland: 1974

	Court of Session	Sheriff courts	All courts Number	All courts Percentage of total number
Duration of hearing		Number of cases		%
Not more than 2 hours	–	4	4	4
Over 2 hours–1 day	13	43	56	60
Over 1 day–2 days	9	16	25	27
Over 2 days–1 week	4	5	9	10
Totals	26	68[1]	94[1]	100

1 One case omitted where duration not known.

Further information

590 In 1974 the Lord Chancellor's Office set up a system for recording on a computer details of all civil actions set down in the High Court in England and Wales. As a result summary information about actions in the High Court, including separate figures for personal injury claims, is now published annually by Her Majesty's Stationery Office in Judicial Statistics.

591 Further particulars of the surveys summarised in this chapter, including copies of the forms used to record the data, are available from the Lord Chancellor's Office, the Scottish Home and Health Department, and the Northern Ireland Office.

CHAPTER 25

Earnings before and after industrial accidents

592   A study of earnings before and after industrial accidents was made by the Department of Health and Social Security. The results were received in November 1975. The study was limited to male employees in Great Britain.

593   It related to injuries in the year June 1969 to May 1970 inclusive. Changes in the earnings of a sample of men who had been injured in that period were compared with changes in the earnings of all male employees. The changes were measured between the fiscal year 1968–69 (which ended two months before the year in which the injury occurred) and two periods after the injury, namely 1971–72 (about two years after) and 1973–74 (about four years after). The sample included men who earned little or nothing in these subsequent years because of sickness or unemployment.

594   Information was compiled separately for those with or without disabilities leading to the receipt of industrial disablement benefit. For those not disabled, who received injury benefit only, a further distinction was made between those involved in one accident only, and those involved in a subsequent accident in any year up to and including 1973–74; and degrees of severity were distinguished in terms of the duration of incapacity. For the disabled, different degrees of disablement were distinguished.

Relative growth of earnings

595   The average earnings of all male employees rose by 46 per cent between 1968–69 and 1971–72, and by 85 per cent between 1968–69 and 1973–74. These figures, used as the basis of comparison, are shown at the foot of the accompanying tables, and are termed the 'control figures'.

596   Percentage increases in the average earnings of the sample of men who had been injured are accompanied in the tables by ranges. There is a 95 per cent probability in each case that the true figure was in the range given. For convenience, asterisks mark cases where the control figure is outside the range shown for the sample; in these cases there is at least a 95 per cent probability that the increase in average earnings of the sub-sample of those injured was in fact less than the control figure representing the increase in earnings of all male employees.

597   The tables show that average increases between 1968–69 and 1971–72 in the earnings of those who had sustained industrial injuries were less than the control figure. This was not always true however of increases between 1968–69 and 1973–74.

598   Table 149 shows changes in earnings for men who drew injury but not industrial disablement benefit. The differences were of greatest significance for the more severe accidents, as measured by the duration of injury benefit following them. The lower increases in earnings could have reflected diminished earning capacity, or greater proneness to spells of sickness following injury. There is no firm evidence that the comparative reduction in earnings persisted to 1973–74, about four years after the accident.

Table 149   Changes in average earnings following industrial accidents in 1969–70

Male employees in Great Britain who received only injury benefit

	Number of cases in sample	Percentage increases in average earnings of sample			
		1968/69 to 1971/72		1968/69 to 1973/74	
		Sample figure	Range	Sample figure	Range
Single accidents	1,011	40*	36–44	85	80–90
Duration of benefit (weekdays)					
1–12	438	43	37–49	91	82–100
13–24	297	40	34–46	83	75–91
25–48	183	41	28–54	78	68–88
over 48	93	28*	19–37	81	69–93
Multiple accidents	609	36*	31–41	82	76–88
Duration of benefit (weekdays)					
1–12	242	45	33–57	92	83–101
13–24	217	35*	29–41	81	72–90
25–48	104	27*	19–35	74	63–85
over 48	46	25*	11–39	65	43–87
All men (control figures)	Over 50,000	46	..	85	..

* Control figure is outside the range: there is at least a 95 per cent probability that average earnings of injured men in these categories increased less than those of all male employees.

599   Those who experienced subsequent accidents appear to have fared worse between 1968–69 and 1971–72 than those with a single accident. The association between comparative loss of earnings and severity of the accident is stronger for the multiple accident group; and there is evidence that for some in this group the comparative reduction in earnings persisted four years after the accident.

600   Table 150 gives comparisons for those who received industrial disablement benefit following injury benefit. It shows that their average earnings rose substantially less than those of the control group. In the group with a 50 per cent disablement assessment or more, they were lower two years after the accident than a year before it. The comparative reduction in earnings persisted four years after the accident.

Table 150 Changes in average earnings following industrial accidents in 1969–70

Male employees in Great Britain who received industrial disablement benefit

	Number of cases in sample	Percentage increases in average earnings of sample			
		1968/69 to 1971/72		1968/69 to 1973/74	
		Sample figure	Range	Sample figure	Range
Disablement gratuity sample	449	28*	23 to 33	73*	66 to 80
Disablement pension sample	654	11*	7 to 15	50*	44 to 56
Percentage assessment					
20	390	22*	17 to 27	61*	54 to 68
30	129	3*	Minus 6 to 12	51*	39 to 63
40	50	2*	Minus 14 to 22	48*	24 to 72
50 or more	85	Minus 22*	Minus 35 to Minus 9	3*	Minus 14 to 20
All men (control figure)	Over 50,000	46	..	85	..

* Control figure is outside the range: there is at least a 95 per cent probability that average earnings of injured men in these categories increased less than those of all male employees.

Sample selection

601 The first part of the sample consisted of men who had drawn injury benefit but not industrial disablement benefit. The initial selection comprised 1 in 200 of those men who had drawn injury benefit owing to an industrial accident in the year June 1969–May 1970. The following were then excluded: those over 60 at 31 May 1970, those who received disablement benefit in the twelve months ending in September 1970, and those who had fewer than 48 insurance contributions as employees paid or credited in any of the years 1968–69, 1971–72 and 1973. The effect of the last exclusion was to remove those who had not been in

185

the working population throughout the period under study or who had been self employed for part of the period, while retaining those who had been sick or unemployed during the years in question.

602   The second part of the sample was drawn from those who had industrial accidents in the year June 1969–May 1970, and who were awarded industrial disablement benefit in the year October 1969–September 1970. It consisted initially of 1 in 100 of those awarded gratuities, and 1 in 10 of those awarded pensions. Similar exclusions were made of those over 60 (at 31 December 1970) and of those without the relevant contributions in the years under study.

603   The whole sample of those injured consisted of 2,723 men.

604   For changes in the earnings of all male employees, the best basis of comparison consisted of the DHSS records from which the samples for those injured had been drawn. An analysis is made each year of a large sample consisting of $\frac{1}{2}$ per cent of all employees. For the present purpose, the figures used for each of the three years related to men under 65 with at least 48 insurance contributions as employees. The sample included men who had experienced industrial injury, as well as those who had not, since it was not practicable to exclude the first group. It included those who had been credited with contributions as a result of sickness or unemployment, and whose earnings were lower on that account, in the same way as the samples of those experiencing an industrial accident. It consisted in each year of over 50,000 men.

Qualifications

605   The wide ranges attaching to the results are due to possible sampling error. They reflect the fact that changes in earnings between the specified years showed great variations among individuals, even among those subject to accidents of similar severity. Variations of the same nature occur among men who have not been involved in accidents. The sample from which the control figures were derived was however sufficiently large for the sampling errors attaching to them to be disregarded.

606   A difference between the samples of men who had been injured at work and of all male employees was that the average earnings of those injured, before the year of injury, were about 15 per cent less than those of male employees generally. This difference probably results from men in certain industries and occupations being more likely to suffer injury.

607   The effect of different industrial patterns was tested. It was found that the control figures would have been little different in 1971–72, but about one percentage point lower in 1973–74, if the proportions of men included for each industry had been the same as in the sample of men who had been injured.

CHAPTER 26

Surcharges in Ontario

608 Following the visit to Canada in 1974, an investigation was made of the operation of the provisions for imposing penal surcharges on firms with bad accident records. The investigation was made with the assistance of the Secretary of the Workmen's Compensation Board of Ontario, and of the staff of its Finance Department.

609 Professor Atiyah of Oxford University, who has also studied the Ontario system, was consulted about the interpretation of the results of the investigation, although he bears no responsibility for the conclusions.

The Ontario system

610 Workmen's compensation in Ontario is financed by assessments on employers under a system of differential rating for different groups of industries. The assessments are broadly the equivalent of premiums on employers' liability policies paid by employers in the United Kingdom. Rates vary widely; for example, in 1974 the rate for lumbering was 50 times the rate for accountants.

611 Under legislation dating from 1964, the Board is given wide discretion to increase the assessments of employers with accident costs and incidences of work injury above the average for the industry in which they are engaged. The Board's powers now derive from section 86(7) of the Workmen's Compensation Act 1970 and from regulations made under it. The surcharges serve as a penalty on firms with poor records rather than as a means of raising additional revenue.

612 Regulations provide that increased assessments shall be levied where the employer:

i   has incurred in two of the last three complete years of operation a deficit accident cost experience, including his proper share of administration, safety and other expenses; and

ii has incurred a 'lifetime' deficit accident cost experience, including his proper share of administration, safety and other expenses; and

iii has incurred during two of the last three complete years of operation a frequency rate of compensable accidents at least 25 per cent higher than the average rate in the industry in which he is classified.

613 All three conditions have to be satisfied. If they are, the assessment may initially be increased by 100 per cent. The Board, however, has discretion not to

187

impose the surcharge, or it may be cancelled on appeal, made through the machinery used for appeals for compensation, concluding with appeal to the Board itself.

614 It is believed that the financial penalties, together with the assistance provided by the safety associations, who receive lists of all delinquent employers, are effective in inducing managements to pay more attention to safety. There remains the question whether they are effective also in leading to a reduction in accidents, and it was to this question that the investigation was directed.

Results of the investigation

615 It was thought best to direct the investigation to employers who were in the same industry group, and therefore engaged in broadly similar activities. The metal working group of industries was chosen since it involved a fair degree of risk, and contained an adequate number of firms, most of which would have been in existence throughout the period studied. Comparison was made between the accident experience of all firms in the group and that of firms listed as delinquent in 1969. Numbers of accidents were extracted for that year and for three years before and after, and expressed as incidence rates per million man hours.

616 The main results are set out in Table 151.

Table 151 Trends in accident rates in metal working industries in Ontario

	Number of firms	1966	1967	1968	1969	1970	1971	1972
		Number of accidents per million man hours						
All firms	3,067 in 1966 increasing to 3,807 in 1972	35·1	33·0	32·4	39·4	39·4	36·5	38·4
All firms listed as delinquent in 1969	159	79·8	74·6	66·5	62·4	55·9	46·3	47·5
Of which:								
Surcharge not imposed	53	81·0	81·5	59·6	54·5	52·4	45·5	52·7
Surcharge remitted on appeal	34	71·4	60·9	59·7	55·1	44·7	35·4	40·9
Surcharge paid	72	85·4	78·8	79·6	75·6	67·9	55·5	47·7

617 The results show a decline in the incidence of accidents for the firms listed as delinquent whether or not they were required to pay a surcharge. The decline was, however, most marked for those paying the surcharge. Except for one group in one year, the accident rates remained above those of all metal working firms, suggesting either that remedial measures had not been fully effective, or that the activities of the listed firms involved a degree of risk greater than for other metal working firms.

618   The results provide *prima facie* evidence that the Ontario system may lead to lower accident rates, although to determine conclusively how much effect it has would require a much fuller analysis.

619   Two qualifications deserve mention. The first is, that since the data analysed in this study related to numbers of accidents, they mainly represented minor injuries; no account was taken of the degree of severity of the accidents recorded. There must sometimes have been doubt whether particular minor accidents should be recorded, although there is no evidence that eligible accidents were unrecorded. The Workmen's Compensation Board receive reports from doctors and hospitals, and from trade unions, as well as from employers.

620   The second qualification concerns the possible effect of random variations in the incidence of accidents. Among those with a 'lifetime' deficit with the Board, there might have been some with bad accident records in two of the three years qualifying them for listing as delinquent which were the consequence of bad luck rather than bad management. This might have occurred in particular with small firms, where one or two accidents in a year would take them above the average incidence rate, and put them in deficit with the Board; the average number of accidents in a year in all firms in the metal working industries was less than four, and in the delinquent firms less than nine.

621   Where such cases could be identified, the Board would impose no penalty, and they are likely to be included among those listed as delinquent without being required to pay a surcharge. This category includes also some firms surcharged in previous years, but not in 1969, since a good safety programme had been adopted.

622   The figures may reflect these factors, for example, in showing lower accident rates for delinquent firms, which were not surcharged, in 1968 than in 1966 and 1967. Also, if some firms had high accident rates from 1966 to 1968 as a matter of chance, one would expect their figures to revert to a lower average level from 1969 on – as appears to have happened with the group of 53 firms on whom a surcharge was not imposed. It is less easy to use the element of chance to explain the continuing decline from 1969 to 1972 in the average accident rate for the group of 72 firms which were surcharged.

PART IV

Technical aspects of the assessment of compensation

CHAPTER 27

Calculations made by consulting actuaries

623 This chapter discusses some of the results of illustrative calculations commissioned from Duncan C. Fraser & Co., a firm of consulting actuaries who have developed a computer programme to make detailed calculations of lump sums payable in compensation in varying circumstances, and on varying assumptions.

624 The calculations they were asked to make were selected so as to illustrate a wide range of possibilities. The examples chosen were therefore not limited to typical cases, or to the conditions thought most likely to prevail in the future, but included some extreme values. Only a selection from the results is given here.

625 All the calculations related to a man assumed to be wholly incapacitated, with a wife and two children. The calculations related to net earnings levels of £2,000, £5,000 and £10,000 a year. They showed the effect of full offsetting of existing social security benefits throughout the period of incapacity.

626 Alternative assumptions were made about future average annual rates of return on capital, and rates of inflation of earnings. The first assumption, representing a return to the kind of conditions which have prevailed in the past, was for rates of 6 per cent and 3 per cent respectively. The second, a more pessimistic one, was for rates of 8 per cent in each case; that is to say, a zero real rate of return was assumed.

Some results of the calculations

627 A selection from the results is set out in Table 152, where they are compared with the sums which might be awarded under the present system of assessment. Since these are not based on actuarial calculations, they were estimated independently.

628 The results show the very much larger sums that might be claimed on the basis of full theoretical allowance for the combined effects of tax and inflation. They show also how much they could vary with different assumptions about future rates of return and of inflation – on the alternative assumptions used here by a factor of 2 or more.

629 The results show also that, when earnings are low, social security benefits can go a long way towards replacing them, leaving limited scope for tort compensation if benefits were fully offset. In the example chosen of a man with net

earnings of £2,000 a year, the benefits received would have been greater than his earnings as long as they included allowances for both his children; only after the first child had grown up would there have been any net loss, after deduction of benefits, to be made good. The calculation allowed accurately for this situation by including nothing for the first few years, but allowing for the net losses in the later years.

Table 152 Estimated capital sums showing effect of offsetting existing social security benefits

Married man aged 35, wholly incapacitated, with wife and two children aged 10 and 8

	£ a year	£ a year	£ a year
Gross earnings	2,170	6,793	20,944
Net earnings	2,000	5,000	10,000
Social security benefits			
At start	2,066	2,066	2,066
After 10 years	1,445	1,445	1,445
Average[1]	1,632	1,632	1,632
Annual loss[2]	368	3,368	8,368
Estimated capital sums	£'000	£'000	£'000
6% and 3% assumption[3]			
Without offset	35·4	123·7[4]	429·5[5]
Implied multiplier[6]	(18)	(25)	(43)
With full offset	5·3	81·7[4]	372·1[5]
Implied multiplier[7]	(14)	(24)	(44)
8% and 8% assumption[3]			
Without offset	60·8	252·9[4]	1,280·5[5]
Implied multiplier[6]	(30)	(50)	(128)
With full offset	8·2	164·4[4]	1,147·3[5]
Implied multiplier[7]	(22)	(49)	(137)
Present basis			
Without offset	30·0	75·0	150·0
Multiplier	(15)	(15)	(15)
With partial offset[8]	25·9	70·9	145·9

1 Including an appropriate proportion of the benefits for the children.
2 Net earnings less average benefits.
3 Assuming investment income taxed as unearned income.
4 Allowance made for lost pension.
5 Allowance made for lost pension and for gross earnings increasing at 3 per cent more than the rate of inflation of earnings generally.
6 Capital sum divided by the net earnings.
7 Capital sum divided by the annual loss.
8 After deducting half the initial benefits of £39·60 a week for 208 weeks – assuming that of the five years in respect of which deduction is made, one had elapsed by the time of award or settlement.

630   The other two examples considered were of earnings above the average level of about £4,000 a year in January 1977. For them, the effect of the full offset of social security benefits was less marked, though still appreciable. In these cases, however, it was outweighed by the effect of making full allowance for tax and inflation, and even on the more conservative assumptions about rates of return and rates of inflation, the calculated capital sums were greater than under the present system. For the extreme case of net earnings of £10,000 a year and rates of return and of inflation both of 8 per cent a year, the capital sum required was estimated to be over £1 million.

631   Table 153 compares estimates of the capital sums required on different assumptions about taxation. The first calculation in each case related to the normal situation in which the tax on invested income was subject to the investment.

Table 153   Estimated capital sums with different taxation arrangements

Married man aged 35, wholly incapacitated, with wife and two children aged 10 and 8. No deduction made for social security benefits.

	£	£	£
Annual net earnings to be replaced	2,000	5,000	10,000
Estimated capital sum	£'000	£'000[1]	£'000[2]
6% and 3% assumption[3]			
Investment income taxed as unearned income	35·4	123·7	429·5
Investment income taxed as earned income	34·8	112·6	359·3
No tax on investment income; withdrawals taxed as earned income	38·1	126·7	543·5
8% and 8% assumption[4]			
Investment income taxed as unearned income	60·8	252·9	1,280·5
Investment income taxed as earned income	55·8	206·6	942·1
No tax on investment income; withdrawals taxed as earned income	53·6	182·8	832·9

1 Allowance made for lost pension.
2 Allowance made for lost pension and for gross earnings increasing at 3 per cent more than the rate of inflation of earnings generally.
3 Rate of return 6 per cent a year, rate of inflation of earnings 3 per cent a year.
4 Rate of return 8 per cent a year, rate of inflation of earnings 8 per cent a year.

income surcharge. The second assumed that investment income was taxed at earned income rates – comparison with the first calculation then showing the effect of the investment income surcharge. The third assumed that income from the invested fund was free of tax, but that the withdrawals made each year were taxed as earned income.

632   The results indicated that the investment income surcharge had an appreciable effect only at the higher levels of income. The establishment of a tax free fund would increase the capital sums required on the more conservative assumption about rates of return and of inflation, as a result of tax being imposed on withdrawals from capital as well as from the income of the invested funds. If a higher rate of inflation were assumed, however, the capital sums required might be reduced as the result of tax not having to be paid on the whole of the investment income.

633   Table 154 gives details, for a single example, of the year by year calculation of the value of the fund, the income derived from it, the tax payable, and the amount withdrawn. It is for the case of net earnings of £5,000 a year, with rates of return and of inflation both of 8 per cent per year and without deduction of social security benefits.

634   Provision was made to compensate for a lost pension assumed to be at half the rate of the earnings at age 65, not indexed. It is because of the addition to the lump sum in respect of the lost pension that the income provided is estimated to continue until after retirement age. Had it not been for this addition, the allowance made for the possibility of death or incapacity if the injury being compensated had not occurred would have meant that payments would have ceased earlier. The implied multiplier, obtained by dividing the capital sum by the net income lost, is just over 50.

635   The table shows that the tax on the investment income starts at over 65 per cent, and then steadily decreases until in the last three years no tax is paid.

636   In this example, the net income of the fund after payment of tax is greater in the early years than the amount withdrawn; and consequently the fund is built up in the earlier years, only starting to be drawn down in the 13th year. This can happen when the multiplier and the rate of return are both large.

Details of the calculations

637   The calculations relate to a married man aged 35 at the time the compensation is assessed, with a wife aged 33, and two children aged 10 and 8.

638   Net earnings were assumed to be £2,000, £5,000 and £10,000 per year. In the case of the £5,000 and £10,000 earnings levels, a loss of pension from age 65 was assumed, at the rates of one half and two thirds respectively of gross earnings in the 65th year, not subject to indexation. In the £10,000 a year case, allowance was made for an annual increase in gross earnings on account of age, experience and promotion, over and above the effects of inflation, at the rate of 3 per cent a year in gross earnings.

Table 154 Example of a step by step calculation

Married man aged 35, wholly incapacitated, with wife and two children aged 10 and 8. Net income £5,000 a year; pension one half of earnings in 65th year. Rate of return 8 per cent per year. Rate of increase of earnings 8 per cent per year. No deduction made for social security benefits.

Year	Fund at start of year £	Gross income of fund £	Tax Amount £	Tax Rate %	Net income of fund £	Amount added to or withdrawn from fund £	Total withdrawn £
1	252,889	20,231	13,245	65·5	6,986	+1,987	5,000
2	254,876	20,390	12,962	63·6	7,428	+2,013	5,414
3	256,889	20,551	12,676	61·7	7,875	+2,027	5,848
4	258,916	20,713	12,343	59·6	8,370	+2,037	6,333
5	260,953	20,876	12,060	57·8	8,816	+1,976	6,840
6	262,929	21,034	11,740	55·8	9,294	+1,907	7,387
7	264,836	21,187	11,380	53·7	9,807	+1,810	7,997
8	266,646	21,332	11,050	51·8	10,282	+1,645	8,637
9	268,291	21,463	10,658	49·7	10,805	+1,458	9,348
10	269,749	21,580	10,310	47·8	11,270	+1,173	10,096
11	270,922	21,674	9,941	45·9	11,733	+ 830	10,904
12	271,752	21,740	10,036	46·2	11,704	+ 266	11,438
13	272,017	21,761	9,675	44·5	12,086	− 267	12,353
14	271,750	21,740	9,800	45·1	11,940	− 977	12,916
15	270,773	21,662	9,434	43·6	12,228	−1,721	13,949
16	269,052	21,524	9,066	42·1	12,458	−2,608	15,065
17	266,444	21,316	8,696	40·8	12,620	−3,650	16,271
18	262,794	21,024	8,368	39·8	12,656	−4,916	17,572
19	257,878	20,630	7,999	38·8	12,631	−6,347	18,978
20	251,531	20,122	7,559	37·6	12,563	−7,934	20,496
21	243,597	19,488	7,042	36·1	12,446	−9,691	22,136
22	233,906	18,712	6,438	34·4	12,274	−11,633	23,907
23	222,273	17,782	5,740	32·3	12,042	−13,777	25,820
24	208,496	16,680	4,937	29·6	11,743	−16,142	27,885
25	192,354	15,388	4,018	26·1	11,370	−18,746	30,116
26	173,608	13,889	2,975	21·4	10,914	−21,612	32,525
27	151,996	12,160	1,924	15·8	10,236	−24,892	35,128
28	127,104	10,168	744	7·3	9,424	−28,513	37,938
29	98,591	7,887	−	−	7,887	−33,086	40,973
30	65,505	5,240	−	−	5,240	−39,011	44,251
31	26,494	2,120	−	−	2,120	−22,272	24,391[1]
32	4,222						

1 Pension that would have been received.

639   The method used was to multiply the value of a future payment by the probability that it would become payable, and to discount it to a present value at the given rate of return. The probabilities used allowed for the possibility that the injured man might have died or become incapacitated had he not been injured.

640   Alternative assumptions about rates of return and rates of inflation were:

	Per cent per year	
	i	ii
Rate of return	6	8
Rate of inflation of earnings	3	8

Investment income was calculated by applying the given rate of return to the estimated value of the fund at the start of each year.

641   Tax was calculated at the rates of the fiscal year 1976/77. Allowance was made for the investment income surcharge where it was applicable, and for tax allowances in respect of the children until they reached the age of 21. In the conversion from net earnings to gross earnings, no adjustment was made for social security contributions, or for the tax clawback on the family allowance payable in 1976/77 in respect of the second child.

642   Where allowance was made for the full offset of long term benefits for loss of earnings the assumed benefits were as follows:

	£ a week
Invalidity pension	15·30
Invalidity allowance (assuming age 34 at the time of injury)	3·20
Increase for wife	9·20
Increase for each child	5·95

643   The child allowance of £5·95 a week represents £7·45 less an assumed child benefit of £1·50 a week for each child. It was assumed to continue until the children reached the age of 18, and consequently the benefits deducted were:

Years	£ a week
1 to 7	39·60
8 to 9	33·65
10 to 30	27·70

Further information

644   The full report is available from Duncan C. Fraser & Co., 24–28 Cheapside, London EC2V 6AB.

CHAPTER 28

The inflationary background

645 In the discussion which follows, the term inflation is used to mean an increase in the general level of prices.

Rates of inflation

646 Historically, prices have tended to rise over time, but often by no more than 2 or 3 per cent a year; and there have been periods, as in the nineteenth century, when prices fell rather than rose. Large price increases occurred only when the normal relationship between supply and demand was disrupted – for example by harvest failures, pestilence or war.

647 The recent acceleration of inflation, which started in the late 1960's and has affected most countries in the world, was not due to this cause, and there is no general agreement as to why it occurred. It has been accompanied lately by a reduction in economic activity and increased unemployment – a combination which is quite new, at least in modern times.

648 Recent rates of inflation have been higher in the United Kingdom than in most other industrial countries, as is shown in Table 155; the annual rates of 20 per cent or more which have been recorded are probably unprecedented in peace time.

Rates of return on capital

649 In ordinary times, the rate of return on capital is greater than the rate of inflation, and the real rate of return – measured approximately by the difference between the two – is positive. In the last few years however this normal relationship has not held.

650 Table 156 gives estimates of average real rates of return, on both equities and bonds, for the period from 1950 to 1974 inclusive, which is sub-divided into five 5-year periods. The rates allow for the re-investment of dividends and interest, and are given both before and after taking account of income tax at the standard rate. They are based on data published by Nicholas Barr.[31] The present estimates differ from his in relating to different periods, and in making allowance in respect of equity investment for capital appreciation on reinvested dividends as well as on the original investment. The estimates show how an investment would have built up over time assuming no withdrawals, rather than the rate of withdrawal which could have taken place without eroding the real value of the original capital.

Table 155 Comparative rates of inflation since 1967

Percentage changes in index numbers of retail prices from January of the year stated to January of the following year

	1967	1968	1969	1970	1971	1972	1973	1974	1975	1976
United Kingdom	2·6	6·2	5·0	8·5	8·2	7·7	12·0	19·9	23·4	16·6
All OECD countries[1]	..	..	..	..	5·3	4·7	8·0	13·6	11·4	8·6
France	4·0	5·4	6·1	4·7	5·7	6·6	10·3	14·5	9·6	9·0
Germany F.R.	1·7	2·0	3·4	3·7	6·3	6·3	7·4	6·2	5·3	4·1
Italy	2·3	1·0	4·4	5·3	4·6	8·1	13·2	24·1	11·0	22·3
Netherlands	4·0	7·2	3·3	6·4	9·1	7·9	8·1	10·7	9·1	7·6
Sweden	3·1	1·6	5·1	7·8	7·3	5·9	8·0	10·2	10·7	9·0
Switzerland	3·6	2·4	2·3	6·2	6·1	7·4	11·6	7·2	3·4	0·9
United States	3·5	4·6	6·2	5·2	3·4	3·7	9·4	11·7	6·8	5·2
Canada	4·5	3·8	4·6	1·6	4·9	5·6	9·1	13·1	9·6	6·1
Australia[2]	3·3	2·9	3·2	4·9	7·2	5·6	13·6	17·6	13·3	13·6
New Zealand[2]	4·9	5·5	4·8	10·3	8·5	5·9	10·3	13·2	17·1	13·7

1 24 countries, including the major Western industrial countries.
2 Percentage changes from first quarter of year stated to first quarter of following year.

Source: Based on OECD statistics.

651 Since capital appreciation represents part of the return which is sought from equity investment, the rates of return on equities which include capital appreciation are the more significant of those shown. The after tax returns on equities are on the high side in that allowance has been made only for income tax, not for capital gains tax.

652 The last 5-year period differed in character from the previous ones. Dividend and interest rates failed to match the rate of inflation. Dividends did so by the wider margins, reflecting Government controls on the distribution of profits. At the same time, ordinary share prices fell to an abnormally low level, and there were capital losses, not capital gains. In consequence, all the rates averaged over the period from 1970 to 1974 are negative. Before 1970, dividend and interest rates kept ahead of inflation, except in 1951 and 1952, when prices shot up as the result of the Korean war and the return on bonds was less than the rate of inflation.

653 The exceptional circumstances prevailing in the five years 1970 to 1974 inclusive brought down the rates for the whole period 1950 to 1974 as well as for that 5-year period. An alternative set of figures has been calculated for the period 1955–1969, when there were no abnormal circumstances. In that period, real rates of return after tax were for the most part positive, although those relating to bonds were all less than $\frac{1}{2}$ per cent.

Table 156 Real rates of return on capital

Annual averages   Percentages

| | Equities | | | | Bonds[1] | |
| | With capital appreciation | | Without capital appreciation | | | |
	Before tax	After tax[2]	Before tax	After tax[2]	Before tax	After tax[2]
1950–1954	10·9	8·1	0·5	−2·0	−1·5	−3·1
1955–1959	14·3	11·7	2·8	0·4	1·9	−0·1
1960–1964	2·7	0·8	1·7	−0·1	2·5	0·4
1965–1969	8·1	6·1	0·5	−1·4	2·9	0·1
1970–1974	−19·5	−21·1	−5·5	−7·3	−0·7	−4·5
1950–1974	2·5	0·4	0	−2·1	1·0	−1·5
1955–1969	8·3	6·1	1·7	−0·4	2·5	0·1

1 Medium term Government bonds.
2 Standard rate of income tax (unearned income rate up to 1973). No allowance has been made for capital gains tax.

Source: Based on data published by Nicholas Barr.

Average tax rates

654 As incomes rise, average tax rates increase unless personal allowances and the levels at which higher rates of tax become payable are increased correspondingly. This is the phenomenon known as 'fiscal drag'. By a provision of the Finance Act 1977, personal allowances are from 1977–78 to be increased by not less than the rate of inflation in the previous calendar year, unless Parliament decides otherwise. The provision does not however extend to the higher tax bands.

655 Partly because of fiscal drag and partly because of changes in the tax structure, rates of tax increased appreciably from 1972 to 1977. Table 157 shows how they have changed during the last eight years for men with average earnings, and with three times average earnings.

Assumptions as to the future

656 As there is no certainty as to what caused the recent upsurge of inflation, there can equally be no certainty as to the level at which it will be brought under control. No attempt has been made to forecast the future rate of inflation, but in the consideration of how lump sum compensation should be assessed, account has been taken of at least a strong possibility that it will be appreciably higher than it used to be before the late 1960's.

Table 157 Average rates of tax on earned income

Tax as a proportion of income[1]   Percentages

		Single person		Married couple with no children	
		Average earnings[2]	Three times average earnings	Average earnings[2]	Three times average earnings
Earnings in	*Tax year*				
April 1970	1970–71	23·40	29·81	19·66	28·56
April 1971	1971–72	22·78	28·30	19·61	27·24
April 1972	1972–73	20·80	27·87	17·96	26·92
April 1973	1973–74	21·81	28·71	19·33	27·61
April 1974	1974–75	24·68	33·55	21·49	32·01
April 1975	1975–76	27·53	39·65	24·43	37·88
April 1976	1976–77	28·11	41·54	24·83	39·51
April 1977	1977–78[3]	26·14	38·57	21·90	36·08

1 With no allowances other than the personal allowance.
2 New earnings survey estimates of the average earnings at April of each year of full time adult male workers in all occupations, manual and non-manual.
3 Rates introduced in November 1977.

657 The underlying assumption made in this context about average long term rates of return on capital was that they would be higher than the rate of inflation, although probably not a great deal higher than the rate of inflation of earnings. Again, no forecast was attempted; the wide range of rates shown in Table 156 indicates the difficulty of choosing past rates which might serve as a guide to the future.

658 In respect of tax, the choice of January 1977 as the basis for value figures led to the use of 1976–77 tax rates, which were the highest of those shown in Table 157. In view of past trends, it may not be unreasonable to apply these to the future, even though tax rates may be somewhat lower in the next year or two.

PART V

Costs

CHAPTER 29

Cost of the present systems of compensation

659   The cost estimates presented here and in the following chapter represent the totals of payments made in a year to the injured, or to the dependants of those who have died following injury, together with the administrative expenses involved in making these payments. Costs in this sense are those most directly affected by the recommendations made. The effect of the recommendations on public expenditure, for example, will be measured by the change in social security payments and related administrative expenditure.

660   The estimates include injuries outside as well as inside the terms of reference, although separate figures are given for injuries and deaths at work, and for those caused by motor vehicles.

661   The estimates of present costs of tort compensation given in this chapter are based on fuller information than was available when previous estimates[2] [32] were made. Even so, the present estimates, especially those for services to the injured, and for the cost of administering the tort system, are subject to wide margins of error, for reasons explained at the end of the chapter.

662   The tables bring together payments of different kinds. Some social security payments for injury are short term, and relate to injuries sustained in the current or previous year; but rather more in terms of the value of payments are long term in character, and may relate to injuries or work illnesses dating from many years back. A small proportion, consisting of gratuities for minor disabilities incurred at work, represents compensation in the form of a lump sum for impairments whose effects will continue to be felt in the future.

663   Payments of tort compensation include provision for future disability, although they partly represent recompense for losses already incurred by the time of payment. It normally takes longer to obtain payment on a tort claim than on a claim for social security benefit, and a small proportion of the tort payments made in any year will relate to claims first made several years earlier.

664   Estimates of compensation payments made in a year may differ from estimates of compensation accruing for injuries occurring in that year for two reasons: first, because some payments would be made earlier in time, and so at a lower price level; secondly, because of changes in the incidence of injury. However, since the incidence of injuries of all kinds is fairly stable, the values of compensation paid and of compensation accruing, at a given price level, may not be widely different.

665   Social security benefits for loss of earnings are paid only after a minimum of three days' incapacity. But there can be entitlement to tort compensation even when there has been no interruption of work or other activities, and the same is true of industrial disablement benefit. Medical services may be called on for minor as well as major injuries, and their cost includes that of first aid treatment by general practitioners, out-patient departments or factory sick bays.

666   Most social security benefits paid in consequence of injury are free of tax, but some are taxable, in particular widows' benefits. Tort payments are tax free, but other payments from private sources may be taxable. No estimate has been made of the tax which may be recouped by the state from recipients of compensation which is subject to tax.

667   Nor has any attempt been made to estimate the impact of injuries on the national economy, for example through reductions in output; still less to estimate the value of non-economic losses in the form of suffering and bereavement. Estimates covering both economic and non-economic loss have been made elsewhere for two of the classes of accident within the terms of reference – work and road.[33][34][35]

668   The present estimates have been made by the secretariat with help from the Government Actuary on social security benefits. Details of sources and dates, with other technical notes, are given at the end of the chapter.

The main forms of compensation

669   The estimated total of compensation payments given in Table 158 is £827 million at January 1977 price and benefit levels. Of this total, roughly half is provided by social security, a quarter through tort, and the remaining quarter from various sources, mainly private, of which the most important are occupational sick pay and personal accident insurance.

670   The different kinds of compensation are not mutually exclusive, but overlap considerably. Some injuries, especially injuries to employees, are compensated from several sources. The figures set out separately in the table represent forms of compensation which are largely independent of each other, but by no means represent flows of payments to distinct groups.

671   The estimate for non-contributory invalidity pension is for housewives incapacitated through injury as distinct from disease, together with others of working age who were not covered by national insurance when they were injured, for example during childhood. Pensions paid in respect of incapacity arising from congenital injury are not included.

672   Estimates are not included in Table 158 for payments on life insurance policies, since there is insufficient information about the proportion of those who die following injury who hold life policies, and the average amounts received on policies of different kinds.

Table 158 Provision for injury, industrial disease and death

United Kingdom: Based on data for 1971–1976

	Estimated value £ million a year at January 1977 prices		Reliability[1]
Social Security			
Industrial injuries benefits			
Injury benefit	61		A
Industrial death benefit[2] [3]	14		A
Industrial disablement benefit			
Pensions and gratuities	109		A
Special hardship allowance	73		A
Other allowances	2		D
Total industrial injuries benefits		259	A
Sickness benefit	71		B
Invalidity benefit	42		B
Widow's national insurance benefits[2] [3]	25		D
Supplementary benefit	13		D
Unemployment benefit	1		D
Attendance allowance	3		D
Mobility allowance[2] [4]	3		D
Non-contributory invalidity pensions	4		D
Total social security benefits		421	B
Social security administration		47	C
Tort compensation			
Paid by insurers	188		D
Paid by organisations carrying their own insurance	14		D
Total tort compensation		202	D
Tort administration		175	D
Other payments[5]			
Employers' sick pay[2]	125		D
Occupational pensions[6]	5		D
Personal accident insurance[6]	50		B
Permanent health insurance[6]	1		D
Criminal injuries compensation	17		B
Rent and rates rebates	1		D
Trade unions, friendly societies and charities[6]	5		D
Total, other payments		204	D
Other administration		..	
Total compensation payments[5]		827	C
Public services[7]			
Hospitals and community health services	390		D
Family practitioner and other health services	120		D
Personal social services	50		D
Central and miscellaneous services	15		D
Total public services		575	D
Private services[7]			
Employers' medical services		50	D
Total value of services		625	D

Notes appear overleaf.

Notes to table 158

1 There is a 90 per cent probability that the figures given do not differ from the true figures by more than: 2 per cent (A); 5 per cent (B); 10 per cent (C); or 25 per cent (D).
2 Taxable.
3 For widows over retirement age, only any excess over entitlement to retirement pension is included.
4 Estimated cost of a year's allowances for those eligible from age 5 to retirement age.
5 Omitting life insurance payments, for which no estimate could be made.
6 Lump sum payments are usually not taxed; periodic payments are taxable, at least after an initial period.
7 Cost includes cost of administration.

Source: GAD and estimates made by the Commission.

Administration costs

673 The estimates of administration costs included in Table 158 confirm the conclusion reached in earlier investigations that the social security system is relatively cheap to run and the tort system relatively expensive. The estimate for the cost of operating the tort system includes insurers' own costs as well as their payments to others, for example legal fees, and expenses recovered by successful claimants.

Services

674 Table 158 gives broad estimates of the value of assistance to the injured in the form of medical and other services. The estimates were made by taking approximate percentages of total expenditure on these services. The value of services provided by the state appears to be greater than that of all social security benefits in respect of injury.

Table 159 Compensation payments by class

United Kingdom: Based on data for 1971–1976   £ million at January 1977 prices

	Total		Injuries or diseases	Deaths	
Social security	421		382	39	
At work		280	266		14
Motor vehicle[1]		47	33		14
Other		94	83		11
Tort compensation	202		179	23	
At work		69	63		6
Motor vehicle[2]		118	102		16
Other		15	14		1
Other compensation	204		195	9	
Total	827		756	71	

1 Excluding injuries or deaths while at work.
2 Including most injuries or deaths while at work.

Estimates made by the Commission.

Make up of compensation payments

675   Both social security and tort compensation go largely to the working population, but they differ in that 67 per cent of social security benefits for the injured relate to injuries at work, but 58 per cent of tort payments to motor injuries (Table 159). The former proportion is largely explained by the preference given to industrial injuries in the social security arrangements, in particular that benefits for disablement are at present restricted to injuries or diseases incurred at work. The different bias in the tort system is explained by a higher claim rate in respect of motor than of work accidents and a higher average payment, and because most motor injuries in the course of work give rise to tort claims under motor rather than employers' liability policies.

676   In all, deaths account for about 11 per cent of tort compensation, 10 per cent of social security payments and 4 per cent of compensation of other kinds, excluding life insurance.

Technical notes

677   The estimates are based on data for varying dates, converted to a common price basis. For some compensation payments and for costs of tort adminis-tration, the only available source was a set of cost estimates relating to 1972 prepared by HM Treasury and other Departments, and presented as evidence in 1975.

678   The bases of the various estimates were as follows:

Payments of compensation	*Basis*
Industrial injuries benefits	
Sickness and invalidity benefit	Official accounts for 1975–76 (esti-mates made by GAD).
Widows' benefits	
Attendance allowance	
Supplementary benefit	Treasury estimate for 1972.
Unemployment benefit, and rent and rates rebates	Personal injury survey, relating to 1973.
Mobility allowance	12 per cent of a DHSS estimate made in July 1977.
Non-contributory invalidity pensions	Public expenditure forecasts.
Tort compensation paid by insurers	Data from BIA for insurance com-panies in 1975 (employers' liability) or 1974 (motor) and for their market share.
Tort compensation paid by organisa-tions carrying their own risk	Commission's survey of self insurers, relating to 1972 and 1973.
Employers' sick pay	DHSS survey relating to September 1974.
Occupational pensions	GAD survey for 1971.
Personal accident insurance	Department of Trade statistics.

Payments of compensation	*Basis*
Permanent health insurance	10 per cent of a figure provided by the Life Offices Association, up-dated, and rounded up to £1 million.
Criminal injuries compensation	Accounts of the Boards for 1976–77.
Trade unions, friendly societies, charities	Treasury estimates for 1972.
Administration costs	
Social security	Official accounts for 1974–75 and 1975–76.
Tort	Treasury estimate for 1972 based on BIA data, and Commission's survey of self insurers.

679   The estimates relating to tort compensation paid by insurers are subject to a number of qualifications. They are based on data provided by the British Insurance Association for member companies. Because of a different basis of accounting, figures for Lloyd's underwriters could not be included. The figures given, which are representative of the whole insurance market, are based on estimates made by the British Insurance Association of the share of the market held by non-participating companies and by Lloyd's. These estimates are inevitably uncertain.

680   Except for employers' liability insurance, where all payments are for injury, disease or death, insurance covers other risks – in particular, of damage to property; and companies had to estimate the personal injury component within the total provision made for claims. In consequence, the estimates for motor business were less reliable than those for employers' liability. Estimates for products and other liability were still more uncertain.

681   The estimate for tort administration costs suffers from similar drawbacks, with the addition that it is mainly based on data for 1972 – the only year for which information was compiled. It covers commissions on premiums, general administration costs, an allowance for profit margins, and fees recovered by successful claimants, as well as fees and other expenses met by insurers when dealing with claims. The allowance for insurers' profit margins was obtained by constructing a pattern for the periods from receipt of premiums to payment on claims with the help of the British Insurance Association's survey of claims settled in November 1973, and assuming that 7 per cent was earned on accrued funds. Repetition of these calculations for 1973 and 1974 produced results very similar to those obtained for 1972.

CHAPTER 30

Cost of the changes proposed

682 This chapter contains estimates of the costs of the major proposals for change. The figures represent changes in the annual payments made by way of compensation or to meet administrative costs. The former represent a transfer of funds, in one way or another, from the uninjured to the injured; the latter represent a changed demand on real resources.

683 The estimates relating to social security benefits, except for children, were made by the Government Actuary, whose report is reproduced as an annex to this volume. Other estimates, including those relating to children and to tort compensation, were made by the secretariat.

684 Some of the changes would have further financial consequences. For example, any change in employers' costs through changes in insurance premiums could affect prices, profits and payments of corporation tax. In so far as improved social security benefits took the place of occupational sick pay, a higher proportion of the amount received by employees during incapacity would be tax free, if short term benefits continued to be untaxed. No attempt has been made to assess secondary effects of these kinds.

685 In order to present a substantially complete account of changes in costs, it has been necessary to include some estimates which are only indications of likely orders of magnitude, or which rest on arbitrary assumptions. Particular uncertainties attach to the estimates of social security benefits for partial incapacity, and to many of the tort estimates, in particular those relating to costs of administration.

Résumé of proposals

686 The Commission's proposals and the reasons for them are fully described in Volume One. The following is a brief summary of those which would lead to significant changes in costs.

687 No-fault compensation in the form of social security would be improved both by extending the existing schemes to cover additional categories of injury, and by improving the benefits they provided.

688 The improvements would apply to new beneficiaries after the changes had been introduced and not to existing cases, with the exception of children.

689 It is proposed that benefits akin to those now provided by the industrial injuries scheme should be extended to these additional categories:

i Work injuries or diseases of the self employed.

ii Injuries on the way to or from work.

iii Additional cases of industrial disease.

690 A similar scheme would be introduced for injuries involving motor vehicles. As a result, many non-earners injured by motor vehicles would become entitled to benefit for the first time.

691 Benefits following death would be extended to widowers on the same basis as to widows.

692 Those injured by motor vehicles, and the additional categories brought into the industrial injuries scheme, would be entitled to benefits for disablement. Since no specific proposals have been made in respect of partial incapacity, estimates have been included of the cost of extending the present special hardship allowance to these categories, in order to provide some indication of the sums which might be involved. These estimates are on a different footing from the rest, and serve only to indicate a possible order of magnitude for the cost of an extension of provision for partial incapacity.

693 There would be improved earnings related benefits for employees already covered by the industrial injuries scheme as well as for the additional categories. In particular, the new earnings related pensions for widows (and now widowers), and for those receiving invalidity pension during lengthy spells of incapacity for work, would become payable at the maximum rate at an earlier date. There would also be improvements in the earnings related component of retirement pensions for those who had experienced periods of incapacity, and for their widows or widowers.

694 It is proposed that a weekly allowance should be paid for severely handicapped children, and that children should be eligible for mobility allowance from the age of two instead of from five.

695 For some benefits, the full cost would be incurred within the first few years, but for some of the long term benefits, costs would build up gradually over a long period. After that, they would reach approximate stability in real terms, though still fluctuating from year to year in accordance with demographic and other changes. In these estimates, 40 years has been taken as the period needed to reach a fairly stable state.

Changes in tort compensation

696 Social security benefits as extended and improved would be offset in full against any tort compensation payable. Benefits for loss of earnings, to meet expenses, and for non-pecuniary loss would be offset against the corresponding heads of damages, without any carry over from one to the other.

697   There would also be changes in the basis of assessment. There would be a threshold of three months before compensation for non-pecuniary loss was payable. In assessing pecuniary loss extending beyond the date of award or settlement, fuller account would be taken of prospective inflation and the impact of taxation by the introduction of a system of modified multipliers. In some cases, compensation for future pecuniary loss would take the form of periodic payments. The part to be played by such payments is however uncertain and the costings have been prepared as though all this compensation continued to take the form of lump sums. Roughly equivalent amounts should eventually be required whichever form the compensation took.

698   Separate estimates are not given in the tables for other changes in tort compensation, many of which would lead to no more than marginal changes in costs.

699   Changes in tort compensation could be effected quickly, and would start to be reflected in insurance premiums as soon as they came into force. Any claims governed by the old system should be disposed of within three or four years.

Occupational sick pay
700   There are no proposals relating directly to occupational sick pay. But where, as often happens, occupational sick pay is reduced to take account of social security benefits for loss of earnings, any improvement in those benefits would automatically lead to an offsetting reduction in sick pay.

701   Occupational sick pay is predominantly short term in character, and the effect of the reductions would be felt soon after an improved scheme of benefits had come into operation.

The pattern of costs
702   The general picture is of increases in the cost of the social security system accompanied by reductions in the cost of the tort system and – to a minor extent – of occupational sick pay. After 40 years, the annual cost of the state system would have increased by £130 million a year, and the reductions in tort and in sick pay would amount to £89 million, at January 1977 prices. The net cost in total would have increased by £41 million a year (Table 160).

703   After five years, the annual cost of the state system would have increased by £78 million a year against a reduction of £89 million in other compensation costs. The net reduction of £11 million a year would result from an increase of £5 million in the value of compensation and a reduction of about £16 million in costs of administration (Table 161).

Additional social security costs
704   The estimated cost of additional social security benefits represents the difference between the amount to be provided under the proposals and the amount which would be provided in future years under the existing arrangements, including benefits not yet in payment. Possible savings in supplementary benefit were however not taken into account. The discussion which follows

213

concentrates on the costs which would be incurred eventually when the proposals had come fully into effect; the build-up to that point is considered subsequently.

Table 160   Estimates of changes in costs after 40 years

United Kingdom   £ million a year at January 1977 prices

	Total	Work injuries and diseases	Motor vehicle injuries	Other
Social security				
For loss of earnings, or incapacity				
Short term	8	5	3½	
Long term	2	1	½	
Partial incapacity[1]	32	18	14	
Non-pecuniary loss	46	23	23	
Widows' and widowers' pensions[2]	6	1½	4½	
Retirement pensions	5	2½	2½	
Children[3]	16			16
Total, social security benefits	115	51	48	16
Social security administration	15	7	6	2
Total social security	130	58	54	18
Tort[4]				
Full offset of				
Present benefits	−38	−24	−13	−½
Additional benefits	−19	−2	−17	–
Changed basis of assessment				
Pecuniary loss	25	5	18	1½
Non-pecuniary loss	−44	−16	−23	−5
Other changes in tort compensation[5]	15	3	7	5
Total, tort compensation	−61	−34	−28	1
Tort administration	−25	−13	−12	–
Total tort	−86	−47	−40	1
Occupational sick pay	−3	−2	−1	–
All forms of compensation				
Net cost of all proposals	41	9	13	19
Of which, changes in cost of				
Compensation	51	15	19	17
Administration	−10	−6	−6	2

1 Extension of special hardship allowance to additional categories.
2 For those over retirement age, includes only any excess over entitlement to retirement pension.
3 Allowance for severely handicapped children, and entitlement to mobility allowance from age 2. Benefits in respect of motor vehicle injuries are included under benefits for incapacity above.

4 Most injuries in the course of work involving motor vehicles are included under motor vehicle injuries.
5 Broad estimates of maximum cost.

Amounts less than £5 million have been rounded to £½ million.
– means nil, or less than £¼ million a year.

Source: GAD and estimates made by the Commission.

Table 161 Summary of changes in costs after 5 years and after 40 years

United Kingdom   £ million at January 1977 prices

	After 5 years	After 40 years
Social security		
Benefits	69	115
Administration	9	15
Tort		
Compensation	−61	−61
Administration	−25	−25
Occupational sick pay	−3	−3
Totals		
Compensation	5	51
Administration	−16	−10

Source: GAD and estimates made by the Commission.

705 The greater part of the cost would arise from improvements in benefits for work and motor vehicle injuries, which would cost £51 million a year and £48 million a year respectively. Additional assistance to children would cost £16 million a year, and additional costs of administration about £15 million a year.

706 Most of the increased cost of the benefits for work injuries, and the whole cost of those for motor injuries, would result from extending benefits of the kind provided under the industrial injuries scheme to categories of injured people who do not receive them at present. The main category to be brought within the scope of the industrial injuries scheme consists of those injured in commuting accidents. Most of these accidents involve motor vehicles; those injured in this way are treated as receiving benefits under the work scheme, not the motor vehicle scheme.

707 Table 162 gives a breakdown of the estimates of additional cost within the enlarged work injuries scheme.

215

Table 162 Analysis of additional costs of benefits for work injuries and diseases

United Kingdom   £ million a year at Jan. 1977 prices

	Year				
	1 1983/84	6 1988/89	11 1993/94	21 2003/04	41 2023/24
Employees[1]	4½	8	10	12	6
Self employed[1]	3	6	7	10	13
Commuting injuries	6½	11	15	19	23
Motor vehicle	5	9	12	15	18
Other	1½	2	3	4	5
Additional occupational diseases	2	4	5	7	9
Totals	16	29	37	48	51

1 For injuries and diseases of kinds covered by existing schemes.

Source: GAD estimates, rounded by the Commission. The approximate sub-division between motor and other commuting injuries was supplied separately, and is not included in the GAD report in the annex.

708   Many of those in the additional categories would under present arrangements be entitled, now or in the future, to benefits under the general national insurance scheme, including earnings related pensions. Largely for this reason, the additional amounts shown in respect of benefits for loss of earnings are small, in relation either to the cost of other proposals or to costs under present arrangements.

709   The greater part of the additional cost of benefits under both the work and motor schemes relates to benefits for partial incapacity, and benefits for non-pecuniary loss in the form of disablement pensions and gratuities. These are benefits to which there is no equivalent under the existing arrangements so far as the additional categories are concerned. Together, they would account for £78 million out of the eventual increase of £115 million in the annual cost of benefits.

710   The remaining elements of the extra cost of the industrial injuries and motor schemes for the most part represent improvements in existing provision and account for relatively small amounts. The costs for widows and widowers reflect the degree to which the proposed schemes would provide better pensions than the general national insurance scheme, and the treatment of widowers on the same basis as widows; an appreciable proportion is for widowers whose wives had died in road accidents.

711   Additional costs of administration would arise in respect of those becoming entitled to benefits for the first time, and of those entitled to benefits similar to those of the industrial injuries scheme in place of sickness or invalidity benefits, which are less expensive to administer.

712   The build up of the cost of additional social security benefits is shown in Table 163. The full cost of benefits for partial incapacity and for non-pecuniary loss would not be incurred at the start, but would gradually increase over many years as more injured people received them. Most of the other costs would be incurred within the first few years. This is true even of long term loss of earnings benefits and widows' (though not widowers') pensions, since for these benefits the superiority of the proposed arrangements to the existing ones would be reduced as time went on. Costs of administration might be expected to increase in much the same way as the cost of social security benefits in total, except for the initial cost of identifying severely handicapped children and arranging for payment of their allowances.

Changes in tort payments

713   Substantial reductions in the value of tort compensation could be expected as the result of the full offset of social security benefits, and the disregard of non-pecuniary losses within the first three months following an injury. These changes taken together would reduce the annual value of payments by about £100 million.

714   On the other hand, there would be increases in the multipliers used to calculate lump sums paid in compensation for pecuniary losses extending into the future, which – on their own – would result in increases in payments of the order of £25 million a year.

715   For all other proposed changes in tort compensation, provision has been made for a possible increase of £15 million a year. There is no statistical basis on which to estimate the effect of these changes, and this figure reflects a broad judgment that their combined cost would probably be no greater than this. Appreciable additions to tort payments might result from the proposed widening of the scope of strict liability, and from the extension from Scotland to the rest of the United Kingdom of compensation for loss of society; the latter would only partly be offset by the discontinuance of the present conventional awards for loss of expectation of life.

716   The estimate does not allow for the possible consequences of a man made disaster brought within the scope of a tort action by the imposition of strict liability for exceptional risks. The chance of such a disaster is so slight and uncertain, even though it cannot be disregarded altogether, that it would not be realistic to attempt to assess its consequences in terms of an average cost per year. Moreover, because of the limits which often apply to liability insurance, only part of the cost of a disaster might be met through the tort system.

717   The reduction in tort payments would be proportionately greater in employers' liability than in motor insurance, so increasing the disparity between the total amounts paid out under these classes of business (see Table 164). One factor helping to produce this result is that the changed basis of assessment of future pecuniary loss would have a smaller effect in aggregate on work than on motor cases, which tend to be more serious and include many more

fatal cases. Another is that the proposed threshold for non-pecuniary loss is estimated to lead to a larger percentage reduction in cost for work cases, which give rise to a relatively large proportion of small payments under this head.

Table 163   Build up of additional social security costs over time

United Kingdom   £ million a year at Jan. 1977 prices

	Year				
	1 1983/84	6 1988/89	11 1993/94	21 2003/04	41 2023/24
Social security benefits					
Work injuries and diseases					
For loss of earnings					
Short term	7	7	6	6	5
Long term	1	3	3	1	1
Partial incapacity[1]	$\frac{1}{2}$	5	8	13	18
Non-pecuniary loss	7	10	13	18	23
Widows' and widowers' pensions[2]	$\frac{1}{2}$	3	3	2	$1\frac{1}{2}$
Retirement pensions	–	1	4	8	$2\frac{1}{2}$
Total additional cost of benefits for work injuries and diseases	16	29	37	48	51
Motor vehicle injuries					
For loss of earnings or incapacity					
Short term	6	5	$4\frac{1}{2}$	4	$3\frac{1}{2}$
Long term	0	$\frac{1}{2}$	$\frac{1}{2}$	$\frac{1}{2}$	$\frac{1}{2}$
Partial incapacity[1]	1	4	6	10	14
Non-pecuniary loss	8	11	14	18	23
Widows' and widowers' pensions[2]	1	4	6	6	$4\frac{1}{2}$
Retirement pensions	–	$\frac{1}{2}$	3	$4\frac{1}{2}$	$2\frac{1}{2}$
Total additional cost of benefits for motor vehicle injuries	16	25	34	43	48
Children Additional cost	16	15	17	18	16
Social security administration Additional cost	9	9	11	14	15
Total additional cost for social security	57	78	99	123	130

1 Extension of special hardship allowance to additional categories.
2 For those above retirement age, includes only any excess over entitlement to retirement pension.

Amounts less than £5 million have been rounded to £$\frac{1}{2}$ million.
– means nil, or less than £$\frac{1}{4}$ million a year.

Sources: GAD and estimates made by the Commission.

Table 164   Estimated changes in costs after 40 years compared with costs under present arrangements

Social security benefits and tort compensation

United Kingdom   £ million a year at Jan. 1977 prices

	Total	Work injuries and diseases	Motor vehicle injuries	Other
Social security benefits[1]				
For loss of earnings or incapacity				
Short term				
Additional cost	8	5	3½	
Cost of present benefits	83	70	13	
Long term				
Additional cost	2	1	½	
Cost of present benefits	25	22	3	
Partial incapacity[2]				
Additional cost	32	18	14	
Cost of present benefits	72	72	–	
Non-pecuniary loss				
Additional cost	46	23	23	
Cost of present benefits	99	99	–	
Widows' and widowers' pensions[3]				
Additional cost	6	1½	4½	
Cost of present pensions	35	19	16	
Retirement pensions[4]				
Additional cost	5	2½	2½	
Children[5]				
Additional cost	16			16
Cost of present allowances	26			26
Total cost of additional benefits	115	51	48	16
Total cost of present benefits[6]	340	282	32	26
Social security administration				
Additional costs of administration	15	7	6	2
Present cost of administration[6]	40	32	4	4
Total social security				
Total additional cost of social security	130	58	54	18
Present cost of social security	380	314	36	30
Tort compensation[7]				
Change in cost	−61	−34	−28	1
Present cost[8]	202	69	118	15
Tort administration[7]				
Change in cost of administration	−25	−13	−12	–
Present cost of administration	175	50	112	13
Total tort[7]				
Total change in tort costs	−86	−47	−40	1
Present tort costs	377	119	230	28

Notes appear overleaf.

Notes on table 164

1 Costs of present schemes are estimated costs in 2023/24 of benefits under the industrial injuries and national insurance schemes at January 1977 rates and corresponding earnings levels.
2 Special hardship allowance.
3 For those over retirement age, includes only any excess over entitlement to retirement pension.
4 The cost of present provision for retirement pensions for beneficiaries of the proposed work and motor vehicle schemes cannot be isolated.
5 Allowances for handicapped children, excluding proposed benefits in respect of motor vehicle injuries, which are included above under benefits for incapacity. Present allowances are attendance and mobility allowances.
6 Excluding retirement pensions and benefits other than those specified.
7 Most injuries in the course of work involving motor vehicles are included under motor vehicle injuries.
8 Equivalent, at January 1977 prices, of payments in 1975.

Amounts less than £5 million have been rounded to £½ million.
– means nil, or less than £¼ million a year.

Source: GAD and estimates made by the Commission.

Reduction in occupational sick pay

718   Material reductions in occupational sick pay would arise only as offsets to the increases in short term social security benefits for employees, which themselves would not be large. The reduction in aggregate would probably be no more than £3 million a year.

Costs under present arrangements

719   For tort compensation, the figures for present costs given in Table 164 assume no change from the estimates given in Table 159 in the previous chapter; most motor injuries while at work or commuting are classified as motor vehicle, not as work, injuries. For social security, fresh estimates were made for 2023/24, with a different coverage from those in Table 159; in particular, they do not cover injuries to adults other than work or motor vehicle injuries; motor vehicle injuries while at work or commuting are included under work, not under motor vehicle injuries.

Methods of estimation

Social security
720   The methods used in estimating the cost of additional social security benefits, except for children, are described in detail in the Government Actuary's report reproduced as an annex to this volume.

721   For children, the major cost was that of providing an allowance of £4 a week for severely handicapped children aged from 2 to 15, estimated to number 73,000 in 1983–84. To the resultant initial cost of £15 million, £1 million was added in respect of the lowering of the age of eligibility for mobility allowance from 5 to 2; this estimate was supplied by the Government Actuary.

722   Allowance was made for prospective changes in numbers of children.

723   Estimates of additional costs of social security administration were based on ratios of costs of administration to values of benefits in 1974–75 or 1975–76.

Tort

724 Because less information was available, the estimates relating to the tort system are of necessity more uncertain than those relating to social security, and are given in less detail. The estimates are for the full effect of the proposed changes, which would be felt within a few years.

725 The starting point was a set of estimates of the value of tort compensation in the United Kingdom under different heads at January 1977 price and earnings levels. These estimates were based on aggregate values of payments in 1975, assumed to be made up in the same way as in the analysis of insurance claims in 1973.

726 Consistency with the social security estimates was secured as far as possible. Estimated reductions in tort payments on account of the full offsetting of benefits were based on the Government Actuary's estimates for the social security proposals at maturity. Allowance was made where necessary for cases where the values of benefits might be greater than the corresponding tort values, for example where benefits plus allowances for dependants exceeded take home pay before the injury, or cases settled on the basis of partial liability.

727 The estimates for the offset of benefits include the effect of making the present deduction for industrial disablement benefit from compensation for non-pecuniary instead of for pecuniary loss.

728 For future loss of earnings, detailed calculations were made to estimate the effects of the use of modified multipliers. In order that these might be distinguished from those of the full deduction of social security benefits, comparison was made between four sets of estimates of compensation for future loss of earnings:
 i Present multipliers, with present deductions.
 ii Present multipliers, with full deduction of existing benefits.
 iii Present multipliers, with full deduction of proposed benefits.
 iv Modified multipliers, with full deduction of proposed benefits.

729 The effect of fully offsetting present benefits was assessed by comparing ii with i. The effect of fully offsetting the additional benefits proposed was assessed by comparing iii with ii. The effect of the change to a system of modified multipliers was assessed by comparing iv with iii.

730 An approximation to the present basis of assessment was made by using multipliers obtained by discounting future years' losses at $4\frac{1}{2}$ per cent a year. The modified multipliers were obtained by assuming a rate of return of 9 per cent and a rate of growth of earnings of 8 per cent a year; approximate account was taken of taxation at different income levels, assuming that tax rates remained the same as in 1976–77, and that tax bands were adjusted every year to allow for inflation.

731 For each injury type, calculations were made in detail for different sex, age and income groups. For each group, average amounts of compensation, allowing for the effect of tax and for the offset of social security benefits, were calculated on the four bases set out in paragraph 728. For each basis, the results

for the different groups were combined into a weighted average, the weights used being in proportion to the numbers in each group expected to obtain tort compensation for future loss of earnings following personal injury. Proportionate changes in the values of compensation on the revised bases, ii–iv, compared with the existing arrangements, basis i, were calculated from the ratios of the corresponding weighted averages. The values themselves were derived by applying these ratios to the estimated total sums of compensation for future loss of earnings under existing arrangements.

732   Estimates relating to future expenses were made on similar lines to those for future loss of earnings, though in less detail.

733   The calculations using multipliers represented an approximation to the outcome of awards made by the courts. It was assumed that the relationship between out-of-court settlements and court awards would be the same under the changed basis of assessment as at present.

734   The calculations were for compensation in the form of lump sums. The capitalised values of compensation in the form of periodic payments on the same assumptions about interest and inflation were assumed to be of a similar order of magnitude.

735   The estimate for the reduction resulting from disregard of non-pecuniary loss during the first three months is an approximate one. A ceiling of five times average annual full time male earnings would affect only $\frac{1}{4}$ per cent of awards, and its effect on cost would be negligible.

736   The estimate of the reduction in the cost of administering the tort system is one of the least reliable. Present administration costs were analysed on the assumption that they were made up in the same way, as estimated by the BIA for 1972. It was assumed that the total cost of commissions and insurers' margins would be reduced by the same percentage (30 per cent) as tort payments. Claims handling costs – which represent no more than 12 per cent of all administration costs – were assumed to be reduced by one third, in line with a similar estimated reduction in the number of claims. No allowance was made for any reduction in general administration costs, since the number of policies would not be materially affected by the changes proposed. In total, administration costs were estimated to be reduced by 14 per cent.

Occupational sick pay
737   It has been estimated that at any time within six months of injury, 40 per cent of employees would be receiving sick pay from their employers, usually after taking account of social security benefits receivable for loss of earnings. If short term benefits for employees were increased, there would be some corresponding reduction in sick pay. It would be less than 40 per cent of the increased payments, partly because benefits are not invariably deducted, and partly because of cases where benefits either already were or became greater than the entitlement to sick pay. The estimated reduction in sick pay is based on the arbitrary assumption that 30 per cent of increased short term benefits to employees for loss of earnings would be offset in this way. Reductions in long term sick pay would be negligible.

Report by the Government Actuary

Report by the Government Actuary on the cost of schemes of compensation for work and motor vehicle injuries

To the Chairman and Members of the Royal Commission on Civil Liability and Compensation for Personal Injury.

As requested, I have made estimates of the cost of schemes of compensation on a 'no fault' basis covering (i) persons injured at work or on the way to and from work or suffering from a disease as a result of their work, and (ii) persons injured in road accidents involving a motor vehicle in other circumstances, and submit the following report.

1 Particulars of the schemes to be costed were supplied by the Commission's Secretary. Subject to certain modifications the proposed benefits are similar in form to existing industrial injuries and national insurance benefits, a summary of which is given in an annex to the first volume of the Commission's report, and reference to these benefits is made in the summary of the proposed schemes given below. Although the finances of the former industrial injuries and national insurance schemes have been merged and the benefits are now prescribed under the Social Security Act 1975, which has replaced the National Insurance and National Insurance (Industrial Injuries) Acts, for convenience the terms 'industrial injuries scheme' and 'national insurance scheme' have been retained for the present report to denote respectively those benefits specifically confined to cases arising from employees' accidents at work or prescribed occupational diseases, and the other benefits under the present arrangements.

SUMMARY OF THE PROPOSALS

2 The benefits would be modelled on the present industrial injuries scheme (which would be replaced by the new work injuries scheme) but the scheme would be extended to include a long-term loss of earnings benefit on the lines of national insurance invalidity benefit. As under the present industrial injuries scheme, title to benefit would not be dependent on the fulfilling of any contribution conditions.

Work injuries
Coverage
3 The present industrial injuries scheme covers employees who have an accident at work or suffer from a prescribed occupational disease and, as a result, become disabled or incapable of work. The proposed new scheme would include the self-employed and would extend cover to accidents on the way to and from work, but the self-employed would not be eligible for any earnings-related benefits while they remained excluded from such benefits under the national insurance scheme. In addition, benefit in respect of occupational diseases would not be limited to the present list of prescribed diseases but would be extended to all cases where it could be shown that the disease was due to and was a particular risk of the occupation.

225

Short-term loss of earnings benefit

4   The present flat-rate injury benefit, payable during periods of incapacity for work for a maximum of 6 months, would be retained. This benefit is payable at a higher rate than flat-rate national insurance sickness benefit but for some years the differential has remained fixed at £2·75 a week. It is proposed that it should continue to be held at this level with the result that, as benefit rates are increased over the years with rises in the general levels of prices and earnings, the margin would steadily decline as a proportion of the total benefit. Allowances for adult and child dependants would be payable at the same rates as for sickness benefit.

5   At present persons fulfilling the necessary contribution conditions receive the earnings-related supplement to sickness benefit in addition to injury benefit. This supplement, which is payable only after the first two weeks of incapacity, is based on the average weekly earnings (taken as 1/50th of the annual earnings) falling between certain limits in the tax year ending in the calendar year preceding the date on which incapacity for work commenced. For example, the weekly rate of benefit based on the 1975–76 tax year is one-third of the average weekly earnings in that year in the range £11 – £30 and 15 per cent of the earnings in the range £30 – £69 a week. A similar benefit is included in the proposed scheme but the percentage of earnings in the upper range would be increased from 15 per cent to 25 per cent. As at present, the payment of earnings-related supplement would be limited to the amount that would bring the total benefit up to 85 per cent of previous earnings.

6   Apart from the improvement in the rate of earnings-related supplement, the main change from the benefits payable at present would be that the preferential rate of flat-rate benefit would apply to those, like the self-employed and persons injured on the way to and from work, to whom cover is being extended, instead of the sickness benefit to which most of them would otherwise be entitled. The disappearance of the qualifying contribution conditions for the earnings-related supplement and for title also to flat-rate benefits for those to whom cover is being extended, would benefit persons unable to fulfil the contribution conditions for sickness benefit. These would include not only recent entrants to the work force but also married women and widows who have exercised an option to pay national insurance contributions at a reduced rate and forgo title to benefits in their own right.

Long term loss of earnings benefit

7   The scheme would provide flat-rate benefits with allowances for dependants, payable after a period of incapacity for work had lasted more than 6 months, identical to the invalidity pension and invalidity allowance benefits under the national insurance scheme. The absence of any qualifying contribution conditions would again benefit married women optants and others who could not satisfy the conditions for invalidity benefits.

8   In addition to the flat-rate invalidity benefits under the national insurance scheme, from April 1978 employees will build up title to an earnings-related benefit based on the earnings on which contributions have been paid. This will be calculated as 25 per cent of the average earnings falling between a base level approximately equal to the flat-rate pension in force at the beginning of a tax year and the ceiling for contribution liability of about 7 times that amount. For the purpose of calculating the average, the relevant earnings in a tax year would be revalued in step with the movement of national average earnings up to the last complete tax year before the invalidity benefits become payable. The average will be taken over the best 20 years but earnings before April 1978 will not be taken into account, so that the benefit will build up

gradually over a 20-year period at a rate of $1\frac{1}{4}$ per cent of relevant earnings a year, with the first additional components at the full 25 per cent rate not being awarded until after April 1998.

9   An earnings-related benefit calculated in similar lines would be provided under the proposed scheme but from the outset benefit would always be awarded at the full 25 per cent rate, average earnings being calculated for this purpose over the actual years in employment after April 1978 when this was less than twenty.

10   The increase in benefit over the existing scheme would be greatest during the early years after 1978, but even after April 1998 (when the earnings-related component of invalidity pension can be at the full 25 per cent rate) there would be enhancement of pension for persons incapacitated before they had completed 20 years in employment.

Non-pecuniary loss
11   Compensation for non-pecuniary loss would be provided by benefits depending solely on the degree of disablement, identical to the disablement pensions and gratuities under the present industrial injuries scheme. The effect would be to extend eligibility for such benefits to categories, like the self-employed and persons injured on the way to and from work, who would be included in the proposed scheme but are outside the scope of the present industrial injuries scheme.

Partial loss of earnings
12   The scheme would provide compensation for partial loss of earnings but the proposals in this regard have not been specified in detail. For this reason, and on account of the very limited information available at present as to the effect on earnings in the longer term of accidents at work and of industrial diseases, it has not been possible to make any estimates of the likely cost of such provision.

13   The special hardship allowance under the present industrial injuries scheme constitutes a limited form of benefit for partial loss of earnings. Allowances are currently in payment to about 40 per cent of disablement pensioners; in addition a further substantial number of allowances are in payment where a disablement gratuity has been paid in lieu of a pension. The total expenditure on special hardship allowances represents about 65 per cent of the expenditure on disablement pensions and gratuities.

14   In order to give some indication of the possible cost of a partial loss of earnings benefit, estimates have been included for the cost of providing for a benefit on the lines of the present special hardship allowance under the proposed scheme, though I understand that it is not the Commission's view that any provision for partial loss of earnings should necessarily be modelled on this allowance.

Widow's benefits
15   Widow's benefits under the present industrial injuries scheme are in some respects more favourable than the corresponding national insurance benefits payable, in general, on death in other circumstances, namely, (i) the main rate of industrial widow's pension is 55p a week higher than the national insurance widowed mother's allowance or the maximum rate of national insurance widow's pension, though this differential has remained unaltered in money terms for many years; (ii) if an industrial widow is over age 40 when she ceases to qualify for benefit as a widow with children, pension at the full-rate continues to be payable, whereas the national insurance widow's pension is awarded at a reduced rate on a sliding scale if the widow is aged between 40 and 50 when title to widowed mother's allowance ceases; (iii) where the age or other requirements for title to a full-rate widow's pension are not satisfied, an industrial widow receives a pension at a reduced rate (£4·59 a week at the beginning of 1977), but there is no corresponding benefit under the national insurance scheme.

227

16 It is proposed that these preferential provisions under the present scheme should be abolished and the flat-rate benefits for widows in all respects brought into line with national insurance widow's benefits except that no qualifying contribution conditions would be applied. Benefits in payment at the time the proposed scheme took effect would, however, continue to be governed by the old provisions. The provision for a gratuity of a year's pension when benefit ceases on remarriage, which also has no counterpart where death is outside the scope of the industrial injuries scheme, would be retained and extended to the additional categories brought within the work injuries scheme.

17 Earnings-related additions to widow's allowance, payable for the first 26 weeks of widowhood, on the basis of the husband's earnings, would be calculated in the same way as the proposed earnings-related supplement to short-term loss of earnings benefit. Similarly an earnings-related addition to the widow's pension or widowed mother's allowance would be calculated on the lines of the corresponding addition to long-term loss of earnings benefit and would be reduced on a sliding scale in the same way as the flat-rate benefit if the widow was between 40 and 50 at widowhood or when title to widowed mother's allowance ceased. Subject to the effect of these provisions, the margins over the corresponding national insurance benefits would be similar to those which have been described for earnings-related additions to short and long-term loss of earnings benefit respectively.

18 In estimating the cost of the proposed scheme it has been assumed that a provision would be included to ensure that, as under the national insurance scheme, on a widow's attaining pension age the retirement pension awarded would not be less than her widow's pension.

19 Benefit would be payable to widowers on the same basis as for widows.

Credited earnings
20 Credits would be awarded on the basis of the earnings level at the time of the accident or commencement of incapacity for work as a result of industrial disease, so that title to earnings-related additional components of retirement pension would continue to accrue as if employment had continued during the period of incapacity. This is in contrast to the position at present, where only actual earnings on which contributions have been paid are taken into account and credits during periods of incapacity for work are awarded only to the extent necessary to bring the earnings in a tax year to the minimum level required for that year to count for the purpose of entitlement to flat-rate pension. Earnings would not be credited, however, for married women and widows who had chosen to pay contributions at a reduced rate and were thus not building up entitlement to any earnings-related pension in their own right.

Miscellaneous benefits
21 The provisions for constant attendance allowance and exceptionally severe disablement allowance under the present industrial injuries scheme may result in payments at higher rates than national insurance attendance allowance, and similar benefits would be included under the proposed scheme. However it is intended that the rates at which these benefits are paid should be frozen at the levels applying when the proposed new scheme takes effect, and that this should apply to allowances in payment as well as to new awards. As a result it is to be expected that in time even the maximum combined rate of constant attendance allowance and exceptionally severe disablement allowance would fall below the level of national insurance attendance allowance, so that these special benefits would gradually be phased out.

228

22 A benefit corresponding to the hospital treatment allowance under the present industrial injuries scheme would be included in the proposed scheme, but the present unemployability supplement would be superseded by the proposed long term loss of earnings benefit.

Motor vehicle injuries

23 The proposed scheme would cover road injuries involving motor vehicles, other than those occurring in circumstances to be covered under the work injuries scheme. Injuries sustained on the road but not involving a motor vehicle would not be covered.

24 For persons in employment or self-employment the benefits would be virtually identical to those to be provided under the proposed work injuries scheme and the improvements in benefits resulting from the proposals would be the same as described above in relation to categories, like the self-employed or persons suffering accidents on the way to or from work, who would be covered under the proposed work injuries scheme but who are outside the scope of the present industrial injuries scheme. As for the work injuries scheme, some arbitrary allowance for the cost of partial loss of earnings benefit has been included on the basis of the cost of applying the provisions for special hardship allowance under the present industrial injuries scheme to the accidents to be covered under the proposed scheme.

25 For non-earners a flat-rate benefit would be payable during periods of incapacity, at the same rate as the flat-rate short-term loss of earnings benefit for persons in employment or self-employment, except that for children under 16 the benefit would be at the reduced rate of £4 a week. The benefit would cease at pension age (65 for men and 60 for women) and non-earners at above these ages would not be eligible.

26 In addition, all persons other than children under age 12 would be eligible for compensation for non-pecuniary loss, according to the degree of disablement, on the lines of the disablement benefits under the present industrial injuries scheme.

THE BASIS OF THE ESTIMATES

27 It has been assumed that the provisions of the proposed schemes would not be applied retrospectively, so the expenditure on the long-term benefits would only build up gradually over a long period from the date when the schemes took effect. The additional costs resulting from the proposals, compared with the present arrangements, can thus only be brought out by means of projections of expenditure for many years ahead. Accordingly estimates have been made for the first year of the scheme, taken to be the financial year 1983–84, and for selected years up to 40 years thereafter.

Allowance for the effects of inflation

28 There is a requirement under the Social Security Act 1975 for the main flat-rate benefits to be reviewed at least once a year and increased at least in step with the movement of earnings or prices, whichever is the greater, in the case of long-term benefits, and at least in step with the movement of prices in the case of short-term benefits. It is assumed that similar provisions would apply in regard to the benefits under the proposed schemes.

29 Although there is no requirement for short-term benefits to be increased more than in line with the movement of prices, if in the future, as in the past, earnings were to rise significantly faster than prices, increases at this minimum level would result in a steady fall in the value of the benefits in relation to earnings and sooner or later the point would be reached where the benefits would cease to fulfil their function as a replacement for earnings during periods of absence from work on account of, for example, sickness or injury. Accordingly, it would not be realistic to base long-term

estimates on the assumption that upratings would always be less than in proportion to the increase in earnings and for the present estimates it has been assumed that short-term as well as long-term benefits would rise in step with increases in the general level of earnings. To the extent that the increases were less than on this assumption, the cost of short-term loss of earnings benefit would be lower than shown in this report, but the effect on the extra costs arising from the Commission's proposals would be small.

30   Although it must be assumed that benefit rates will be increased at regular intervals, projections of cost which made explicit allowance for this feature on the basis of an assumed average rate of increase would show steadily rising monetary amounts which would be meaningful only if set against corresponding estimates of, for example, the gross national product or tax and contribution yields, for the years in question. For this reason, in order to obtain a true picture of the development of the costs over the years, it is best to express the estimates for future years in equivalent present-day terms. Accordingly all the estimates in the present report are shown on the basis of flat-rate benefits at the rates which took effect in November 1976, with earnings-related benefits calculated on the earnings levels corresponding to these benefit rates on the basis of the long-term average rate of earnings inflation assumed. The costs on this basis may be regarded as making explicit allowance for future increases in earnings and benefit rates but with the resulting estimates for a future year in money terms reduced in the ratio of the rates of benefit in the base year to the corresponding rates assumed for the year in question, so as to obtain meaningful estimates in present-day terms.

31   If all benefits were increased precisely in line with changes in the level of earnings, the resulting estimates in present-day terms would be the same whatever the rate of increase in earnings assumed. However it is intended that the margin of preference in the rates of certain industrial injuries benefits, which are to be carried over to the proposed new schemes, should be frozen in money terms. The level of these benefits would therefore fall in relation to earnings, to an extent depending on the rate at which earnings increase. Also, the new earnings-related components of national insurance invalidity and widows' pensions and the corresponding benefits under the proposed schemes will be increased only in line with the movement of prices once they are in payment. To the extent that earnings increase faster than prices, therefore, the cost of these benefits will also rise less steeply than earnings. Thus, to make allowance for these and similar features an assumption must be made about the average future rate of increase in earnings and about the margin in the rate of increase in earnings over the rate of increase in prices, and for the purpose of the estimates it has been assumed that earnings will, on average, increase at a rate of 8 per cent per annum, representing a margin of 2 per cent over the rate of increase in prices. The extra costs of the proposed schemes compared with the present arrangements will not, however, be sensitive to variations in the rates of increase assumed.

Rates of claim and amounts and durations of benefit
32   Estimates of future expenditure must be based on assumptions about factors such as numbers of accidents falling within the provisions of the schemes and the resulting rates of claim to benefit, durations of incapacity, degrees of disablement and reductions in earnings. For accidents and diseases covered by the present industrial injuries scheme relevant statistics for past years are for the most part available on which the assumptions for the future could be based. For categories to which entitlement to benefits, other than those available generally under the national insurance scheme, would be extended for the first time under the proposals, eg the self-employed, persons injured on the way to and from work or in other motor accidents, the assumptions had to be deduced indirectly from data from a variety of sources and the resulting estimates are inevitably

subject to a considerable margin of uncertainty and should be regarded more as indications of orders of magnitude rather than precise estimates of future costs. Particulars of the assumptions underlying the estimates and the methods by which these were derived, and corresponding estimates of future numbers of beneficiaries are given in an appendix.

33   On the Commission's instructions, it has been assumed for the purpose of the costings that the proposed extension of the provisions in regard to incapacity arising from occupational diseases would ultimately result in a doubling of the costs arising in respect of prescribed diseases, other than pneumoconiosis, under the present industrial injuries scheme.

ESTIMATES OF FUTURE COSTS

34   The estimated benefit expenditure under the present arrangements in respect of injuries (or incapacity due to occupational diseases) to be covered under the proposed schemes, together with the extra costs resulting from the proposed changes, are shown in Tables 1(a) and 2. An analysis of the extra costs for the proposed work injuries scheme, showing separately the amounts relating to persons covered under the present industrial injuries scheme and to each of the categories to which cover is being extended, is shown in Table 1(b). The costs of the present scheme shown in the tables represents the estimated expenditure on national insurance or industrial injuries benefits (other than mobility allowance) in respect of cases where a benefit would be payable under the proposed new schemes, if these had been in force at the time of the accident. All the estimates relate to the United Kingdom.

35   For the effects of the proposals on retirement pensions which result from the provisions in regard to the crediting of earnings during periods of incapacity or as a consequence of the improvements in widows' benefits, only the extra costs are shown, as the amounts of expenditure resulting from the corresponding provisions under the present arrangements cannot be isolated.

Table 1(a) Estimated cost of work injuries scheme

£ million

	1983–84	1988–89	1993–94	2003–04	2023–24
Short-term loss of earnings benefit					
Cost of present scheme	66·8	67·5	67·5	69·5	70·1
Extra cost	6·6	6·5	6·1	5·8	5·4
Total proposed scheme	73·4	74·0	73·6	75·3	75·5
Long-term loss of earnings benefit					
Cost of present scheme	16·9	17·3	17·8	20·4	22·0
Extra cost	1·1	3·3	2·2	1·3	0·8
Total proposed scheme	18·0	20·6	20·7	21·7	22·8
Non-pecuniary loss					
Cost of present scheme	102·9	101·0	99·3	98·1	99·2
Extra cost	7·2	10·2	12·7	17·5	23·1
Total proposed scheme	110·1	111·2	112·0	115·6	122·3
Partial loss of earnings benefit					
(Special Hardship Allowances:)					
Cost of present scheme	67·9	66·0	65·1	66·0	71·7
Extra cost	0·7	4·8	8·0	12·8	17·8
Total proposed scheme	68·6	70·8	73·1	78·8	89·5
Short-term benefits for widows and widowers					
Cost of present scheme	1·7	1·7	1·7	1·8	1·9
Extra cost: widows	–	0·1	0·1	0·1	0·1
widowers	0·1	0·1	0·1	0·1	0·1
Total proposed scheme	1·8	1·9	1·9	2·0	2·1
Long-term benefits for widows and widowers					
Cost of present scheme[1]	12·7	12·7	13·3	16·1	17·4
Extra cost: widows	0·3	2·1	2·3	1·2	0·7
widowers	–	0·5	0·6	0·8	0·8
Total proposed scheme	13·0	15·3	16·2	18·1	18·9
Total cost of work injuries scheme					
Present scheme	268·9	266·2	264·7	271·9	282·3
Extra cost:					
(i) as set out above	16·0	27·6	32·8	39·6	48·8
(ii) retirement pensions due to earnings credited during incapacity for work	–	0·5	2·5	5·0	1·5
(iii) retirement pensions of widows and widowers	–	0·6	1·8	2·9	0·9
Total extra cost	16·0	28·7	37·1	47·5	51·2

1 Including only the cost of benefits in excess of any entitlement to retirement pension in respect of widows over 60 and widowers over 65.

Table 1(b)   Work injuries scheme   Analysis of extra costs under proposed scheme

£ million

	1983–84	1988–89	1993–94	2003–04	2023–24
Employees: accidents and diseases covered under industrial injuries scheme at present					
(i) Short-term loss of earnings	3·3	3·6	3·6	3·7	3·7
(ii) Long-term loss of earnings	0·9	2·7	2·4	1·1	0·7
(iii) Non-pecuniary loss[1]	–	−0·4	−0·6	−0·6	−0·6
(v) Short-term benefits for widows	–	0·1	0·1	0·1	0·1
(vii) Long-term benefits for widows[2][3]	0·2	1·2	1·2	0·3	−0·1
(ix) Retirement pensions due to credited earnings	–	0·4	2·0	4·2	1·2
(x) Retirement pensions to widows	–	0·4	1·3	2·2	0·6
Total extra cost	4·4	8·0	10·0	11·0	5·6
Self-employed: accidents and diseases covered for employees under industrial injuries scheme at present					
(i) Short-term loss of earnings	0·6	0·5	0·5	0·4	0·3
(ii) Long-term loss of earnings	–	–	–	–	–
(iii) Non-pecuniary loss	2·5	3·8	4·8	6·6	8·7
(iv) Partial loss of earnings (Special Hardship Allowance)	0·2	1·2	2·0	3·2	4·4
(v) Short-term benefits for widows	–	–	–	–	–
(vii) Long-term benefits for widows[3]	–	–	–	0·1	0·1
(ix) Retirement pensions due to credited earnings	–	–	–	–	–
(x) Retirement pensions to widows	–	–	–	–	–
Total extra cost	3·3	5·5	7·3	10·3	13·5
Occupational diseases not covered under industrial injuries scheme at present – employees and self-employed					
(i) Short-term loss of earnings	0·4	0·4	0·3	0·3	0·2
(ii) Long-term loss of earnings	–	0·1	0·1	–	–
(iii) Non-pecuniary loss	1·1	1·6	2·0	2·6	3·4
(iv) Partial loss of earnings (Special Hardship Allowance)	0·2	1·4	2·3	3·7	5·3
(v) Short-term benefits for widows	–	–	–	–	–
(vii) Long-term benefits for widows[3]	–	0·1	0·1	–	–
(ix) Retirement pensions due to credited earnings	–	–	0·1	0·2	0·1
(x) Retirement pensions to widows	–	–	0·1	0·2	0·1
Total extra cost	1·7	3·6	5·0	7·0	9·1

1 Saving from freezing the rates of Constant Attendance Allowance and Exceptionally Severe Disablement Allowance at the rates in force at the end of March 1983.

2 Net of savings from bringing the flat-rate benefits into line with those payable under the national insurance scheme.

3 Excluding the extra cost for widows over 60 which is included under retirement pensions.

Table 1(b) *(Contd.)*

£ million

	1983–84	1988–89	1993–94	2003–04	2023–24
Widowers: accidents and diseases other than accidents on the way to and from work					
(vi) Short-term benefits	–	–	–	–	–
(viii) Long-term benefits	–	0·1	0·1	0·2	0·2
(xi) Retirement pensions	–	–	–	–	–
Total extra cost	–	0·1	0·1	0·2	0·2
Accidents on the way to and from work – employees and self-employed					
(i) Short-term loss of earnings	2·3	2·0	1·7	1·4	1·2
(ii) Long-term loss of earnings	0·2	0·5	0·4	0·2	0·1
(iii) Non-pecuniary loss	3·6	5·2	6·5	8·9	11·6
(iv) Partial loss of earnings (Special Hardship Allowance)	0·3	2·2	3·7	5·9	8·1
(v) Short-term benefit for widows	–	–	–	–	–
(vi) Short-term benefit for widowers	0·1	0·1	0·1	0·1	0·1
(vii) Long-term benefit for widows[1]	0·1	0·8	1·0	0·8	0·7
(viii) Long-term benefit for widowers	–	0·4	0·5	0·6	0·6
(ix) Retirement pensions due to credited earnings	–	0·1	0·4	0·6	0·2
(x) Retirement pensions to widows	–	0·2	0·4	0·5	0·2
(xi) Retirement pensions to widowers	–	–	–	–	–
Total extra cost	6·6	11·5	14·7	19·0	22·8
Summary by type of benefit					
(i) Short-term loss of earnings	6·6	6·5	6·1	5·8	5·4
(ii) Long-term loss of earnings	1·1	3·3	2·9	1·3	0·8
(iii) Non-pecuniary loss	7·2	10·2	12·7	17·5	23·1
(iv) Partial loss of earnings (Special Hardship Allowance)	0·7	4·8	8·0	12·8	17·8
(v) Short-term benefit for widows	–	0·1	0·1	0·1	0·1
(vi) Short-term benefit for widowers	0·1	0·1	0·1	0·1	0·1
(vii) Long-term benefit for widows	0·3	2·1	2·3	1·2	0·7
(viii) Long-term benefit for widowers	–	0·5	0·6	0·8	0·8
(ix) Retirement pensions due to credited earnings	–	0·5	2·5	5·0	1·5
(x) Retirement pensions to widows	–	0·6	1·8	2·9	0·9
(xi) Retirement pensions to widowers	–	–	–	–	–
Total extra cost	16·0	28·7	37·1	47·5	51·2

1 Excluding the extra cost for widows over 60 which is included under retirement pensions.

Table 2 Estimated cost of motor vehicle injuries scheme   £ million

	1983–84	1988–89	1993–94	2003–04	2023–24
Short-term loss of earnings benefit					
Cost of present scheme	12	12	12½	12½	13
Extra cost	6	5	4½	4	3½
Total proposed scheme	18	17	17	16½	16½
Long-term loss of earnings benefit					
Cost of present scheme	2½	2½	2½	3	3
Extra cost	–	½	1	½	½
Total proposed scheme	2½	2½	3½	3½	3½
Non-pecuniary loss					
Cost of present scheme	–	–	–	–	–
Extra cost	8	11	14	18	23
Total proposed scheme	8	11	14	18	23
Partial loss of earnings benefit *(Special Hardship Allowance)*					
Cost of present scheme	–	–	–	–	–
Extra cost	½	4	6	9½	13½
Total proposed scheme	½	4	6	9½	13½
Short-term benefits for widows and widowers					
Cost of present scheme	1	1	1	1	1
Extra cost: widows	½	½	½	½	½
widowers					
Total proposed scheme	1½	1½	1½	1½	1½
Long-term benefits for widows and widowers					
Cost of present scheme[1]	10	10½	11	12½	14½
Extra cost: widows	–	2	3	3	1
widowers	½	2	3	3½	3½
Total proposed scheme	10½	14½	17	19	19
Total cost of motor vehicle injuries scheme					
Present scheme	25½	26	27	29	31½
Extra costs:					
(i) as set out above	15½	25	32	39	45½
(ii) retirement pensions due to earnings credited during incapacity from work	–	–	½	1	–
(iii) retirement pensions to widows and widowers	–	½	2	3	2½
Total extra cost	15½	25½	34½	43	48

1 Including only the cost of benefits in excess of any entitlement to retirement pension in respect of widows over 60 and widowers over 65.

36   The cost after 40 years, in the year 2023–24, may be regarded as close to the ultimate cost when the proposed schemes are fully mature. For that year, the extra costs for the two schemes combined total £99 million, representing an increase of nearly a third in the amounts of benefit that would be payable if the present arrangements were to continue. Of the total of £99 million, £46 million arises in respect of benefits for non-pecuniary loss and a further £31 million represents the notional allowance included for the cost of partial loss of earnings benefits, which together amount to over three-quarters of the total extra cost. This reflects the fact that under the present arrangements no benefits of this nature are available in respect of injuries or diseases not covered by the industrial injuries scheme, whilst in regard to loss of earnings during incapacity for work and widows' benefits the great majority of persons at the working ages will be covered for benefits under the general national insurance scheme. Only £6 million of the extra cost relates to accidents and diseases for which benefit is payable under the industrial injuries scheme at present.

37   The pattern of the build-up of the extra cost over the years varies greatly according to the nature of the benefit. For short-term loss of earnings benefit most of the cost arises already in the first year, and for disablement gratuities paid as compensation for non-pecuniary loss a high proportion of the ultimate cost is also reached within a year or two. The cost of disablement pensions, on the other hand, builds up gradually over a long period as a significant proportion of awards remain in payment for life.

38   For long-term loss of earnings benefit and widows' pensions the extra cost rises to a peak after five or ten years; it then declines, because the margin of the proposed earnings-related benefits over the corresponding new national insurance benefits gradually falls as the latter build up to their full rate over a twenty-year period from April 1978. A similar pattern applies to the extra cost of retirement pensions, though here the peak is not reached for some twenty years.

39   The result is that in round figures the estimated total extra annual cost builds up from about £30 million in the first year, to about £50 million after 5 years, about £70 million after 10 years and about £90 million after 20 years. The ultimate extra cost is estimated to be about £100 million a year.

E. A. JOHNSTON

Government Actuary's Department
London
January 1978

APPENDIX: THE BASIS OF THE ESTIMATES

1 This appendix gives particulars of the methods and assumptions adopted in obtaining the cost estimates shown in the report. In the main the estimates were based on statistics obtained from the working of the existing national insurance and industrial injuries schemes but in costing the proposed extensions of cover these had to be supplemented by data obtained from other sources. Allowance was made for the effects of future changes in the size of the population and its distribution by age and sex by reference to the most recent projections of the population available at the time the estimates were made, particulars of which are published in a booklet entitled 'Population Projections, 1975–2015' (HMSO).

2 It was assumed for the purpose of the costings that the provisions of the proposed schemes would apply to benefits for loss of earnings and non-pecuniary loss awarded after 31st March 1983 and to benefits to widows and widowers in respect of deaths occurring after that date.

3 In estimating the extra cost of the proposed schemes compared with the cost of the benefits payable under the existing arrangements, account was taken of the changes in the national insurance scheme resulting from the Social Security Pensions Act 1975–in particular, the gradual introduction of earnings-related additions to long-term benefits and the phasing out of the option currently exercised by a majority of married women in employment to pay reduced contributions and forgo cover for national insurance benefits in their own right.

4 The costs shown in the report relate to the United Kingdom and were based on detailed estimates for Great Britain with overall additions varying according to the type of benefit and category of injury within the range 1·4 per cent–3·7 per cent, to allow approximately for costs arising in Northern Ireland.

5 Estimates of numbers of beneficiaries after 40 years when, for practical purposes, the scheme may be regarded as fully mature are shown in Table 12 at the end of this appendix.

THE WORK INJURIES SCHEME

Employees' accidents at work and present prescribed diseases

6 For accidents and diseases falling within the scope of the present industrial injuries scheme, the only contingency to be covered under the proposed scheme not covered under the existing scheme is loss of earnings resulting from incapacity for work lasting more than 6 months. Subject to this and also to the proposal that the lower rate of widow's pension (£4·59 per week at the beginning of 1977) should be withdrawn

237

for new widows, the numbers who would be entitled to benefit under the Commission's proposals would be exactly the same as if the present industrial injuries scheme had continued.

7 The methods for estimating these numbers, using statistics collected from the working of the industrial injuries scheme, is largely unaltered from that described in the report by the Government Actuary on the Third Quinquennial Review of the Industrial Injuries Scheme (H.C. 226 of 1964–65), though the various rates of award etc assumed have been revised in the light of the experience over recent years. Briefly, the method for injury benefit is to compare the number of days of benefit paid in past periods, broken down by age and sex and distinguishing between accidents and prescribed diseases, with the employed work force and to deduce average numbers of days of benefit per employee which are then applied to estimates of the employed work force in future years to obtain the days of benefit to be paid in those years.

8 For disablement pension, disablement gratuity, special hardship allowance and widow's pension, award rates per head of the employed work force are determined in a similar way to days of injury benefit. For the continuing benefits, the future numbers in payment are then obtained by applying probabilities of continued receipt of benefit according to duration since award, derived from the experience of the scheme, to existing beneficiaries and to new awards. The number of remarriage gratuities is equal to the widows' pensions ceasing because of remarriage.

9 For accidents the days of injury benefit per employee and the award rates of the other benefits have exhibited a downward trend over a period of years. Much of the decline may be attributed to the fall in the numbers employed in coal mining and a reduced level of activity in the construction industry in recent years, but there has been some fall also in the rates obtained when these industries are excluded. In deriving the assumptions for the future allowance has been made for these trends to continue for a further two or three years, with the rates taken as constant for all future years thereafter. The rates assumed for injury benefit, for disablement benefits and for widows' benefits are shown in Tables 1, 2 and 3 respectively.

Table 1   Injury benefit – assumed average annual number of days of benefit per 1,000 employees

Ages nearest birthday at date of award	Accidents		Prescribed diseases	
	Men	Women	Men	Women
16 – 19	550	160	20	20
20 – 24	600	100	20	10
25 – 29	650	130	20	20
30 – 34	750	180	20	20
35 – 39	900	220	25	20
40 – 44	850	240	25	30
45 – 49	850	260	30	30
50 – 54	850	290	30	20
55 – 59	750	290	35	20
60 – 64	850	} 220	35	} 10
65 and over	250		10	

Table 2   Disablement benefits (accidents and prescribed diseases other than pneumoconiosis) – assumed annual rates of award per 1,000 employees

Ages last birthday at date of award	Disablement pensions		Disablement gratuities[1]	
	Men	Women	Men	Women
16 – 19	0·25	0·05	4·0	1·0
20 – 24	0·45	0·05	5·0	1·0
25 – 29	0·55	0·10	6·5	2·0
30 – 34	0·80	0·20	9·0	2·5
35 – 39	1·00	0·25	10·5	3·5
40 – 44	1·05	0·35	11·0	4·0
45 – 49	1·25	0·50	12·0	4·5
50 – 54	1·20	0·55	12·0	5·0
55 – 59	1·15	0·50	10·5	5·0
60 – 64	1·35	0·50	9·5	4·5
65 and over	0·70	0·35	5·5	2·5

1 Including awards on reassessment from a previous disablement pension or gratuity.

Table 3   Death benefit – assumed annual number of deaths giving rise to awards of
widows' pension per 1,000 male employees

Ages last birthday at date of death	Accidents	Prescribed diseases (other than pneumoconiosis)
16 – 19	·002	–
20 – 24	·020	–
25 – 29	·035	–
30 – 34	·050	–
35 – 39	·055	–
40 – 44	·060	·002
45 – 49	·065	·004
50 – 54	·070	·006
55 – 59	·080	·010
60 – 64	·090	·020
65 – 69	·080	·050
70 – 74	·055	·090
75 and over		·050

10   On the basis of the experience in recent years, the proportions of disablement
pensions remaining in payment, by durations since award, assumed for the future were:

Duration since award (years)	$\frac{1}{2}$	$1\frac{1}{2}$	$2\frac{1}{2}$	$3\frac{1}{2}$	$4\frac{1}{2}$	5
Proportions remaining in payment (per cent)	71	39	32	29	28	28

Long-term loss of earnings benefit

11   The present industrial injuries scheme does not provide a long-term loss of
earnings benefit, though most persons covered by the scheme who are still incapable
of work after 6 months when injury benefit ceases would be eligible for national
insurance sickness or invalidity benefit. Statistics are available of annual numbers
of awards of these benefits immediately following payment of injury benefit but there
are no reliable data about the duration of benefit in such cases. Statistics of sickness
and invalidity benefits in payment at the end of each statistical year, analysed by duration since onset of incapacity, are available from which rates of termination of benefit

can be estimated, but the breakdown by cause of incapacity does not extend to work accidents as such but only to the wider category comprising all accidents, poisonings and violence. In the absence of other data it was assumed that the rates of termination of sickness or invalidity benefit awarded following an accident at work will be similar to those for this wider category as a whole, which implied that about 40 per cent of men and 20 per cent of women in receipt of benefit after more than 6 months in this category would have suffered their accidents at work.

12 For convenience of calculation, the numbers of beneficiaries obtained on this basis (for whom there is no age distribution) were compared with the corresponding numbers of disablement pensioners, and the following factors derived for obtaining future numbers qualifying for long-term loss of earnings benefit resulting from accidents at work from the projected numbers of disablement pensioners.

Duration since award of disablement pension (years)	Proportion of disablement pensioners aged under 65 (60 for females) disabled as a result of accidents at work assumed to be in receipt of sickness or invalidity benefit	
	Males	*Females*
0–1	·300	·190
1–2	·210	·125
2–3	·150	·115
3–4	·110	·090
4–5	·070	·075
5–10	·045	·060
10–15	·015	·030
15+	·005	–

13 In applying these proportions in future years the rates for women were gradually increased, ultimately by about 100 per cent, to allow for the phasing out of the married women's option to forgo cover for benefits in return for the payment of contributions at a reduced rate. In addition, in determining the cost of benefit under the proposed scheme allowance was made for an assumed 2 per cent of men and 5 per cent of women who would not satisfy the contribution conditions for invalidity benefit but would be entitled to the long-term loss of earnings benefit under the proposed scheme.

14 A similar method was applied for benefit arising from pneumoconiosis, where however the total numbers of days of sickness or invalidity benefit due to this cause are available; rather arbitrary methods were used to obtain estimates of future numbers of beneficiaries suffering from other prescribed diseases, but the numbers involved are relatively small.

Earnings-related benefits

15 For short-term loss of earnings benefits, on the basis of the recent experience the following proportions of employees entitled to flat-rate injury benefit under the present industrial injuries scheme were assumed to have entitlement to earnings-related supplement:

Males   – 0·67
Females – 0·23

As the minimum earnings to provide a benefit under the formula for earnings-related supplement are also sufficient to satisfy the present contribution conditions for entitlement to benefit, the proportion for men may be assumed to apply unaltered to the proposed scheme also. For women it is estimated that the proportion would have increased from 0·23 to 0·31 for awards in 1983–84 and would ultimately have become 0·42 due to the phasing out of the married women's option. Under the proposed scheme the benefit would no longer be dependent on the satisfying of contribution conditions and the proportion of 0·42 has been assumed to apply from the outset.

16   The amount of earnings-related benefit, for those who are entitled, is based on the earnings of manual workers in April 1975, including those whose earnings were affected by absence in the relevant pay period, as shown by the Department of Employment survey of earnings at that date. This distribution, suitably adjusted so that it gives earnings over a 12-month period rather than in one pay period, was found to be broadly consistent with amounts of earnings-related supplement actually paid to recipients of injury benefit. The earnings distribution was adjusted at the lower end so as to simulate the effect on the supplements of the rule that the flat-rate benefits and the supplement together must not exceed 85 per cent of earnings in the relevant year. The resulting costs were adjusted to the level of earnings in terms of which the estimates are shown in the report.

17   The earnings-related short-term benefits to widows were calculated on a similar basis; it was assumed that 80 per cent of new widows under 60 receiving flat-rate benefits would be entitled to an earnings-related addition.

18   The earnings-related additions to long-term loss of earnings benefit and to pensions to widows and widowers were also calculated on the basis of the average earnings of manual workers. In calculating the benefit that would become payable under the existing scheme it was assumed that earnings would be at this average level in all years relevant for the purpose of calculating benefit.

Retirement pensions arising from credited earnings

19   The new earnings-related additional components of long-term benefits under the national insurance scheme will be calculated as 1¼ per cent of relevant earnings for persons within 20 years of pension age in April 1978 and as 25 per cent of the average relevant earnings in the best 20 years for younger contributors. Accordingly in costing the proposal that earnings should be credited during periods of incapacity for the purpose of calculating these benefits, it was assumed that for age groups substantially more than 20 years below pension age in April 1978 the effect would be negligible but that for those within 20 years of pension age all credited earnings would give rise to corresponding increases in pension benefit. The earnings distribution of all manual workers was again used for this purpose, except that those whose earnings were affected by absence during the relevant pay period were excluded.

Self-employed accidents at work and present prescribed diseases

20   The method of determining the number of self-employed who would benefit from the Commission's proposal to extend to them the flat-rate benefits that are proposed for employees was similar to that described for employees. Little information is available about the incidence of accidents at work and occupational diseases for self-employed persons and, as explained in detail below, the rates of claim to the various benefits assumed in costing the proposals were obtained on the assumption that the self-employed would experience the same rates of accidents etc as for employees in the same industry. On this basis the days of short-term loss of earnings benefit per self-employed person and the rates of award of the other benefits were derived as a proportion of the corresponding days or rates per employed person of the same age.

21   The proportions adopted were:

	Males		Females	
	Accidents	Prescribed diseases (other than pneumo-coniosis)	Accidents	Prescribed diseases (other than pneumo-coniosis)
Short-term loss of earnings benefit:	0·90[1]	0·50[1]	1·00[1]	0·50[1]
Disablement pension:	1·05	0·50	1·05	0·25
Disablement gratuity:	0·90	0·45	1·00	0·25
Special hardship allowance:	0·70	0·40	0·70	0·20
Widow's pension:	1·10	0·50	–	–

1 Before adjustment for lower rates of take-up of benefit.

22   The assumed number of days of short-term loss of earnings benefit per self-employed person and the assumed award rates for the other benefits were then applied to estimates of the numbers of the self-employed in future years. For the pension benefits the same probabilities of continued receipt of benefit were used as for employees. The rates of claim to national insurance sickness benefit in respect of short spells of incapacity are substantially lower for self-employed persons than for employees. It seems likely that some difference in the propensity to claim benefit for minor injuries would be found under the proposed scheme also and the days of short-term loss of earnings benefit obtained on the basis of the factor shown in the table were reduced by 10 per cent to allow for this feature.

23   The method of deriving the proportions shown above is described in detail for short-term loss of earnings benefit. The statistics of injury benefit from the present industrial injuries scheme give days of incapacity in twelve-month periods split by industry, between accidents and prescribed diseases, and between males and females. These days for each industry were adjusted to exclude waiting days and divided by the number of employees in that industry given by the Department of Employment's count of employees in employment each June, counting half for those employed part-time, to obtain the average number of days of benefit per employee in that industry. These averages for employees were then weighted by the number of employers and self-employed in the same industry as shown on page 1347 of the Department of Employment Gazette of December 1976 to obtain an overall average number of days of benefit per self-employed person. This average was then expressed as the proportion of the corresponding average for employees and is the basis for the proportions shown in the table above.

24   No industrial analysis of new awards of disablement pension or special hardship allowance is available and it was therefore necessary to base the proportion of award rates for employees to be assumed for the self-employed on the awards in force per person in the industry. In the absence of relevant data, largely arbitrary assumptions had to be made in regard to awards of disablement gratuities and also for special hardship allowances in the case of women.

25   The estimated number of self-employed who would receive long-term loss of earnings benefits was obtained by a similar method to that described above for employees. In estimating the cost of benefits under the present arrangements it was assumed that 95 per cent of men would satisfy the contribution conditions for national insurance sickness and invalidity benefits and for pensions for their widows. For women the proportion gradually increases, with the phasing out of the married women's option, to 29 per cent for awards in 1983–84 and 45 per cent ultimately.

Occupational diseases not covered under present industrial injuries scheme

26   On the Commission's instructions it was assumed that the proposal to extend cover to all diseases which could be shown to be due to and a particular risk of the occupation would result in a doubling of the rates of award for the various benefits in respect of prescribed diseases, other than pneumoconiosis, qualifying for benefit under the industrial injuries scheme at present.

Accidents on the way to and from work

27   The numbers of injuries and days of incapacity resulting from accidents on the way to and from work involving motor vehicles are derived in the course of the costing of the proposed motor vehicle injuries scheme described in a later section of this appendix and, as set out below, these formed the basis of the estimates of the costs arising in respect of such accidents.

28   However the Commission's proposals cover all accidents on the way to and from work and not just those involving motor vehicles. The Personal Injury Survey, referred to in paragraph 35 below, implied that about 40 per cent of all accidents on the way to and from work do not involve motor vehicles, but no information is available about the nature of these accidents nor of the extent of the resulting injuries. It is reasonable to assume, however, that in general the injuries resulting from accidents not involving motor vehicles will be very much less serious than from those involving motor vehicles and the costs in respect of the latter were increased arbitrarily by 50 per cent for short-term loss of earnings benefit, 25 per cent for long-term loss of earnings benefit, disablement benefits and special hardship allowance and 10 per cent for widows' and widowers' benefits to make allowance for accidents not involving motor vehicles.

Loss of earnings benefits

29   The number of days of short-term and long-term loss of earnings benefit, analysed by age and sex, in respect of accidents on the way to or from work involving motor vehicles were obtained by applying the factors in Table 6 to the numbers of days shown in Table 11. These benefit days, which were assumed to apply to the 12-month period June 1973 to May 1974, were related to the corresponding numbers in the work force at that time, to obtain factors which were then applied to estimates of the work force in future years.

30   The assumptions as to the proportions of the resulting days for which sickness or invalidity benefit would be paid in any event under the national insurance scheme are the same as those described above in the sections on work accidents for employees and the self-employed respectively. The earnings distribution adopted for the calculation of earnings-related benefits was that for all employees and not that for manual workers. In other respects the estimates follow those for accidents at work.

Disablement benefits and special hardship allowance

31   No detailed information is available about the degrees of disablement resulting from motor vehicle injuries and any estimates of the likely cost of benefits for non-pecuniary loss and special hardship allowance (costed in lieu of a partial loss of earnings

benefit) in respect of motor vehicle injuries under the proposed schemes must be subject to a considerable degree of uncertainty. On the basis of a tabulation of cases in the Personal Injury Survey where there was at least a possibility that some permanent disability or disfigurement would result from the accident, broken down between work, transport and other accidents, it was assumed that ultimately the expenditure on benefit for non-pecuniary loss and special hardship allowance arising from accidents on the way to and from work involving motor vehicles would be 10 per cent of the corresponding expenditure in respect of accidents at work. It was also assumed that the pattern of build-up over the years would be broadly the same as that for new awards in respect of accidents at work after March 1983.

Widows and widowers

32 Details of deaths as a result of road accidents, including a breakdown by age and sex, are given in the statistics produced by the Department of the Environment. It was assumed that at the working ages the proportions of deaths in accidents involving a motor vehicle which occurred on the way to and from work would be the same as the proportions for all such accidents given in Table 6 below. On this basis, using the statistics for 1975, rates of award of widows' and widowers' pensions were obtained by applying proportions married from the 1971 Census to the deaths, and relating the resulting numbers to the corresponding numbers in the work force in 1975. These rates were then applied to the projected work force in future years to obtain new awards of widows' and widowers' pensions. The subsequent numbers remaining in payment were obtained on the same assumptions as regards rates of termination as for the corresponding benefits arising from employees' accidents at work.

33 The earnings distribution assumed for the calculation of earnings-related benefits was again that for all employees and not just that for manual workers.

THE MOTOR VEHICLE INJURIES SCHEME

34 Unlike the position with the work injuries scheme there is no existing scheme specifically covering motor vehicle injuries to provide statistics on which the cost estimates for the proposed scheme could be based. The following paragraphs describe in detail the sources of data and the methods used in obtaining estimates of the numbers of injuries, durations of incapacity and the numbers of deaths that would be covered under the proposed scheme. The final stage of deriving benefit costs is described only briefly as it generally follows the methods and assumptions employed in making the corresponding estimates for the work injuries scheme.

Statistical information about injuries resulting from accidents

35 *The Personal Injury Survey* (*PIS*) was carried out by the Office of Population Censuses and Surveys partly for the purpose of deriving the relevant statistics for the costing of the benefits under the proposed scheme. As a consequence the information was made available in the most suitable form with differentiation by sex, age, type of accident, marital status, size of family and duration of incapacity. The results related to all accidents, not only to motor vehicle accidents, for a sample of the whole population, and when rated up to take account of the sampling fraction covered a total of about 230,000 persons injured in motor vehicle accidents in a year and a total of 1,900,000 persons injured in all types of accidents, of whom 1,200,000 were at the main working ages[1]. The survey covered injuries leading to four or more days incapacity for work or other normal activities, and the totals thus include some persons who were absent from work for less than four days.

---

1 16–64 (men), 16–59 (women), denoted by the abbreviated form 16–64/59 hereafter.

36   Unfortunately the survey suffered from the disadvantage that the respondents were asked to disclose accidents and injuries that might have occurred over a year before the interview and also that occurred to a member of the household other than themselves. As a consequence there was a considerable understatement in the number of cases, particularly the less serious ones. Injuries resulting in incapacity for work for more than three months were two to three times as frequent, relative to less serious cases, in the survey than in comparable national insurance statistics. It will be seen below that those statistics suggest that there are about 2·2 million persons injured in accidents at the main working ages – about 80 per cent more than the number shown in the PIS.

37   However, while the PIS figures as absolute quantities are therefore not directly serviceable as a basis for costing, figures for the proportion of non-motor vehicle accidents, of accidents occurring at work, occurring while on the way to and from work, etc can be derived and applied to the more reliable total accident figures obtained from other sources to give estimates for the separate categories.

38   *The social security statistics* produced by DHSS are undoubtedly the most reliable and most accurate relevant figures available. Figures are available separately for accident victims receiving sickness benefit or injury benefit under the national insurance and industrial injuries schemes, grouped according to both age and nature of injury. These figures have the further advantage that they relate to benefit paid and, in particular, allow for non-payment of benefit for the first three days of incapacity which would also be a feature of the proposed scheme. They show that about 1·7 million new claims are made annually, of which 1·1 million are for sickness benefit and 0·6 million are for injury benefit.

39   It is not possible, however, to base the costings directly on these figures as the statistics cover all accidents, with no separate breakdown of motor accidents, and relate only to the age band 16 to 64/59 and, within this band, only to those covered for benefit under the national insurance and industrial injuries schemes. These statistics, therefore, have to be used in conjunction with those from other sources to obtain the estimates required.

40   *The Hospital In-Patient Enquiry* (HIPE) statistics collected by DHSS provide figures showing the number of in-patients by age and nature of injury for road traffic accidents, home, and other accidents separately, the average in-patient durations by nature of injury for road traffic accidents, home, and other accidents separately, and the average duration by nature of injury and age for all accidents together. These statistics cover all age groups and suggest that 80,000 persons injured in road traffic accidents are admitted to hospital in a year, as compared with the total for all types of accident cases admitted of about 500,000.

41   The major limitation of the HIPE statistics is that they relate to only a section of the total accident experience, that is those admitted to hospital, and the durations quoted are durations of in-patient stay and not the complete period of incapacity for which benefits under the proposed scheme might be payable. Accordingly there is no way in which they would serve directly in estimating the cost of benefits. Another deficiency is that the 'road traffic accidents' they purport to record are not identical with the category of motor vehicle accidents which would be covered by the proposed scheme.

42   These statistics are of value, however, in that they give a breakdown of the total accident figures between road traffic accidents and other categories, by age and by nature of injury. Admittedly this breakdown is directly applicable only in respect of hospital in-patient cases, but if the appropriate assumptions can be justified this

245

breakdown can be extended more generally to estimate the proportions of all accidents in these categories. It would therefore appear that if acceptably accurate figures of the total accident cases by nature of injury could be obtained from other sources, the HIPE could be of value in deriving the motor accident cases and, more particularly, in deriving duration statistics which would be used in conjunction with the number of cases.

43   *The Department of the Environment* (DOE) Road Traffic Accident statistics offer the best available national count of the numbers of persons injured on the roads, although they are far from ideal as a basis for estimates of the amount of incapacity. They show 345,000 persons as injured in 1973, of which 90,000 were regarded as serious i.e. where the person was detained in hospital as an in-patient or in any case if he suffered from fractures, concussion, internal injuries, crushings, severe cuts and lacerations or severe general shock. (Such injuries as sprains and bruises are regarded as slight injuries.)

44   When using these statistics it has to be borne in mind that two major adjustments are needed; first, an addition of about 30 per cent for the large number of accidents not reported to the police – for with many accidents there is no compulsion to do so – and, secondly, an adjustment because perhaps 60 per cent of those treated in hospital have what are clinically regarded as only minor injuries so that about half of the casualties may be expected to be back at work within four days. There is useful information on the size of these adjustment factors in sample surveys done in certain hospitals by Bull and Roberts[1] and Grattan and Keigan[2].

45   Thus the DOE statistics suggest that there are probably around half a million road casualties a year which require medical attention or for which some personal injury is reported, but the number with incapacity for more than three days is probably round about 350,000. This estimate has been taken into account when considering the more detailed statistics obtained from the national insurance scheme and the HIPE.

The calculation of the numbers of accidents

Base year of the calculations

46   It was decided to take the year 1973 as the base year for the estimates of numbers of accidents even though many of the statistics related to some period other than this calendar year. For such statistics the choice was either to bring them back to the calendar year by interpolation, or to use the statistics as they stood, accepting a possible slight error resulting from the non-coincidence of data periods. In view of the broad methods which necessarily had to be adopted in the calculations, it was considered justifiable to use the statistics as they stood without adjustments for any changes after 1973, and to assume that the level of accidents would vary thereafter only as a result of expected population changes.

Numbers of accident cases

47   The statistics for numbers of accidents in various categories are more extensive than those for the numbers of days of incapacity and therefore estimates of the numbers of persons injured and who would benefit from the scheme have been made first and then used in analysing and extending the incapacity statistics.

---

1 Bull and Roberts. *Accid. Anal. & Prev.* Vol. 5 pp 43–53. 1973.

2 Grattan and Keigan. Patterns and Severity of Injury in a Hospital Sample of Road Traffic Accident Casualties. Transport and Road Research Laboratory. 1975.

48   The social security statistics of sickness benefits, injury benefits and invalidity benefits due to accidents were taken as the starting point for the calculations, in particular the tables showing by sex and age group the number of new spells by cause in the year. The number of new spells was taken as identical to the number of new injury cases, although the definition of 'new spell' might include a recurrence under an old injury and hence lead to an overstatement of the true number of new injuries. It was, however, considered that this possible overstatement could be neglected.

49   To obtain the costing basis it was then necessary to transform the social security statistics by estimating the road traffic accident component of the totals for all accidents and then extending the figures to cover the total population and not merely the insured. This required the application of both HIPE figures and the DOE figures.

50   The principle adopted in the first place was that for any given age and nature of injury the proportion of the social security cases which related to road traffic accidents would be the same as amongst the in-patients. Since the HIPE figures give the proportion of road traffic accident cases to total cases for each sex and each age group and by nature of injury, applying these proportions to the totals given by the social security statistics would give the number of road traffic accident cases by age, sex and nature of injury for which benefit was payable.

51   Before this calculation of road traffic accidents as proportions of all accidents could be carried out, it was necessary to adjust the social security figures because, first, in a few cases the nature of injury heads in the tables were wider than those in the HIPE tables, and, secondly, there were large groups under the head 'injuries not further specified' where only the part of the body injured was indicated. To deal with these points the number of cases in the social security tables was split in proportion to those in the HIPE tables and the unspecified cases were allocated in proportion to the specified ones.

52   It was then necessary to effect the extension from the insured population to the total population figures. This is essentially two distinct calculations; the adjustment of the age groups of the insured population (i.e. 16 – 64 (men), 16 – 59 (women)) and the extrapolation to include the young and old outside those age groups. The first of these was carried out by scaling up the figures for a five-year age group by the ratio of the number in the population to the number insured. For women over 25 there is some evidence that those at work have relatively more accidents than those not in employment, even when accidents at work are excluded. For this reason at ages 25 – 34 a 15 per cent reduction was made in the figures that were obtained by strict proportion and at ages 35 – 59 a 20 per cent reduction was made. This extension of the accident numbers for each cause and age-group from the insured population is primarily of significance for the youngest ages for men (where the highest rates of motor vehicle injury occur) and for women. It gave a total of 2·2 million accidents as compared with only 1·7 million in the insured population.

53   Applying proportions varying with age and nature of injury based on the HIPE figures as outlined in paragraph 50 a total of 287,000 road accident cases is obtained; this represents only 13 per cent of the total of 2·2 million accident casualties, although as many as 20 per cent of admissions of accident victims as in-patients to hospitals at ages 16–64/59 are road traffic casualties. The discrepancy reflects the tendency for the more serious accidents to have taken place on the roads and, other things being equal, for casualties being more likely to be taken to hospital if the accident occurs away from the home or work place.

54 Although the assumption of proportionality is applicable with a high degree of reliability for injuries such as fractures of the lower limbs for which so large a proportion of victims will be admitted to hospital that the proportion arising from road accidents amongst all with that category of injury can be reliably inferred, the same is not true for some of the more common and less serious of the 20 injury categories for which the statistics are available, such as sprains and bruises. For this reason and because the results are then more in accord with the DOE statistics the numbers obtained were reduced by 15 per cent to give an adjusted figure of 245,000 road traffic casualties a year at the working ages incapacitated for more than three days, or about 11 per cent of the 2·2 million such cases arising from all causes. The adjusted numbers are given in Table 5. The corresponding DOE count is 258,000 persons slightly or seriously injured at these ages but this is subject to the adjustments discussed in paragraph 44 above. It must be admitted that it is impossible to estimate with certainty the number of road injuries which might give rise to claims under the proposed scheme, but the exact number of borderline, less serious, cases is not crucial to the costing of the scheme: the main problem lies in the costing of the benefits payable to the more serious cases.

55 Having obtained estimates of the number of road injuries at the working ages that might qualify for benefit under the proposed system (whether under the motor vehicle scheme or the work injury scheme) it is then necessary to consider the number of cases at the non-working ages, namely children and pensioners, where the criterion of incapacity for work is not normally strictly applicable but where incapacity in a general sense must inevitably be the basis of any scheme of compensation. The available statistics of persons injured in road accidents for these age groups are shown in Table 4.

Table 4 Data on number of persons injured in road accidents aged under 16 and over 64/59[1]

thousands

	Males ages 0–15	Females ages 0–15	Men aged 65 and over	Women aged 60 and over	Total
PIS[2]	34	27	7	21	89
DOE:					
seriously injured	10	5	4	7	26
slightly injured	25	13	8	12	58
Total	35	18	12	19	84
Hospital in-patients	12	6	3	5	26

1 Over 64 men (estimated), over 59 women.
2 Without adjustment for under-reporting.

56 Similar considerations apply to these sources of statistics for children and pensioners as do for persons of working age, but with the added difficulty that there is no simple criterion of incapacity which can be applied. However, relying on the numbers of cases reported in the PIS, rated up for unreported cases in the same pro-

portions as has been estimated as applicable at the main working ages, gives some 90,000 children and 40,000 pensioners a year as incapacitated. These numbers, broken down by sex, are also shown in Table 5.

Table 5   Estimated number of persons incapacitated in road accidents

thousands

Sex		Age group					over	Total
	0–15	16–19	20–25	25–34	35–44	45–64/59	60/65	
Male	50	40	33	35	25	37	10	230
Female	40	13	13	14	14	21	30	145
Total	90	53	46	49	39	58	40	375

57   The total estimate of 375,000 persons a year incapacitated in road accidents is thus little different from the broad estimate of some 350,000 obtained on the basis of the DOE statistics mentioned above.

58   The final stage in deriving the number of accidents for the costing of the scheme was to subdivide the road accident figures according to whether the accident occurred whilst at work, on the way to or from work, or at any other time. Also allowance had to be made for the fact that the scheme was to cover all motor vehicle road accidents, not just those on the public highway but also those on other roads to which the public has access and including those involving stationary vehicles but, on the other hand, was not to cover road accidents only involving bicycles and other non-motor vehicles. These two factors are of uncertain importance and it was thought reasonable to assume that for persons of working age they roughly offset each other. So on the basis of the statistics from the PIS the following division of the total road accident figures (now assumed to represent all motor vehicle accidents) was made for persons at the working ages.

Table 6   Proportions of motor vehicle accidents at various times at ages 16–64/59

	Men	Women	Total
At work, during working hours	30%	10%	25%
Whilst on the way to or from work	28%	15%	25%
At other times	42%	75%	50%
	100%	100%	100%

59   For children and pensioners many of the road accidents do not involve motor vehicles or would not result in benefit being paid and on the basis of the available data the numbers of cases obtained above were reduced by 50 per cent for children and by 75 per cent for pensioners, though these estimates are inevitably very tentative.

60. The resulting numbers of injuries assumed to be covered by the motor vehicle scheme, allowing for the fact that injuries involving motor vehicles sustained in the course of work or on the way to or from work are to be covered under the work injuries scheme, are shown in Table 7.

Table 7   Estimated number of injuries covered by proposed motor vehicle scheme

thousands

Sex	0–15	16–19	20–24	Age group 25–34	35–44	45–64/59	Over 60/65	Total
Males	25	17	14	15	11	16	2	100
Females	20	10	10	10	11	16	8	85
Total	45	27	24	25	22	32	10	185

The calculation of the durations of incapacity

61   In order to derive the expected aggregate numbers of days for which incapacity benefits would be payable under the scheme it was first necessary to obtain the average durations of incapacity for each accident category according to the nature of injury and age. As no analysis of days of benefit by age and nature of injury is available for injury benefit, the averages had to be based on statistics relating to national insurance sickness and invalidity benefits. For the main categories of injuries the mean durations obtained ranged from 7 days for most types of sprains and strains at ages under 20, to 110 days for fractures of lower limbs for men over age 45.

62   The method of arriving at these averages, however, implicitly assumed that the duration of incapacity of an injury of a specified nature at a given age is independent of the initial cause of the accident. Examination of the HIPE figures showed that for in-patient stay this assumption was not justified and that for some injuries the duration of stay following a road accident was significantly greater than that following apparently the same type of injury arising through other causes. It seemed reasonable to assume, therefore, that a difference would also exist for these injuries in the average days of incapacity for work. With no other indication of the extent to which this differential in respect of days of incapacity might exist, the most reasonable course appeared to be to increase the average number of days of incapacity for those injuries showing this feature, in the ratio of average in-patient (HIPE) stay for road accident cases to that for all cases. These 'severity factors' are given in Table 8.

Table 8   Addition to average duration to allow for greater severity of road accident cases for certain injuries

Nature of injury	Men	Women
Fracture of skull	+40%	+20%
Fracture of spine and trunk	+40%	+20%
Fracture of upper limb	+75%	+50%
Intracranial injury	+60%	+15%
Laceration of lower limb	–	+50%

63   The average durations for each type of injury and age were then applied to the corresponding numbers of motor injuries and it was found that on this basis the 170,000 men injured at the working ages had just over 7 million days of incapacity (excluding the first three days) and the 75,000 women had nearly 2½ million days of incapacity. The average durations for various age groups are given in Table 9. The averages are considerably greater for men than for women, and this is compatible with the DOE statistics, which show a larger proportion of serious casualties (as compared with all casualties) for men than for women.

Table 9   Average days incapacity for motor vehicle injuries

	Age group					
	0–15	16–19	20–24	25–34	35–44	45–64/59
Males	42	29	32	35	44	70
Females	31	22	23	27	33	44

64   For costing it is necessary to break down the total days of incapacity benefit paid into short-term and long-term. The basis for this split was again the national insurance statistics which give for age and cause of injury the days of sickness benefit and invalidity benefit separately, summed over all accidents. These cover all accidents since the national insurance scheme began in 1948 for which benefit is still being paid and hence represent the situation when the proposed scheme will have been in operation for nearly 30 years. No data are available as to whether the ratio of sickness benefit to invalidity benefit days is the same for motor vehicle accidents as for all other accidents but, in view of the findings above on the 'severity factor', it is reasonable to assume that some differential will apply. Accordingly the ratios of invalidity benefit days to all days were increased by one-tenth for all age groups to give the proportions shown in Table 10.

Table 10 Invalidity benefit days as proportion of all days of benefit

Age	16–24	25–34	35–44	45–64/59
Men	·029	·116	·150	·277
Women	·034	·131	·117	·240

65   Applying these proportions to the total days previously derived, the figures for short- and long-term incapacity in Table 11 were obtained. These exclude the first three days of incapacity for which no benefit is normally payable. The figures relate to all motor vehicle injuries and the proportions in Table 6 were applied to give a breakdown according to whether the injury was sustained in the course of work, on the way to and from work, or in other circumstances.

66   From the days of incapacity shown in Table 11 (estimated with the population as it was in 1973) the average durations per person in each sex and age group were found. These averages were then applied to the estimated populations in various future years to obtain the days of incapacity for which benefit would be payable in those years.

Table 11 Aggregate duration of incapacity for motor vehicle injuries divided into short- and long-term

thousands of days

		Age 16–19	Age 20–24	Age 25–34	Age 35–44	Age 45–64/59	Total
Men:	Total days	1,130	1,040	1,200	1,120	2,570	7,060
	Short-term	1,100	1,010	1,060	950	1,860	5,980
	Long-term	30	30	140	170	710	1,080
Women:	Total days	280	300	380	460	930	2,350
	Short-term	270	290	330	410	710	2,010
	Long-term	10	10	50	50	220	340

67 There still remained the costing of the accidents to children in the group aged 0–15 for whom a flat-rate benefit is envisaged. The numbers arising in this group have already been estimated (Table 7), but there are no data on which estimates of the duration of incapacity can be directly based. Examination of the HIPE figures, however, shows that for certain accident causes the average in-patient stay for the age group 0–15 is only slightly less than the average for all ages. It was therefore decided that for children the duration of incapacity be taken as the average figure for adults in Table 9. The conditions for benefit are bound to some extent to differ from those for adults and in the absence of detailed criteria the costs for children must be regarded as very tentative.

Estimation of the cost of benefits

68 Having obtained the numbers of days of short- and long-term incapacity for each sex and age group the cost of the loss of earnings benefits was then obtained using methods similar to those used for the work injuries scheme. For benefit for non-pecuniary loss and special hardship allowance (costed in lieu of partial loss of earnings benefit) the level of claims to be expected is very uncertain and it was not possible to make meaningful calculations for each sex and age group. The benefit cost were therefore calculated by reference to the corresponding estimates for accidents on the way to and from work under the work injuries scheme (see paragraph 31), having regard to the relative proportions shown in Table 6. For benefit for non-pecuniary loss additions were made in respect of benefit to children and for persons injured over pension age rising to £1 million and £3 million respectively when the scheme is fully mature.

Benefits for widows and widowers

69 The numbers of deaths due to accidents are given in the road traffic accidents statistics of the Department of the Environment referred to in paragraph 43 and in the mortality statistics of accidents and violence published by the Registrars General, who also publish statistics from which the proportions married and the ages of husbands and wives amongst those killed can be assessed. The present national insurance scheme provides information on other dependants. The only point at which there was some doubt in the making of the estimates of the benefit costs was the assumption as to the proportions of motor vehicle accident widows and widowers whose spouses died respectively in accidents at work, on the way to or from work,

252

or at other times. What information there was indicated that the proportion of motor accidents which were fatal was less for accidents at work than for other accidents and it was assumed that 55 per cent of widows widowed as a result of motor accidents would be covered under the motor vehicle injuries scheme and 45 per cent under the work injuries scheme.

ESTIMATED NUMBER OF BENEFICIARIES

70   Table 12 shows for the main benefits under the proposed scheme the estimated numbers of beneficiaries after 40 years, when for practical purposes the scheme may be regarded as fully mature.

Table 12 Estimated average numbers of benefits in payment at any point in time in the year 2023–24

thousands

	Loss of earnings benefit		Non-pecuniary loss		Death benefits[2]	
	Short-term	Long-term	Pensions	Gratui-ties[1]	Widows	Widowers
Work injuries scheme						
Employees: accidents and diseases covered by industrial injuries scheme at present	47	11	174	179	9	–
Self-employed: accidents and diseases covered for employees under industrial injuries scheme at present	4	1	15	16	1	–
Occupational diseases not covered under industrial injuries scheme at present	2	1	6	9	–	–
Accidents on the way to and from work	11	2	20	23	6	1
Total work injuries scheme	64	15	215	227	16	1
Motor vehicle injuries scheme	28	5	38	46	10	4
Total	92	20	253	273	26	5

1 Estimated number awarded during the year.
2 Excluding widows over age 60 and widowers over age 65.

Note: For loss of earnings and widows benefits the majority of beneficiaries not covered under the industrial injuries scheme at present shown in the table would be eligible for benefit under the national insurance scheme.

Glossary

This glossary contains brief descriptions of the sense in which terms are used in this volume.

Attempt to claim	Any move towards claiming in tort, even discussion of the possibility with someone else.
Average	Arithmetic mean.
Birth injury (or birth trauma)	Injury to a baby during childbirth.
Casualty	Injury, or death following injury.
Claim, tort	A formal request for tort compensation.
Commuting injury	See '*Injury, commuting*'.
Damages, special	Damages for past pecuniary loss, that is, for loss of earnings and additional expenses incurred since the date of injury.
Damages, general	Damages other than for past pecuniary loss, comprising damages for future pecuniary loss and for non-pecuniary loss.
Defender (Scot.)	Defendant.
Differential rating	A system under which insurance premiums are varied according to estimated degrees of risk for different groups of policyholders.
Disability	Functional impairment, whether or not leading to absence from work or restriction of activities.
Discount rate	The rate of interest, or rate of return on capital, used to determine the present sum equivalent to a sum or series of sums to be paid in the future.
Family expenditure survey	A continuing survey of the patterns of expenditure of a sample of households, carried out for the Department of Employment.
Family Fund	A fund established by the Government and administered by the Joseph Rowntree Memorial Trust from which payments are made to assist families with very severely disabled children.
General damages	See '*Damages, general*'.
General household survey	A continuing general purpose household survey carried out for the Central Statistical Office.
Grossing up	Multiplying the numbers derived from a sample survey to obtain estimates for the whole population sampled.

254

Housewife	A married woman under 60 not at work.
Incapacity	Inability to work or to engage in other activities.
Industrial injuries scheme	That part of social security which relates to employees' injuries at work and industrial diseases.
Inflation	An increase in the general level of prices or earnings.
Injury	*In summary statistics (for example, in chapter 2)* Injury leading to four or more days off work, or of an equivalent degree of severity. *For which sickness benefit paid, or resulting in death* Cases classified to the ICD heading 'Accidents, poisonings and violence', except that deaths identified as suicides are excluded. *Personal injury survey* Injury leading to four or more days' incapacity for any activity normally engaged in. The range of injuries is slightly wider than the ICD heading 'Accidents, poisonings and violence'.
Injury, at work	*Social security* Injury arising out of and in the course of work. *Personal injury survey* Injury arising from work or occurring during working hours. *Tort* Injury arising out of and in the course of work. Claims for most such injuries involving motor vehicles are made under motor policies, and consequently classed as relating to motor vehicle, not work, injuries.
Injury, commuting	Injury on the way to or from work.

Injuries, motor vehicle	*Personal injury survey*
	Injuries involving:
	  i Motor vehicles moving on the road
	  ii Motor vehicles designed for road use when moving in car parks, drives or the like
	  iii Stationary motor vehicles.
	
	Cost of proposed scheme of compensation
	Injuries involving motor vehicles, whether moving or stationary, on the road or on land to which the public has access, but excluding injuries at work or while commuting.

Injury, work	*Personal injury survey* Injury at work, commuting injury, and injury at the place of work outside working hours. *Cost of proposed work injuries scheme* Injury at work and commuting injury (including injury of either of these kinds involving a motor vehicle. *Cost of tort compensation* Same as injury at work.

255

Insurance, first party	Insurance against loss resulting from injury to the person insured.
Insurance, third party	Insurance against a liability to make good losses to persons other than the person insured.
Insurance survey	A survey of insurance claims disposed of in November 1973 carried out by the British Insurance Association with the participation of Lloyd's.
International classification of diseases	A classification prepared by the World Health Organisation, used to classify causes of sickness or death.
Investment income surcharge	Additional tax levied on investment income of more than a specified annual amount.
Median	The value which divides a distribution into two halves, with as many below it as above it.
Motor vehicle injury	See 'Injuries, motor vehicle'.
Multiplier	The factor by which expected future annual pecuniary loss is multiplied to determine lump sum tort compensation payable.
New earnings survey	A survey of the earnings in April of each year of a sample of employees subject to PAYE, carried out by the Department of Employment since 1968.
Non-pecuniary loss	The intangible results of injury, often summarised as 'pain and suffering and loss of amenity'.
Partial incapacity	Partial loss of earnings.
Personal injury survey	A survey of injured people in a sample of households in Great Britain carried out for the Commission by the Office of Population Censuses and Surveys. The main results of the survey relate to injuries in 1973.
Pilot survey	A preliminary survey carried out in advance of a main survey to test questions and methods.
Prescribed disease	An occupational disease prescribed under the industrial injuries scheme for which benefits can be claimed.
Proof (Scot.)	Trial.
Pursuer (Scot.)	Plaintiff.
Sampling fraction	The proportion of units in a population or a stratum selected for inclusion in a sample.
Sampling, standard error of	A measure of the extent to which an estimate derived from a sample is likely to vary from the true value. If E is the estimate and e the standard error, there is about a 95 per cent probability that the true value is in the range from $(E-2e)$ to $(E+2e)$.
Sample, stratified	A sample obtained by taking random samples from each of a number of parts, or strata, into which the population being sampled is divided.
Self insurers	Organisations carrying their own risk of liability to pay tort compensation for personal injury.
Skew distribution	A distribution which is not symmetrical.
Socio-economic group	A grouping of households based on the nature of the occupation of the head of the household, broadly reflecting social characteristics and levels of income.

Special damages	See '*Damages, special*'.
Spell of incapacity	An unbroken period of incapacity, especially for work. An injury or illness may be followed by more than one spell of incapacity, if there is a temporary return to work.
Standard error of sampling	See '*Sampling, standard error of*'.
Standard industrial classification	A classification of establishments engaged in economic activities of all kinds, prepared by the Central Statistical Office. The classification was last revised in 1968.
Stratified sample	See '*Sample, stratified*'.
Taxed costs	Legal costs approved by the court, as is necessary, for example, where they are paid from legal aid funds.
Work injury	See '*Injury, work*'.

Abbreviations

BIA	British Insurance Association.
DHSS	The Department of Health and Social Security (for Great Britain) and/or the Department of Health and Social Services (Northern Ireland).
DOE	Department of the Environment.
GAD	Government Actuary's Department.
HIPE	Hospital In-patient Enquiry
ICD	International Classification of Diseases
NI	National Insurance.
OECD	Organisation for European Co-operation and Development
OPCS	Office of Population Censuses and Surveys.
PIS	Personal Injury Survey.

List of references

1   HARTZ S. J. A Road Accident Survey. New Law Journal. 1969.
2   ISON T. G. The Forensic Lottery. Staples Press. 1967.
3   LORD JUSTICE WINN. Report of the Committee on Personal Injuries Litigation. HMSO. 1968.
4   CONARD A. F. AND OTHERS. Automobile costs and payments: studies in the economics of injuries reparation. University of Michigan Press. 1974.
5   UNITED STATES DEPARTMENT OF TRANSPORTATION. Automobile insurance and compensation study: economic consequences of automobile accident injuries. Volume 1. 1970.
6   MORRIS C. AND PAUL J. C. N. The Financial Impact of Automobile Accidents. University of Pennsylvania Law Review. 1962.
7   LINDEN A. M. Report of the Osgoode Hall study on compensation for victims of automobile accidents. Toronto. 1965.
8   ZANDER M. Cost of litigation—a study in the Queen's Bench Division. Guardian Gazette. 25 June 1975.
9   Report on a survey of occupational sick pay schemes. HMSO. 1977.
10 Occupational Pension Schemes 1971: Fourth survey by the Government Actuary. HMSO. 1972.
11 Social Trends No. 7, table 2.22. HMSO. 1976.
12 Report of the Chief Registrar of Friendly Societies for the year 1975. Part 1. HMSO. 1976.
13 Annual Report of H.M. Chief Inspector of Factories 1973. HMSO.
14 HALE A. R. AND HALE M. A review of the industrial accident research literature. HMSO. 1972.
15 GRATTAN E. AND KEIGAN M. E. Patterns and Severity of Injury in a Hospital Sample of Road Traffic Accident Casualties. Transport and Road Research Laboratory. 1975.
16 Drinking and Driving. Report of the Departmental Committee. HMSO. 1976.
17 Accidents to Aircraft on the British Register. Civil Aviation Authority. Published annually.
18 Casualties to Vessels and Accidents to Men. HMSO. Published annually.
19 Report of the Working Party on Water Safety. HMSO. 1977.
20 Report to the Secretary of State for Transport on the Safety Record of the Railways in Great Britain. HMSO. Published annually.
21 The Home Accident Surveillance System. A report of the first six months' data collection. HMSO. 1977.
22 Whooping Cough Vaccination. Review of the evidence on whooping cough vaccination by the Joint Committee on Vaccination and Immunization. HMSO. 1977.
23 BUTLER N. R. AND ALBERMAN E. D. Perinatal Problems. Livingstone. 1969.
24 OPCS Monitor MB 3. HMSO. Published quarterly.
25 DAVIE R., BUTLER N. R. AND GOLDSTEIN H. From Birth to Seven. Longman. 1972.

26 ALBERMAN E. D. AND GOLDSTEIN H. The 'At Risk' Register: A statistical evaluation. Brit. J. Prev. Soc. Med. 1970.
27 CHAMBERLAIN R. AND OTHERS. British Births, 1970. Volume I, The first week of life. Heinemann. 1975.
28 BRADSHAW J. Examining benefits for families with handicapped children. DHSS Social Security Research Seminar paper No. 7. HMSO. 1975.
29 Road Accidents Great Britain. HMSO. Published annually.
30 KALTON G. AND LEWIS S. The General household survey 1972, Chapter 7. HMSO. 1975.
31 BARR, NICHOLAS. Real rates of return to financial assets since the war. The Three Banks Review No. 107. September 1975.
32 LEES D. AND DOHERTY N. Compensation for Personal Injury. Lloyds Bank Review No. 108. April 1973.
33 Safety and Health at Work. Report of the Robens Committee. HMSO. 1972.
34 DAWSON R. F. F. Cost of road accidents in Great Britain. Road Research Laboratory, Ministry of Transport. 1967.
35 DAWSON R. F. F. Current costs of road accidents in Great Britain. Road Research Laboratory, Department of the Environment. 1971.

Printed in England for Her Majesty's Stationery Office by Oyez Press Limited
Dd 291044   K32   3/78